The Magic of Stories

Literature-Based
Languag

Carol J. Strong, Ed.

Thinking Publications • Eau Claire, Wisconsin

04   03   02   01   00   99   98   10 9   8   7   6   5   4   3

Library of Congress Cataloguing-in-Publication Data

Strong, Carol J.
    The magic of stories: literature-based language intervention / Carol J. Strong, Kelly Hoggan North.

          p.   cm.

    Includes bibliographical references.

    ISBN 0-930599-36-5 (pbk.)
    1. Learning disabled children—Education—Utah Language arts (Elementary)   2. Storytelling.   3.   Literature—Study and teaching (Elementary)—Utah.   I. North, Kelly Hoggan. II. Title.
LC4704.85.S78 1996
371.91'42—dc20

                                                                                          95-44015
                                                                                          CIP

Printed in the United States of America

Cover Design and Illustrations: Kris Madsen

THINKING PUBLICATIONS®
A Division of McKinley Companies, Inc.

424 Galloway Street
Eau Claire, WI 54703
(800) 225-GROW • FAX (800) 828-8885
E-mail: custserv@ThinkingPublications.com
www.ThinkingPublications.com

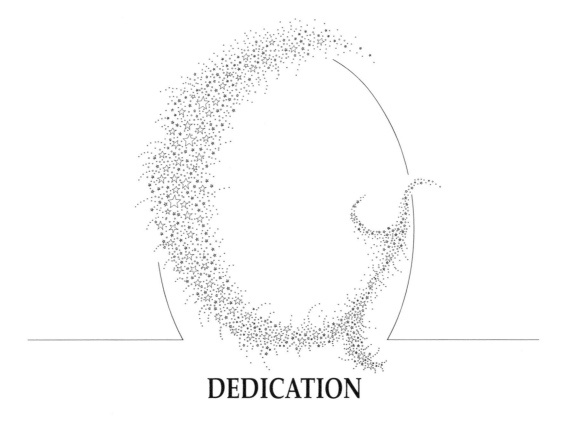

DEDICATION

For our parents, who helped us discover the magic of stories.

And for our children and grandchildren, as they discover that same magic.

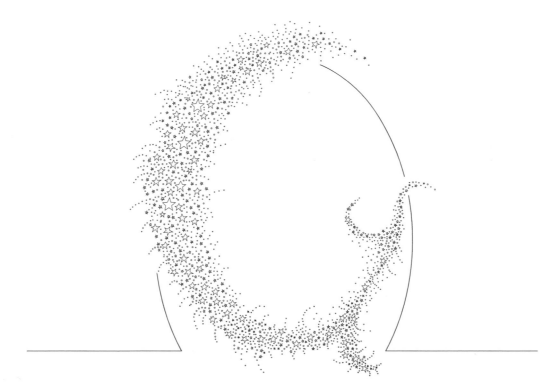

TABLE OF CONTENTS

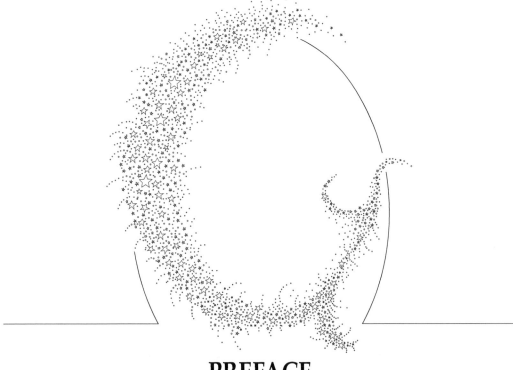

PREFACE

The Magic of Stories was conceived nearly a decade ago. In 1985, a group of intelligent and dedicated professionals—special educators and speech-language pathologists—met weekly to study the needs of school-age students with language impairments. The special educators sought information about language impairment—how to identify students with such problems and how to integrate language instruction into their teaching plans. The speech-language pathologists wanted to alert and inform other school professionals about students with language impairments and to coordinate language intervention with the efforts of those other professionals.

The teachers asked some tough questions during our 10 weeks together: How can we engage students in meaningful language activities that integrate a variety of objectives? How can we teach students all that they need to learn about language and communication in isolated, infrequent remedial sessions that focus on specific objectives? How can we work together cooperatively to support the critical language and communication skills that students need for school success? We didn't answer all of those questions, but

we did embark on a professional journey that continues today. *The Magic of Stories* is but one stage of that journey.

By the end of the first 10 weeks, to sustain the bonds that had been forged, these school professionals formed a journal-reading group and continued the quest for answers to their questions. Since then, the group has met monthly to read about and discuss language impairment in school-age students. One important step in the journey occurred in 1989–90, when many of the school speech-language pathologists learned procedures for testing their students' narrative skills. These assessments revealed both diagnostic and programming information that could not be obtained from standardized tests or conversational language samples. Moreover, the speech-language pathologists quickly learned that by teaching language skills in a meaningful and interesting context (in the context of a story that had not been used for assessment), they could integrate a wide variety of needed language skills.

At this stage, members of our group began, seriously, to teach vocabulary, morphology, and syntax in the context of stories. We also began devising ways to teach narrative skills, for our assessment results had informed us that students' pragmatic skills (summarizing, perspective taking, and asking and answering questions) and general knowledge of literate language (cohesion and story grammar) were also weak. As individual clinicians began integrating narrative skills into their teaching, they devised unique approaches for using stories as a basis for language intervention. What they lacked was a theoretically sound teaching model for their diverse practices.

In 1992, *The Magic of Stories* coauthor Kelly Hoggan, then an energetic and creative graduate student, developed an interest in the theoretical underpinnings of literature-based language intervention. She sought to identify a wide range of narrative-teaching practices in the published language arts and reading literature, to document their intended purposes and the rationales for their use, and to integrate this information into a functional teaching approach for educators. The result of this effort was her master's thesis. For her public-school practicum, Kelly fortuitously worked with Tobey Fields, a charter member of the journal-reading group and one who was pursuing ways to integrate language intervention into meaningful contexts. In this collaboration between student

and cooperating teacher, the union between practice and theory was nurtured. An article titled "The Magic of 'Once Upon a Time'...Narrative Teaching Strategies," published in *Language, Speech, and Hearing Services in Schools* (Hoggan and Strong, 1994), was an extension of this collaboration. Happily, the article received the Editor's Award at the 1995 American Speech-Language-Hearing Association Convention; equally important, it served as the foundation for our collaboration in this book.

Since 1993, a number of experienced and creative clinicians who work throughout Utah have developed narrative-teaching units. Additionally, *The Magic of Stories* coauthor Carol Strong now requires graduate students enrolled in a seminar on language impairments in school-age students to develop teaching units. Many of the units found in *The Magic of Stories* were developed by these master clinicians and graduate students working at various levels of elementary and middle-school education.

The Magic of Stories is divided into three parts. Chapter 1, "Storybook Magic," provides the theoretical basis for and the advantages of using literature-based language intervention. Chapter 2, "Narrative-Teaching Strategies," guides you through the 22 narrative-teaching strategies that can be used in literature-based language intervention. Because the narrative-teaching strategies may be new for your clinical or classroom work, we recommend that you spend a few minutes with both Chapters 1 and 2 and that you refer to Chapter 2 frequently as you begin to use the strategies in your work. The section titled "Narrative-Teaching Units," provides carefully planned narrative-teaching units for 30 children's storybooks—10 at each of three grade levels (early elementary, middle elementary, and upper elementary/middle school).

The narrative-teaching strategies included in the 30 story units are useful for reinforcing both oral and written language. The more we can link spoken and written language, and the more students can participate in such a linkage, the better they will be able to function in the classroom. We urge you to select storybooks other than the 30 featured here and to experiment with the teaching strategies to identify those combinations of strategies that appeal to students. We also suggest that if you are working collaboratively with classroom teachers, you will find the narrative-teaching units especially useful.

As indicated earlier, this book is but one stage of a journey directed at integrating students' language objectives into meaningful contexts and working collaboratively with other professionals in the schools. Our journey continues. If you discover interesting ways to record and document progress in language development, we would enjoy hearing from you. We also welcome any narrative-teaching ideas that you might wish to share with us and other educators.

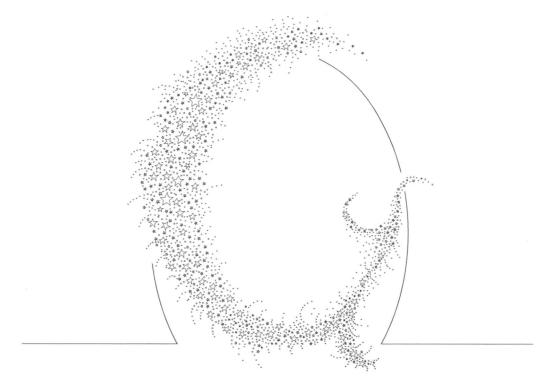

ACKNOWLEDGMENTS

This book is the product of many hands and minds. We are pleased that Thinking Publications has added *The Magic of Stories* to its collection of titles that focus on the academic and communication skills of young children and adolescents with communication impairments.

We want to acknowledge first our colleagues at Utah State University and surrounding schools—Judy Armstrong, Anne Elsweiler, Tobey Fields, Janet Jensen, and Ann McKeehan—all of whom helped develop teaching units included in *The Magic of Stories.* We also appreciate the teaching-unit contributions of graduate students—Jennifer Abbott, Jillyn Abel, Shelly Anderson, Susan Bartholomew, Kimberly Buckner, Rod Bullock, Kevin Costa, Kari A. Fabrizio, Janell Frost, Dawn Gummersall, Maggie S. Harris, Gina A. Hollinger, Kelly Majeroni, Heather Moran, Cathy Nuttall, Jill Palmer, Janette Robinson, Mary P. Scotese, Shannan Smith, Lisa Stott, Curtis G. Thomas, Jill S. Turnier, Kristin L. Walton, Shwu-Jiuan Wang, and Susie Yoakum. Thanks to the students in the elementary and middle schools in northern Utah who participated in field trials of the units.

We especially value the support of Nancy McKinley, Editor in Chief at Thinking Publications, and Linda Schreiber, Senior Editor. This is a better book because of their guidance, insight, and attention to detail. We are delighted with Kris Madsen's creative illustrations and graphic-organizer designs. The seasoned advice and spirited encouragement of the reviewers—Val Erickson, Meg Farrington, LaRae McGillivray, Linda Miller, Fran Neilitz, and Peg Reichardt—also improved *The Magic of Stories.*

Finally, thanks to Karen Casadaban and Elsha Young for their library assistance, to Marcus North for his good humor and patient support throughout this project, and to William Strong for his advice on the manuscript, for his suggestions on story-generation and journal guidelines, and for his celebration of this accomplishment.

Carol J. Strong

Kelly Hoggan North

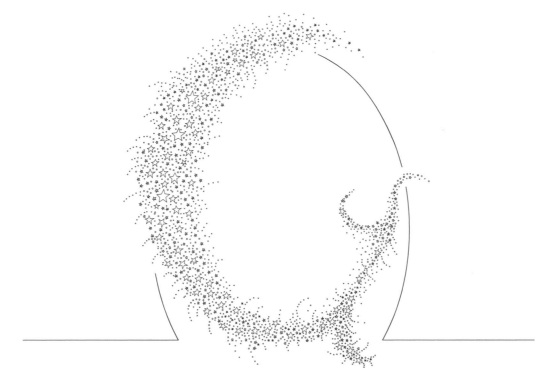

ABOUT THE AUTHORS

Carol J. Strong, an associate professor in the Department of Communicative Disorders and Deaf Education at Utah State University, teaches courses in language assessment and intervention, language disorders of school-age students, language and emergent literacy development, and research in education and psychology. In 1989 she received an American Speech-Language-Hearing Association (ASHA) Foundation research award for new investigators; in 1991 her work was recognized by the Utah Chapter of the American Association of University Women with an emerging scholar award; and in 1995 she received ASHA's Editor's Award for her article in *Language, Speech, and Hearing Services in Schools.*

She now works closely with practicing clinicians on action research projects and continuing education programs. She has published extensively in the areas of early intervention for children with sensory impairments, intervention using sentence combining, and narrative assessment and intervention. Also, she has presented numerous workshops, seminars, and technical papers at state, national, and international conferences

focused on enhancing language and literacy in children with language impairments. In 1994 she was a language arts and children's literature delegate for the Citizen Ambassador Program to the People's Republic of China.

Kelly Hoggan North, a communicative disorders specialist in the Cache County School District in Utah, provides speech and language services to children in elementary and middle schools. She received her bachelor's and master's degrees from Utah State University and was honored as both Outstanding Senior and Outstanding Graduate Student Researcher for the Department of Communicative Disorders and Deaf Education.

Since graduation, she has provided in-service presentations for regional speech-language clinicians and has been a guest lecturer at Utah State University. In April 1994, Kelly published an article describing narrative-intervention strategies in *Language, Speech, and Hearing Services in Schools* for which she received ASHA's Editor's Award at the 1995 ASHA Convention. She also presented this information at the 1994 ASHA Convention in New Orleans.

Chapter 1
STORYBOOK MAGIC

Take a moment to read this list: *Cinderella, The Three Billy Goats Gruff, Hansel and Gretel, The Three Little Pigs*. These stories were likely read to you as a child. As you scan the titles, do characters and imagery come to mind? Can you retell these stories easily? Perhaps stories that you first read independently are even more vividly remembered than these—say, for example, *Charlotte's Web, Little Women, Charlie and the Chocolate Factory, Black Beauty*, or *Old Yeller*. Do such titles evoke memories of exciting plots, distant places, heroic characters, extraordinary events, or intriguing mysteries? Do you recall feelings of jealousy, love, guilt, joy, grief, hope, or despair? Do you remember identifying with the characters and wishing the story would never end?

"The magic of stories" is within reach of all students—even those with severe language-learning disabilities and literacy deficits. Like educators, students are fully capable of becoming engaged in worlds beyond those of the clinic or classroom. Because students are interested in the problems of characters, the story becomes a natural language-learning medium, one that allows educators to guide students through learning activities

that support both oral and written language development concurrently (Teale and Sulzby, 1986). Simply put, stories have sufficient power to transform classrooms from places of skill-and-drill drudgery into places of magic that students enjoy.

OVERVIEW OF THIS RESOURCE

The Magic of Stories: Literature-Based Language Intervention is a resource book for speech-language clinicians, special educators, elementary teachers, and ESL/bilingual specialists who work with students in elementary and middle schools. It provides language-teaching strategies for 30 carefully selected storybooks. As students enjoy the magic of stories, they learn new vocabulary, figurative language, world knowledge, and sentence patterns; and they use language to predict, summarize, problem solve, compare and contrast, retell events, pretend, share feelings, clarify, and answer questions. Moreover, they can be introduced to difficult stories that they are yet unable to read independently. The use of such a literature-based teaching approach assumes that students grasp the meanings, structure, and purposes of language best when they are learned in a meaningful context and that whatever students can do with the support of others, they will eventually be able to do on their own (Vygotsky, 1978).

As indicated previously, a literature-based teaching approach is a means to an end (improved communication and academic skills) not an end in itself. The teaching strategies described in this book provide a kind of "scaffold" (or support) for skill development. Such teaching strategies are consistent with the ideas articulated by Lev Vygotsky (1978), who proposed the concept of a "zone of proximal development" (ZPD). Vygotsky (1962) argued that "the only good kind of instruction is that which marches ahead of development and leads it" (p. 104). He defined the ZPD as the difference between two levels of linguistic (or cognitive) performance—that which the student can do independently and that which he or she can do with the help of an adult or more capable peers. Given Vygotsky's premise, *teaching* is defined here as "assisted performance." With the resources provided in *The Magic of Stories*, students' skill development is supported by thoughtful, caring educators who provide scaffolds for communication and academic learning.

The Magic of Stories focuses on the narrative-teaching strategies most often used in mainstream middle-class families and schools (Schieffelin and Cochran-Smith, 1984). Not addressed are nonmainstream styles of storytelling in which, for example, character qualities and motivation are implied rather than stated, nor nonmainstream styles of learning from print (Heath, 1982; Michaels, 1981). The storybook selections are almost exclusively short fictional stories (i.e., no biographies or nonfiction selections and no chapter books).

The Magic of Stories includes a number of useful features:

1. *A listing of storybooks by grade level*—The list is located in the table of contents and is divided into three instructional levels: early elementary (E), kindergarten through grade 2; middle elementary (M), grades 3 and 4; and upper elementary/middle school (U), grades 5 through 7. This list helps educators locate teaching units at the appropriate grade level for students.

2. *A Thematic/Topical Index*—With a glance, the themes or topics that are treated in specific storybooks can be located using this index. The index begins on page 373.

3. *A Teaching-Strategies Index*—Once a storybook for use in intervention is selected, this index (see pages 378–379) can be scanned to discover which of the teaching strategies are included in the story unit. Alternately, the index may be used to locate the units containing a specific strategy, such as using a semantic-word map, in the event an educator would want to emphasize a particular strategy.

4. *Appendices*—The appendices provide reproducible information for educator convenience. Appendices are perforated and may be removed from the book for ease in duplication. The following appendices are included:

   - Appendix A provides a questionnaire for collecting information about students' classroom language abilities.

   - Appendix B includes examples of individualized educational program (IEP) goals and objectives.

- Appendix C contains graphic organizer master forms (i.e., semantic-word maps, a discussion web, episode maps, a story map, a flow chart, an internal-states chart, a story-grammar cue chart, and a compare/contrast Venn diagram) that can be photocopied for overhead transparencies or for student activity sheets.

- Appendix D provides a vocabulary card illustration for each of the 30 stories, plus illustrations for several art activities.

- Appendix E lists publishers and addresses for the 30 storybooks used in *The Magic of Stories*.

5. *Story synopses*—Found at the beginning of each teaching unit, these synopses provide readily accessible summaries of the stories. The summaries can be used for making decisions about selections as well as for summarizing a specific story for students.

Each of these features is provided to save time and to help educators teach creatively.

GOALS FOR *THE MAGIC OF STORIES*

For educators, the goals for *The Magic of Stories* are to provide:

1. a variety of literature-based language-teaching units at three instructional levels (early elementary, middle elementary, and upper elementary/middle school);

2. descriptions and examples of 22 narrative-teaching strategies and instructions for their use; and

3. tables, indexes, and appendixes that save time.

For students, the goals for *The Magic of Stories* are to provide:

1. meaningful, engaging learning contexts in which oral and written communication can develop and flourish;

2. learning activities that enhance receptive and expressive semantic and syntactic development;

3. opportunities to practice organizing, categorizing, and remembering information;

4. practice in using important academic communicative functions such as predicting, summarizing, comparing, and contrasting;

5. exposure to concepts of print and storybook styles; and

6. a learning environment that fosters a lifelong passion for stories.

RATIONALE FOR USING STORIES IN INTERVENTION

Support for routinely reading aloud to students is widespread (Strickland and Morrow, 1989; Teale, 1984; Trelease, 1989a, 1989b). Interactive reading aloud—the type found in mainstream middle-class homes and schools—engages educators and students in the joint act of reading and talking, allowing professionals to share stories' meanings, provide a positive reading role model, and expose students to difficult print material that they cannot yet read independently (Trousdale, 1990; Whitehurst et al., 1988).

Moreover, as professionals share the magic of storybooks, students learn specific language skills. For example, they learn new vocabulary, concepts, and figurative language; expand their world knowledge; discover, in context, the meanings of complex sentence structures; and become familiar with the structure of stories—the story grammar—so that they can comprehend and recall new stories (Holdaway, 1979; Whitehurst et al., 1988). In addition to the content and form of storybooks, students are repeatedly exposed to concepts of print and to storybook styles (Teale, 1984)—important concepts for academic success.

Support for using narrative-teaching strategies in language intervention is also widespread (Gebers, 1990; Norris, 1991; Westby, 1990). As educators focus on the 22 narrative-teaching strategies described in Chapter 2, students will learn new language content and structures, and they will also use language for important communicative functions. For example, students will use language to predict events from picture clues, summarize a story's events, identify main ideas/themes, compare and contrast information, share ideas and feelings, clarify subtle meanings, retell stories, and/or imagine and create new

stories. Furthermore, students will acquire strategies for organizing and remembering information as they work with tables, diagrams, semantic maps, and charts. These strategies are critical for academic success.

TARGET POPULATIONS

The narrative-intervention units can be used with diverse populations. Students with language disorders, learning disabilities, severe cognitive impairments, and/or other special needs all benefit from language-learning activities that are conducted in a meaningful, literacy-based context (Evans and Strong, in press; Koppenhaver, Coleman, Kalman, and Yoder, 1991). For students who come from disadvantaged circumstances or students who are learning English as a second language, the teaching units in *The Magic of Stories* will be important features of a total language-instruction program (Langdon and Cheng, 1992; McEachern, 1990).

The teaching units target small instructional groups (four to six students), but they can be adapted for individual instruction. The units can also be used by professionals or teachers who work in the classroom providing language instruction to large groups of students. When language intervention is provided for 30 minutes, twice a week, then three to four weeks of instruction to complete each teaching unit are needed.

TARGET STORYBOOKS

The 30 storybooks included in *The Magic of Stories* were selected based upon the authors' experiences with teaching young children and students, their own enjoyment of the books, and their commitment to culturally diverse learners. Storybooks were favored that stimulated students' emotions and imaginations (Trelease, 1989a), inspired students to listen to or read other stories, and had intriguing or appealing illustrations. Selections also had to have clear episodic structure, important vocabulary or figurative language, and themes or messages about positive social interactions.

The stories also had to be short ones that could be dealt with comfortably in a typical 30-minute language-intervention session with a small or large group of students.

Many of the books are popular with elementary- and middle-school students, and all are readily available in school or public libraries. Grade-level ratings were sometimes based on estimates provided by publishers and sometimes on the authors' own experiences with each book. For additional information on the selection of storybooks for teaching specific language targets, consult Gebers (1990), Van Dongen and Westby (1986), and Westby (1991).

GUIDELINES FOR
NARRATIVE-INTERVENTION INSTRUCTION

The 22 narrative-teaching strategies described in Chapter 2 provide an important means for supporting students' oral and written language development within a meaningful, familiar, and interesting context. Educators can use the strategies to enhance a variety of language skills: comprehension of vocabulary, syntax, figurative language, and the story itself; development of specific syntactic structures (e.g., morpheme usage, questions, subordinate clauses); pragmatic skills (e.g., turn taking, topic maintenance, perspective taking); cognitive skills (e.g., compare/contrast, cause/effect, problem solving); discourse skills and general knowledge about literate language (e.g., cohesion and story-grammar components). The following sections describe general suggestions for implementing narrative intervention with students.

Preintervention Assessment

Before beginning intervention using *The Magic of Stories*, conduct a preintervention assessment of each student's narrative skills:

- Collect and analyze samples of students' personal narratives (Hutson-Nechkash, 1990; Lahey, 1988; McCabe and Rollins, 1994), oral and written story retellings (Hughes, McGillivray, and Schmidek, in press; Hedberg and Westby, 1993; Hutson-Nechkash, 1990; Strong, 1994), and self-generated stories (Hughes et al., in press). Complete the Classroom Language Questionnaire provided in Appendix A if you are a classroom teacher, or have a classroom teacher complete one for each student.

- Based on the analyses of the oral and/or written narrative samples and answers to the Classroom Language Questionnaire, write both long-term goals and short-term objectives for students' individualized education programs. Examples of IEP goals and objectives can be found in Appendix B.

Preintervention Planning

After determining students' goals and objectives, create a plan for intervention:

- Select a story by scanning the story titles and synopses within the grade level appropriate for students' needs. Use the Thematic/Topical Index (pages 373–377) to review the stories' themes and topics. Use the Teaching-Strategies Index (pages 378–379) to identify story units that include specific teaching strategies.

- Locate the storybook in the school or public library. Read the book. Practice reading the book aloud to become thoroughly familiar with the pictures and the language.

- Read the narrative-teaching unit provided in this book. Review sections of Chapter 2 related to the teaching strategies that will be used. Become familiar with the graphic organizers necessary for that story (see Appendix C).

- Obtain necessary materials (e.g., music, art supplies, related resource books, photocopies or overhead transparencies of blank graphic organizers [Appendix C], and photocopies of the vocabulary card illustration for the selected story [Appendix D]).

- Establish a portfolio or file for each student.

Intervention

Begin the narrative-teaching unit by following these steps:

- Use the strategies that have been developed or develop additional or substitute intervention activities based on the information in Chapter 2.

- When first using a specific graphic organizer, use an overhead transparency to demonstrate to the entire group how to complete the chart, map, or diagram. Once students have experience with each type of graphic organizer, hand out individual copies of the forms so that students learn to develop the graphic organizers independently.

- Select additional narrative-teaching units from this book, or develop units using the information provided in *The Magic of Stories.* Excellent resources exist for locating storybooks focused on a particular theme or topic, written for students at a specific age level, or representing distinct literary genres (Jensen and Roser, 1993; Morrow, 1989; Trelease, 1989a). For selections of culturally diverse children's literature, see Langdon and Cheng (1992), Rudman (1994), and Slapin and Seale (1992) as well as the *Roots and Wings* book catalog (Boulder, CO). For children's literature about persons with disabilities, see Blaska and Lynch (1993).

- Keep records of completed narrative units and strategies used.

- Maintain each student's portfolio. Add samples of written or tape-recorded oral story retellings, self-generated stories, completed activity sheets, and artwork from each narrative-teaching unit completed. Date each of these samples as they are added to the portfolio.

Postintervention Assessment (End of Year)

At the end of the school year or following intervention with students, conduct a postintervention assessment to determine progress:

- Elicit oral narrative language samples; transcribe and analyze these (Hedberg and Westby, 1993; Hughes, McGillivray, and Schmidek, in press; Hutson-Nechkash, 1990; Lahey, 1988; McCabe and Rollins, 1994; Strong, 1994).

- Collect and analyze written samples of narrative skills (Hedberg and Westby, 1993; Hughes, McGillivray, and Schmidek, in press; Strong, 1994).

- Complete the Classroom Language Questionnaire. Compare the results with the preintervention assessment responses.

- Together with each student, select from the portfolio samples of work and study the changes that have occurred.

- Use all of these data sources combined for evaluating student progress, for providing evidence of progress at staffings, and for making intervention recommendations.

Interesting stories capture the attention of students and strategies help sustain motivation. As the narrative-teaching strategies summarized in the next chapter are used, remember to give the stories a chance to work their magic. The overall goal is increased language competence, and this is best achieved by fostering a lifelong passion for stories. Touching the emotions of students enables educators to awaken their imaginations; and imagination, as we know, has magical power.

Chapter 2
NARRATIVE-TEACHING STRATEGIES

The 22 narrative-teaching strategies described in this chapter were located by carefully searching databases that index and abstract teacher-education reports in the areas of language arts and reading. Such journals as *The Reading Teacher, Reading Research Quarterly*, and *Language Arts* are rich sources of literature-based teaching ideas. Content-area reading and writing texts designed for teacher education are also useful for locating teaching strategies (Brown, Phillips, and Stephens, 1993; Readence, Bean, and Baldwin, 1992; Richardson and Morgan, 1990).

Table 1 on pages 12 and 13 presents 22 categorized strategies so that educators can quickly determine the strategies' usefulness at different story-presentation stages of clinical/classroom work (pre-, during-, or poststory presentation), their language-skill focus (content, form, or use), their suggested grade level (early elementary—kindergarten through grade 2, middle elementary—grades 3 and 4, or upper elementary/middle school—grades 5 through 7), and the teaching context (large group—whole classroom, small group—two to six students, or individual). Recommendations for story-

Table 1

Narrative-Teaching Strategies by Story-Presentation Stage, Language-Skill Focus, Grade Level, and Teaching Context

Strategy	Story-Presentation Stage			Language-Skill Focus			Grade Level			Teaching Context		
	Pre	During	Post	C	F	U	E	M	U	LG	SG	Ind
Art Activities (Berney and Barrera, 1990)	+		+	+	+	+	+	+	+	+	+	+
Compare/Contrast Charts or Diagrams (Wisconsin Dept. of Public Instruction, 1989)	+	+	+	+				+	+	+	+	+
Directed Reading/Thinking Activities (Nessel, 1989)		+		+		+	+	+	+	+	+	+
Discussion Webs (Alvermann, 1991)			+	+		+	+	+	+	+	+	
Dramatic Play (Putnam, 1991)			+	+	+	+	+	+	+	+	+	
Episode Maps (Schmelzer and Dickey, 1990)		+	+	+		+	+	+	+	+	+	+
Extensions (Muma, 1971)		+		+		+	+	+	+	+	+	+
Flow Charts (Geva, 1983)			+	+		+	+	+	+	+	+	+
Internal-States Charts (Dunning, 1992)			+	+		+	+	+	+	+	+	+
Journals (Atwell, 1987; Wollman-Bonilla, 1989)			+	+		+	+	+	+	+	+	+
Music (Barclay and Walwer, 1992)	+		+	+	+	+	+	+	+	+	+	+
Preparatory Sets (Alvermann, Smith, and Readence, 1985)	+			+		+	+	+	+	+	+	+

(continued)

Table 1—*Continued*

Strategy	Story-Presentation Stage			Language-Skill Focus			Grade Level			Teaching Context		
	Pre	During	Post	C	F	U	E	M	U	LG	SG	Ind
Question-Answer Relationships (Raphael, 1986)			+	+		+	+	+	+	+	+	+
Questioning (Panofsky, 1986)		+		+		+	+	+	+	+	+	+
Semantic-Word Maps (Hamayan, 1989)	+		+	+			+	+	+	+	+	+
Story Generation (Trousdale, 1990)			+	+	+	+	+	+	+		+	+
Story-Grammar Cue Charts (Graves and Montague, 1991)			+	+	+	+		+	+	+	+	+
Story Maps (Davis and McPherson, 1989)		+	+	+		+	+	+	+	+	+	+
Story Retelling (Peck, 1989)			+	+	+	+	+	+	+	+	+	+
Summarizing (Panofsky, 1986)	+	+	+	+		+	+	+	+	+	+	+
Think Alouds (Davey, 1983)	+	+	+	+		+	+	+	+	+	+	+
Word Substitutions (Beaumont, 1992)			+	+	+		+	+	+	+	+	+

Note: C = Content   F = Form   U = Use

E = Early Grades   M = Middle Elementary Grades   U = Upper Elementary and Middle School

LG = Large Group   SG = Small Group   Ind = Individual

From "The Magic of 'Once Upon a Time': Narrative Teaching Strategies" by K.C. Hoggan and C.J. Strong, 1994, *Language, Speech, and Hearing Services in Schools, 25*, p. 78. © 1994 by the American Speech-Language-Hearing Association. Adapted with permission.

presentation stages, grade levels, and teaching contexts were based upon guidelines from the research literature and the authors' clinical experiences. A language-skill focus is indicated whenever a language skill (content, form, or use) is emphasized. For example, for the journal strategy, the communication of meaningful thoughts or feelings in written language is the focus, as opposed to written language form. Although form is certainly used by students when writing in their journals, correct form is not emphasized.

The strategies summarized in Table 1 are each followed by a reference. These citations are only examples of researchers or projects that have championed a given strategy. Delving into the references will provide additional information on specific strategies.

In the sections that follow, the strategies used within each story-presentation stage (pre-, during-, or poststory) are summarized using the storybook *Gregory, the Terrible Eater* (Sharmat, 1980) as an example. In this charming story, appropriate for primary-grade students, Gregory the goat is a terrible eater. He won't eat healthy goat food (e.g., paper, cardboard), but he will eat human food (e.g., fruits, vegetables). His worried parents take Dr. Ram's advice and give him one new healthy goat food each day. The strategy works too well—Gregory eats all the healthy goat food in sight. His parents solve the problem by bringing him a huge pile of junk goat food from the town dump. Gregory eats it all at one time and gets a stomachache. From then on, Gregory eats healthy goat food, but he eats it in moderation.

Please note that *Gregory, the Terrible Eater,* a story for early elementary students, is used to illustrate all 22 strategies, including those that typically would not be used during early grade levels. For example, a compare/contrast chart is shown on page 16, even though this type of activity would not normally be done with children until approximately grade 3. The same story was used throughout simply to provide continuity for all examples.

As indicated, the 22 strategies are summarized in the three sections that follow by story-presentation stage (pre-, during-, or poststory). Some of the strategies may be used in more than one stage. For example, three strategies (compare/contrast charts or diagrams, summarizing, and think alouds) are used during all three stages, and five strategies (art activities, episode maps, music, semantic-word maps, and story maps) are

used during two of the stages. For ease of presentation, the 22 strategies are discussed in the sections that follow within a single story-presentation stage; however, remember they may also be useful at other teaching stages. Within each section, the strategies are presented alphabetically. The order of appearance implies neither a sequence in which the strategies are presented to students, nor a developmental hierarchy.

PRESTORY PRESENTATION

Students' prior knowledge about a topic promotes comprehension and learning (Readence, Bean, and Baldwin, 1992). By preparing students for the story (Alvermann et al., 1985), assisting them with organizing their prior knowledge (Ausubel, 1960), modeling learning strategies (Camp and Bash, 1981), or asking prediction questions (Davey, 1983), you encourage active student involvement in the story and facilitate story comprehension as well. Five teaching strategies, presented in alphabetical order, are described in this section:

- compare/contrast charts or diagrams
- music
- preparatory sets
- semantic-word maps
- think alouds

Two or three of these strategies are selected for each of the teaching units found in *The Magic of Stories*.

Compare/Contrast Charts or Diagrams

A compare/contrast chart is an effective way to help students link familiar information with new information (Wisconsin Department of Public Instruction, 1989). For example, the phrase *junk food* will likely have a new meaning for students as they listen to *Gregory, the Terrible Eater*. To clarify their understanding of *junk food* in this new context, use a compare/contrast chart (such as the example chart on the following page) that highlights the two meanings. Develop the people-food half of the chart before story reading by referring to the lists of healthy and junk foods generated during the preparatory set

(see pages 17–19). Conduct a discussion about what might be healthy and junk food for a goat. List students' ideas on the goat-food half of the chart. Tell students that you will use the chart again as the story is read so that they can check their ideas and change their suggestions if needed.

People Food		Goat Food	
Healthy	*Junk*	*Healthy*	*Junk*
fruit	candy	leaves	car
vegetables	fries	bark	violin
bread	pop	twigs	tires
beans	chips	grass	barber pole

Another means of visually comparing and contrasting information is through a Venn diagram (Herrmann, 1994). To construct a Venn diagram, draw two interconnecting circles (or ovals; see the Venn diagram example provided for *Gregory, the Terrible Eater* on the following page). Label each circle with the concept being compared (e.g., *people food* for one circle and *goat food* for the other). Next, list all ideas suggested by students in the appropriate circle. Any suggestions that are common to both circles are written in the overlapping area of the two circles.

Music

Students learn language through the rhythm and lyrics of songs, chants, and rhymes (Barclay and Walwer, 1992; Harp, 1988; McCracken and McCracken, 1986; Strong and Strong, 1995; Zoller, 1991). Music is included in several of the narrative-intervention units found in this book; the music activity is often located before story reading to serve as an extension of the preparatory set. For example, you might play the song entitled "Healthy Food" (Cerf, 1993) from a Sesame Street cassette recording. Write the lyrics from the program notes that accompany the cassette where every student can see them. Have students follow the words as they listen to the song. Discuss unfamiliar words. As the students

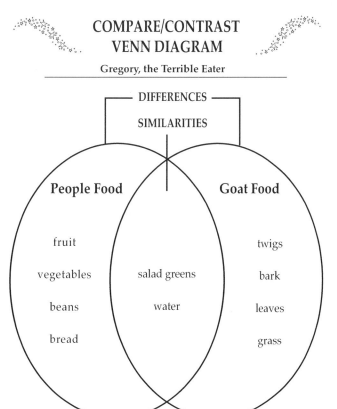

**COMPARE/CONTRAST
VENN DIAGRAM**

Gregory, the Terrible Eater

DIFFERENCES

SIMILARITIES

People Food

Goat Food

fruit

vegetables

beans

bread

salad greens

water

twigs

bark

leaves

grass

become familiar with the song, have them sing along with the tape and follow the written words to facilitate transfer from oral to literate language. Music can be used after the story presentation as well to extend learning and to reinforce concepts introduced during story reading.

Preparatory Sets

A preparatory set triggers students' prior knowledge of the story's topic (Alvermann et al., 1985; Langer, 1984; Pearson, Hansen, and Gordon, 1979). The activity should be interesting and meaningful so that students become engaged in the topic. When using a preparatory set, gear the activity to the students' grade level and ensure that it is culturally appropriate (Hamayan, 1989). For example, before reading *Gregory, the*

Terrible Eater, ask students questions such as "What are your favorite foods?" "What are some foods that you hate?" "What are the names of some junk foods?" and "Can you name some healthy foods?" Make lists of students' responses. Because more than one student will likely love a specific food, count the number of students who love each food and convert those numbers into a simple bar chart. Students can then visually compare the responses and learn about graphing and organizing information as well.

Introduce vocabulary words during the preparatory activity to trigger students' prior word knowledge. Select words for instruction that (1) are conceptually difficult; (2) can be grouped in some way, (3) are important for understanding the storybook, or (4) have wide applicability in general language use (Nagy, 1988). Select 3 to 5 words for early-elementary students, 6 to 9 words for middle-elementary students, and 6 to 12 words for upper-elementary/middle-school students. For *Gregory, the Terrible Eater*, selected words might be *average, revolting*, and *hamper*. Write each of the words on the front of a vocabulary card illustration. If room does not allow, use the back of the card. For this story, see Appendix D for the vocabulary card illustration for *Gregory, the Terrible Eater* [Unit 2E] that can be duplicated and laminated. (Note that the illustration to be used appears on the first page of each unit above the story synopsis.) The cards can be used throughout the story unit for review.

To begin, use the selected words in a familiar scenario. For example, use the information about students' favorite foods to develop their understanding of *average:* "You all said you loved pizza. The average boy or girl in this group loves pizza. Also, you all said you loved French fries. You're an average boy or girl, then, if you love French fries. In the story we're about to read, Gregory says he is an average goat. That means he thinks he's normal or ordinary. But actually, Gregory is not an average goat. He's not normal or ordinary. We'll find out why when we read the story."

Help students develop a definition for each word, using story information, students' background knowledge, and a dictionary (if necessary). Write each definition where all students can see it as well as on a blank vocabulary card.

For review, use the vocabulary and definition cards in a matching activity and have students match each word with its definition. You might also hang the cards in some convenient location. For students in the middle and upper grades, display the definition cards and have students recall and write down their matching vocabulary words. The vocabulary words can be used for spelling practice as well. Read each word aloud so that students can write the word from memory; then reveal the cards so that students can check their own spelling.

Semantic-Word Maps

To further prepare students for story listening and to engage them in the story's topic, use a semantic-word map (Hamayan, 1989; Heimlich and Pittelman, 1986) to provide a graphic display of word/concept relationships. For *Gregory, the Terrible Eater*, obtain a picture book about goats or farm animals from your school library. Have students scan the picture book and identify characteristics of goats. Write these characteristics in a list as

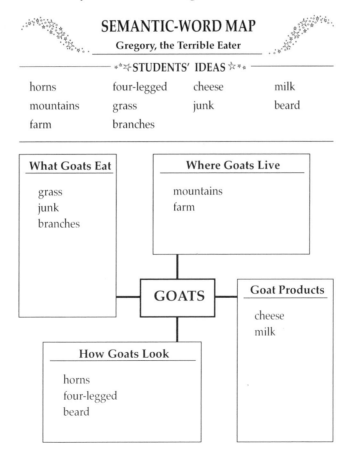

SEMANTIC-WORD MAP
Gregory, the Terrible Eater

STUDENTS' IDEAS

horns	four-legged	cheese	milk
mountains	grass	junk	beard
farm	branches		

What Goats Eat

grass
junk
branches

Where Goats Live

mountains
farm

GOATS

Goat Products

cheese
milk

How Goats Look

horns
four-legged
beard

they are identified. Then help students organize their list of ideas by labeling the categories on a blank semantic-word map (see Appendix C) and sorting their ideas by category. Students who have had experience developing semantic-word maps can work independently or in small groups to categorize the characteristics. Have students share their maps with the class. Refer to and revise the map during story reading. Another option is to use the maps after the story presentation as a guide for summarizing students' initial ideas and for categorizing new information gleaned from story reading. An example of a semantic-word map for *Gregory, the Terrible Eater* is shown on the previous page.

Think Alouds

To further help students with story comprehension, model aloud the kinds of strategies that you use when you begin to read a new book (Davey, 1983). To begin, tell students that they will only look at the pictures (or use the word *illustrations* for older students) for now; you will read the book to them the next time you meet. Point out the author and the illustrator. Take time to ensure that students understand the difference between the two. Then, show the book's cover, read the title, and demonstrate how to make predictions about the book's content. For *Gregory, the Terrible Eater* you might say, "From the cover, I know that this book is about a goat who is thinking about some 'people' foods, not 'goat' foods. How do I know he is thinking? I also know that the goat is surrounded by junk. Because the title is *Gregory, the Terrible Eater*, I predict that this book is about a goat who is not eating what goats usually eat." Or, after showing the cover and reading the title, simply ask, "What do you think the book is about?"

Continue to show the illustrations a page at a time and either think aloud for the students about what you predict will happen and why, or ask a prediction question. Do not correct students' misinterpretations; let them form their own opinions, and write down their predictions so that these can be verified later when the story is read. Stop the think-aloud activity before the story's problem is resolved so that the ending is not revealed. Once students understand how to make predictions from given information, reduce the amount of modeling that you provide and merely ask prediction questions.

During story reading, use the think-aloud strategy in four ways. First, think aloud about confusing information. For example, "I don't understand why Father Goat thinks that fruits, vegetables, and eggs are revolting. This is different from what I would expect. I would expect that some of these foods are good for goats. What would you expect?" Second, talk about the picture you're forming in your head about the story. Show the picture in which Gregory has thought bubbles over his head and say, "Gregory is thinking about vegetables, fish, and butter. I think that his parents look really worried. What do you suppose they are thinking?" Third, link students' prior knowledge with new information found in the story. For example, when Gregory eats too much junk and gets a stomachache, say, "This is like the time I went trick-or-treating and ate all of my candy in one day. I got a terrible stomachache, and I didn't do that again. Have you ever eaten too much and gotten a stomachache?" Finally, model repair strategies: "His parents say that it's all right to eat like a goat, but that it isn't all right to eat like a pig. I don't understand; I'd better read further and see what that means."

After reading the story, use the think-aloud strategy for problem solving. For example, "Gregory was eating everything in sight—clothes, the furniture. I wonder why Gregory's parents decided to bring him more junk to eat." Encourage students to use this prediction strategy whenever they read illustrated stories.

DURING-STORY PRESENTATION

Once you have gained your students' attention, you will want to maintain, nourish, and focus their attention on specific information, events, or relationships within the story. As you read the story aloud, four strategies will be particularly useful for strengthening students' story comprehension:

- directed reading/thinking activities

- extensions

- questioning

- summarizing

Usually, three to four of these strategies are included in each of the teaching units in *The Magic of Stories.*

Directed Reading/Thinking Activities

Encourage active listening and excitement about the story's events and ideas through directed reading/thinking activities (DRTAs) (Nessel, 1989; Nessel, Jones, and Dixon, 1989; Stauffer, 1981). When students raise questions, anticipate outcomes, and interpret implied meanings, they are clearly engaged in learning.

To use a DRTA, present students with a portion of the story and ask them to speculate about the story based on what they know at that point. Have students provide evidence for their opinions. Write down their predictions and then continue reading. Examples for *Gregory, the Terrible Eater* follow. If you did not provide think-aloud models and prediction questions for the book's cover, begin with the cover.

- Show the cover and say, "This goat is surrounded by junk, which goats sometimes like to eat. He has a big smile on his face and he's thinking about something. What do you think this book will be about?"

- Read to where Father and Mother Goat take Gregory to Dr. Ram. Ask, "What do you think Dr. Ram will do to get Gregory to eat right? Why do you think so?"

- Read to where Mother and Father Goat are at the town dump. Ask, "What do you think his parents will do to stop Gregory from eating too much? Why do you think so? What evidence or proof do you have?"

At the story's end, have students reflect on the theme and the actual events versus predicted events. Ask them to determine which predictions were correct; discuss the evidence that was used to make accurate predictions. Encourage students to make predictions during their personal reading. The DRTA not only enhances story comprehension, but it strengthens comprehension monitoring (Dollaghan and Kaston, 1986) in that students learn to detect and respond to comprehension breakdowns.

Extensions

When reading the story, words or phrases whose meanings are not clear to the students are likely to be encountered. Extensions (Barnes, Gutfreund, Satterly, and Wells,

1983; Muma, 1971) are a quick method of clarifying meanings and guiding students to more abstract understandings of particular words. Students have an opportunity to provide examples from their own experiences as well. For example, after reading Dr. Ram's statement, "I've treated picky eaters before…. They have to develop a taste for good food slowly," use the following extension to clarify *develop a taste*: "Dr. Ram says Gregory should try one new goat food each day—maybe he will develop a taste for goat food." Provide an example from your own experience: "When I was little, I hated cheese. I developed a taste for cheese by trying little bites of cheese once in awhile." Then ask the students, "Can you think of something you had to develop a taste for?" Such an extension clarifies the phrase *develop a taste* and prompts students to help with the clarification.

Questioning

Children's storybooks are replete with idiomatic expressions, instances of figurative language and irony, and words with multiple meanings. For students with language impairments, such expressions are particularly difficult to comprehend and use (Nippold, 1985). To support students' understanding, ask questions when the terms occur during story reading (Blank and White, 1986; Norris, 1991; Panofsky, 1986). For example, you might use the compare/contrast chart developed during the prestory presentation activities and ask questions during the story presentation to clarify students' understanding of junk food in the context of *Gregory, the Terrible Eater*. Review students' prior ideas. Then, as the story unfolds, revise or add to the goat-food lists by asking questions that will generate ideas about junk food alternatives for Gregory. Discuss the lists to emphasize their differences.

People Food		Goat Food	
Healthy	*Junk*	*Healthy*	*Junk*
fruit	candy	tin can label	tires
vegetables	fries	newspaper	car
bread	pop	necktie	violin
beans	chips	shoe	wire

The responses to your questions will reveal students' misconceptions so that these can be resolved. Use questioning to prompt predictions, inferences, classification of information (as in the previous junk-food example), justifications, and feelings (e.g., "How would you feel if the doctor said you had to try one new vegetable every day?").

Summarizing

Whenever you have stopped reading to clarify or extend word meanings or provide prediction opportunities, briefly summarize what has occurred thus far so that the flow (or wholeness) of the story will not be interrupted. Moreover, summarizing provides you with an opportunity to reorganize or reduce the story information into comprehensible units for students (Panofsky, 1986; Van Dijk and Kintsch, 1977). Before story reading, summarize the preparatory-set discussion. After story reading, summarize the theme and the episodes, thereby providing students with a model of story retelling.

Assist students in producing their own summaries by using an oral cloze procedure. That is, say part of a sentence, pause and look expectantly, and then have students complete the sentence. For example,

> *Mother and Father Goat thought that Gregory was a terrible* _____
> *(eater). All Gregory wanted to eat was* _____ *(fruits, vegetables, eggs,*
> *etc.). His parents thought he should be eating* _____ *(newspaper,*
> *boxes, rugs, etc.). So his parents took Gregory to Doctor* _____ *(Ram). Dr.*
> *Ram told them to give Gregory one new* _____ *(food) every day until he*
> *ate* _____ *(everything).*

Once students have had experience with producing summaries, have them develop their own.

POSTSTORY PRESENTATION

Once students have listened to the story with the support of the teaching strategies, read the story once again without pausing for questions, extensions, or summaries. Although teacher support is crucial for student understanding, it is equally important

that students hear the story as a whole without interruptions simply for the sheer joy of listening to an interesting story. Then, to extend students' learning beyond the story as well as reinforce concepts introduced within the story, have students participate in three or four additional learning opportunities. The remaining 13 narrative-teaching strategies are often used after the story presentation. They are presented in alphabetical order for easy access:

- art activities
- discussion webs
- dramatic play
- episode maps
- flow charts
- internal-states charts
- journals
- question-answer relationships
- story generation
- story-grammar cue charts
- story maps
- story retelling
- word substitutions

Art Activities

Select an art activity (Bartelo, 1984; Berney and Barrera, 1990) that provides students with a further means of understanding the story and for expressing their understanding. Students at all ability levels benefit from drawing, painting, or creating something associated with the story and then explaining their creations in oral or written form. An art activity may also be used before the story is read to activate students' background knowledge and to encourage active involvement in the story.

For *Gregory, the Terrible Eater*, provide the students with art supplies for making drawings. Have them think of one food that children like and one food that Gregory *developed a taste* for and draw each of these. When completed, have students label their pictures, show them to the group, and describe them. Display all drawings by category (food for people versus food for goats) so that students can compare the two.

Discussion Webs

Discussion webs (Alvermann, 1991; Duthie, 1986) are visual displays of a discussion topic. Successful use of this strategy requires that students participate in cooperative learning groups and that they listen, speak, read, and write during the activity. The discussion-web strategy focuses students less on *what* happened in the story and more on *why* events happened.

After reading *Gregory, the Terrible Eater*, introduce the discussion web with a brief summary of the story followed by a question, such as, "Gregory's parents followed Dr. Ram's advice and gave Gregory one new goat food each day. Gregory developed a taste for goat food. However, he began to eat everything in sight—the clothing and the furniture. Now his parents had a new problem—how to stop Gregory from eating too much

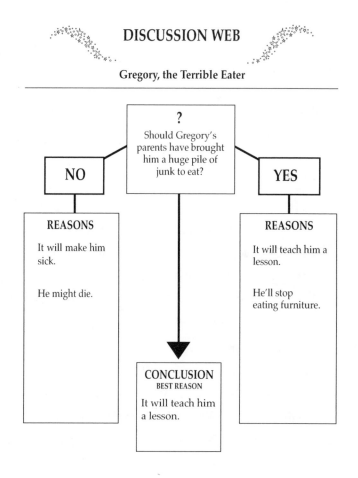

stuff. Should Gregory's parents have brought him the huge pile of junk to eat?" Write the question on a blank discussion-web form (see Appendix C) or develop a similar diagram where all students can see it. The example on the preceding page illustrates a discussion web created for *Gregory, the Terrible Eater*.

At first, support the discussion activity by working with the entire group. Have students identify pro and con reasons for whether Gregory's parents should have brought him the huge pile of junk to eat. Jot key words from their reasons in the appropriate columns. Then help students come to a conclusion and a consensus about whether the parents' solution was a good one and why. Fill in the students' conclusion and their best reason on the discussion web or have students do the writing. Ensure that students know it is acceptable for individual students to disagree with the group consensus (i.e., students have a chance to express dissenting views). Also stress that there is no right answer.

When students in middle and upper grades have had experience with discussion webs on several stories, place them in pairs, give them a discussion-web form, and ask each pair to discuss the pros and cons of the discussion-web question. Have students write down key words in the columns for their pro and con reasons. Then pair one set of partners with another set and ask the two sets to compare their reasons and to come to a consensus for the question. Next, have them decide which of the reasons provides the best support for the group's consensus. Select a spokesperson for the group. This person will present the consensus and the best supporting reason as well as report on any dissenting views. Older students could write their pro and con arguments, conclusions, and best supporting reasons using full sentences. Display their completed work in the room.

Dramatic Play

Dramatic play involves using props and assuming roles to reenact the events depicted in a story (Culatta, 1994). When students participate in dramatic play, they are learning a variety of language and literacy skills. For example, because they are using language to communicate with other students, they practice turn taking and topic maintenance. Within the meaningful reenactment context, they practice emerging syntactic structures and elaborate their semantic knowledge (e.g., greater understanding for the

multiple meanings of *junk food*). Moreover, students learn language and literacy goals concurrently as they associate the print from the story's text with the oral language of the reenactment (Culatta, 1994). Story reenactments provide opportunities for enhancing story comprehension as well as memory for story events (Putnam, 1991).

Reenacting stories may enhance story comprehension more for children in the primary grades than for older students (Christie, 1987). Because young students may lack experience with reenacting stories, some instructions for guiding the dramatization of a story may prove useful (Brown, Althouse, and Anfin, 1993):

1. Retell the story using a flannel board and felt figures (or a cookie sheet and figures with magnets glued on their backs).

2. Have each student adopt the role of a character and have them retell the story together while manipulating the flannel-board figures.

3. Discuss the child-sized props needed and acquire them.

4. Let the students dramatize the story using these props as you tell the story again.

5. Take four or five Polaroid photos of the students as they dramatize the story (or have an older student or aide take the photos while you work with the students). Discuss the photos and put them in sequential order. Under each photo, write related student comments. Then, read the dictated story to the students.

6. Encourage students to reenact the story on their own.

7. Using the photo prompts, have students retell the story into a tape recorder or onto Language Master cards. Let the students listen to their recorded stories.

Begin the story dramatization for *Gregory, the Terrible Eater* by asking students to volunteer for the character roles. After practicing steps 1 and 2, have students discuss the child-sized props needed. Props might include a shoelace and some spaghetti noodles for Mother Goat, an old coat and a newspaper for Father Goat, a banana or carrot for Gregory, and a prescription that says "one new food each day" for Dr. Ram. Once the props are gathered, proceed with steps 4 through 7.

Students at all grade levels enjoy reenacting a story for their parents. Students also benefit from having their reenactments videotaped and from reviewing the video-tape and discussing the performance. Students in middle and upper grades also enjoy reenacting the story for younger students.

Episode Maps

To extend students' story understanding, cooperatively develop graphic displays for teaching the story's events and the relationships among events (i.e., the narrative structure) (Herrmann, 1994). One model that can be used for describing the structure (or grammar) of a story and the order in which the story components typically occur is that of Stein and Glenn (1982). From this perspective, a story, in its simplest form, consists of the following components:

- setting (who, when, where)

- initiating event (a problem, predicament, or goal that the main character attempts to solve or attain)

- internal response (a character's emotional state, goal, or thoughts)

- attempt (an action to solve a problem or obtain a goal)

- consequence (what happened as a result of the action)

- reaction or resolution (the characters' feelings or thoughts about the outcome or story ending)

Using these same components, a more complex story consists of one setting and several episodes, with each episode containing at least one initiating event (or internal response), an attempt, and a consequence (Lahey, 1988; Page and Stewart, 1985).

When children grow up with much experience listening to stories, they internal-ize these story components and acquire a schema for "what a story should include." This internal schema facilitates story comprehension as well as story-retelling and story-gener-ation abilities. Students should have considerable experience listening to stories so that they can internalize their own schema naturally.

One well-known graphic display of a story's grammar is an episode map (Schmelzer and Dickey, 1990). When using episode maps, the focus is on the story's individual episodes. After the story has been read, cooperatively map out the story's episodes by using a blank episode map (see Appendix C) or by constructing a map where all students can see it. Schmelzer and Dickey (1990) included a theme in the map to emphasize the moral (or point) of the story. Two different blank maps are provided in Appendix C (one for a three-episode story and one for a four-episode story). Teach the students each story element on the blank map (problem, theme, setting, episodes, and resolution). The map can be completed as the story is read as well. The following is an example of an episode map for *Gregory, the Terrible Eater*.

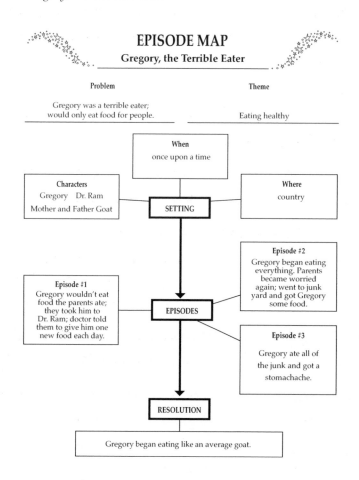

Flow Charts

Flow charts are an alternate means of organizing the story's information visually to demonstrate the interrelationship between ideas and concepts (Geva, 1983; Ollmann, 1989). The flow-chart organization is similar to that described for episode maps. However, Geva limited the story components to setting information, a problem, actions, and consequences.

When developing a flow chart, first encourage students' active participation by having them freely recall the story events. Some students find flow-chart construction less threatening than episode- or story-map construction because of this initial free recall of the story events. Again, the visual display of the story's events and the relationships

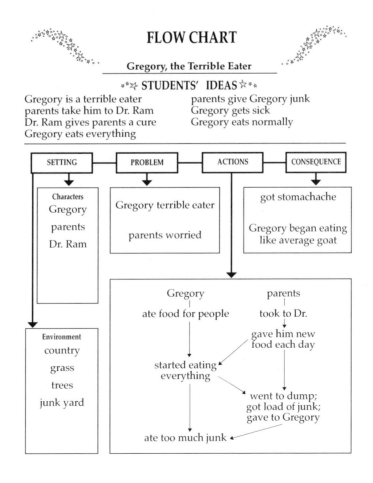

between events supports students' comprehension and their memory for story details when they retell the story.

To construct the flow chart, have students recall any major events from the story. Write their ideas where all students can see them, acknowledge their contributions, and then draw from their list as you construct the flow chart. Verbalize aloud your thought processes as you organize the information on the flow chart. Demonstrate how to use the storybook to check information or to generate any missing information. Once students have experience with developing flow charts, move them toward independent construction. An example of a flow chart for *Gregory, the Terrible Eater* is on the previous page.

Internal-States Charts

Use of the internal-states teaching strategy (Dunning, 1992; Hansen, 1981) allows you to focus your students on the thoughts and feelings of the characters. This subjective approach (Hewitt, 1994) will help students understand causal relationships within the story (why characters behaved in certain ways), thereby leading to better comprehension of the story as a whole. Moreover, a focus on thoughts and feelings emphasizes the need to put oneself in another's place (i.e., perspective taking)—a commonly observed weakness among students with language impairments.

To use the strategy, first encourage students to figure out the characters' feelings and thoughts as you read the story. Then, after story reading, ask questions related to the characters' feelings. For example:

Educator: At the beginning of the story, how did Gregory feel when his parents offered him tin cans and boxes to eat?

Students: He didn't like that kind of food.

Educator: Why didn't he like it?

Students: Because he liked eggs, fruits, and vegetables.

As students respond to the questions, note their responses on the internal-states chart to provide a visual reminder of the relationships among events, feelings, and reasons for

INTERNAL-STATES CHART
Gregory, the Terrible Eater

CHARACTER(S)	WHEN	FEELING	WHY
Gregory	Parents offered him tin cans and boxes	Unhappy	Wanted to eat fruits and vegetables
Mother and Father Goat	Gregory wouldn't eat their kinds of food	Worried	Thought something was wrong
Mother and Father Goat	Gregory ate everything	Worried	Gregory was in house eating like a pig
Gregory	He ate the pile of junk from the dump	Sick	Had eaten too much food

those feelings. As the relationships are clarified, story understanding as well as the ability to retell the story more completely will be enhanced. An example of an internal-states chart for *Gregory, the Terrible Eater* is provided above. To further enhance perspective taking, ask students questions about how they would feel in these same situations.

Journals

Journal writing provides an opportunity for students to express their feelings about or reactions to learning activities. Journal use promotes writing proficiency, positive attitudes toward writing, and the integration of information. Students write in their journals with the understanding that the educator will not comment on the grammatical form or the mechanics of writing, but will respond to the meaning or purpose of the written communication.

Two journal activities are especially useful within the narrative-intervention units. Use of reading/response journals (Wollman-Bonilla, 1989) enhances students' written personal communication about the story and the theme of the story. When using this approach, provide prompts such as the following for each journal-writing episode:

- What did you like or dislike about *Gregory, the Terrible Eater?*

- Do you think Dr. Ram's advice was good? Why?

- Should Gregory's parents have brought him all the junk from the town dump to eat?

As students gain experience with responding to literature selections, phase out the writing prompts.

Dialogue journals (Atwell, 1987; Staton, 1985) provide an opportunity for the student and educator to write to one another about a topic of mutual interest. The topic may or may not be centered on the narrative theme. Some topic examples follow:

- Favorite junk foods

- Recycling junk

- Strange foods that my pet likes

Again, do not correct grammatical form and mechanics; respond to the meaning and communicative intent of the students' writing. Some examples of educators' responses follow:

- What you wrote reminded me of…

- I enjoyed what you wrote because…

- I wondered about…

After responding in such a manner, either ask another question on the same topic or ask about a new topic.

If students do not yet write sentences or paragraphs, have them draw in response to a topic or question prompt and label their drawings. Then have students dictate their responses to someone who can write the responses underneath their drawings.

Vocabulary cards generated during the prestory presentation (see the discussion within the preparatory sets section on page 18) can also be used as a springboard for a weekly journal writing activity. After ensuring that students understand the meanings of the words, each student might select a word that relates to a personal experience. Have

each student briefly tell about the experience, using the selected vocabulary word. If a student fails to use the selected word, demonstrate how it might be used in the scenario. Then have each student write about the experience, using the selected word, as a journal entry for the week.

Question-Answer Relationships

The strategy of question-answer relationships (QARs) is based on the notion that the questions asked are formulated by considering both the story's topic and the listener's background knowledge about the topic (Raphael, 1984, 1986; Raphael and Pearson, 1982). There are four types of QARs. Answers for two of the question types (Right There, Think and Search) are "in the book." For Right-There QARs, the answer is in the story, within a single sentence, and is usually easy to find. For example, ask, "What is the name of one food that Gregory's parents ate?" For Think-and-Search QARs, the answer is also in the story, but the students have to put together information from different parts of the book, and the information is not as easy to find. For example, ask, "Why did Gregory's parents think he was a fussy eater?"

For the two remaining QARs (Author and You, On Your Own), the answers are found "in the students' heads." For Author-and-You QARs, the students must think about what they already know, what the author tells them, and how the two fit together. For example, ask students, "Was Gregory an average goat by the end of the story? Why or why not?" For On-Your-Own QARs, the answer is not in the story. In fact, students can answer this question type without ever listening to the story. They need only rely on their own experiences. For example, ask students, "Why is candy called *junk food?*"

Use the QAR strategy to test for story comprehension. As students improve in their comprehension skills, they will answer the latter two types of questions with increasing skill and confidence.

Story Generation

Because story generation is often a difficult task for students with language impairments (Milosky, 1987; Ripich and Griffith, 1985; Roth, 1986), use story-generation

activities late in the teaching unit. Have students tell/write a personal story or create and tell/write a story. You can support students' self-generated stories a number of ways (Trousdale, 1990). To begin, think of a story prompt. For *Gregory, the Terrible Eater*, have the students create a story about a person who ate too much of one type of food. Provide scaffolds for their stories in the following manner:

- Draw a story line for *Gregory, the Terrible Eater* where all students can see it. As a group, recount what happened in the story. Draw or write on the story line, moving from left to right. For example, at first, Gregory's parents tried to get him to eat newspaper and tin cans, but he wouldn't eat them, so "Gregory won't eat goat food" is written first on the story line. An example story line follows:

Gregory won't eat goat food	Parents take him to Dr. Ram	Tries one new goat food per day	Gregory eats everything		
1	2	3	4	5	6

- Model a brief story of your own (two to three episodes) about a person (or animal) who ate too much of one type of food.

- Draw a story line for your model story where all the students can see it.

- As a way to prepare students for writing and to generate ideas, have students think of their favorite junk foods. List their favorite foods underneath their names where everyone can see them. Have them select/identify the one junk food they like best and allow them to say why.

- As further preparation for writing, have each student list words on a sheet of paper related to the selected junk food; help students cluster their ideas (taste, size, cost, why the food is a favorite) on their papers. A semantic-word map can be used for clustering the ideas.

- Have students draw their own story lines on sheets of paper and use these lines to plan their own brief stories (i.e., only two or three episodes).

- Using their story lines, have students work in pairs and tell their stories to their partners before they start to write.

- Have students write their brief stories (or dictate their stories to an older student or aide).

- Have students read their stories aloud to their partners, edit, and revise. Then have students read their stories to the group.

- As students become more independent with generating stories, reduce the use of scaffolds.

Story-Grammar Cue Charts

The story-grammar cue chart (Graves and Montague, 1991) provides organizational support for students as they write the target story. As was the case with episode maps and flow charts, the story-grammar model used in this strategy is based on that developed by Stein and Glenn (1979). Again, each episode has an initiating event or internal response, plus an attempt, plus a consequence. The component "internal response" has been included within each episode to remind students to emphasize the characters' emotional states, goals, or thoughts. Use the story-grammar cue chart as a prompt for writing activities. When students can check off key elements as they write, they are better able to recall, organize, and develop the story parts in their writing. If necessary, provide a demonstration of how to add words, sentences, or paragraphs to the information on the chart to create a story.

To use the story-grammar cue chart, provide a brief review of the story-grammar components: The setting is when and where the story takes place, and it provides an introduction to the characters in the story; the problem is something that happens in the story that needs to be solved; the episodes include the actions that happen during the story, the consequences of those actions, and the internal responses of the characters (i.e., the characters' emotional states, goals, or thoughts); the ending is how the problem is solved; and the reaction is how the characters feel about the ending. Give students blank story-grammar cue charts (see Appendix C) for use while they plan their stories. Assist students with completing the information for their charts; have them use words or phrases, not full sentences, when filling in the information. Then, as they write their stories using sentences and paragraphs, direct them to check off the story parts they have included. An example story-grammar cue chart for *Gregory, the Terrible Eater* appears on the next page.

STORY-GRAMMAR CUE CHART

Gregory, the Terrible Eater

STORY GRAMMAR	STORY	CHECK-OFF
Setting:		☐
When:	Once upon a time	
Where:	In the country	
Who:	Gregory, Mother and Father Goat, Dr. Ram	
Problem:	Gregory was a terrible eater; Gregory wouldn't eat same food as parents; parents worried	☐
Episode #1:	Parents took Gregory to doctor; Dr. Ram said to give him one new food each day; Gregory began trying their food	☐
Internal Response:	Parents relieved	
Episode #2:	Gregory began eating everything in sight	☐
Internal Response:	Parents worried	
Episode #3:	Parents got a load of junk at dump; Gregory ate all	☐
Internal Response:	Got stomachache	
Episode #4:		☐
Internal Response:		
Ending:	Gregory began eating like an average goat	☐
Reaction:	Parents relieved; Gregory happy	

Story Maps

Story maps (Beck and McKeown, 1981; Davis and McPherson, 1989; Idol, 1987; Idol and Croll, 1985; Reutzel, 1984, 1986) provide another means (in addition to episode maps, flow charts, and story-grammar cue charts) for teaching the story's events and the relationships among events. When using story maps, the focus is on the total structure of the story and less on the individual episodes. After reading the story, cooperatively develop the story map where all students can see it, or photocopy the blank story map provided in Appendix C for each student. The story map can be completed as the story is read as well, providing a visual summary of the story that students can refer to as a reminder of previous events. An example story map, created for *Gregory, the Terrible Eater*, follows on page 39.

STORY MAP

Gregory, the Terrible Eater

SETTING

WHEN   One day

WHERE   In the country

WHO   Gregory, Mother and Father Goat, Dr. Ram

PROBLEM

Gregory was a terrible eater; wouldn't eat food
parents ate; Mother and Father Goat worried

EPISODE   Parents took Gregory to doctor; prescription: Give him
one new food each day until he eats everything

EPISODE   Gregory began eating everything; parents worried; went
to town dump and got some junk food

EPISODE   Gregory ate all the junk; got a stomachache

EPISODE

EPISODE

ENDING

ENDING   Gregory started eating like an average goat

REACTION   Gregory's parents pleased and not worried anymore

Story Retelling

Story retelling provides students with practice at organizing the story into a coherent whole and presenting it in an interesting manner (Morrow, 1985; Peck, 1989; Trousdale, 1990). When students have extensive experience with story retelling, they develop narrative-discourse skills as well as story-comprehension skills. With the development of these skills, students can better benefit from extended discussions, reports, explanations, retellings, and stories when in the classroom (Nelson, 1988).

Graphic support for students' story retellings may be available from an episode map, story map, or flow chart that was developed during previous sessions. Initially,

model a retelling of the story for the students using the map (or chart). Then, provide support for a group retelling of the story by using a cloze procedure, as in the example provided for the summarizing strategy on page 24. During small-group instruction, have individual students retell the story or place students in pairs to practice retelling the story into a tape recorder and to listen and self-evaluate their retellings. For large-group instruction, a shared retelling will likely be more efficient. For example, assign a key part of the story to each student. Then, have the retelling proceed in sequence with each student adding his or her part. Alternatively, have students write their retellings individually and have selected students read their retellings to their classmates.

When students are instructed to retell the entire story individually, assist them to rely on the graphic organizers developed during the unit. If students make sequencing errors during the retelling, guide them to use the correct sequence by referring to a map and/or chart available for the story.

Word Substitutions

To expand students' vocabulary beyond the words found within the storybook, use the word-substitution strategy (Beaumont, 1992). Select a sentence from the book that includes a difficult vocabulary word. Write the sentence where everyone can see it, emphasize the target word, and read the sentence stressing the target word, as in the following example sentence:

"Gregory was a *terrible* eater."

terrible (synonym)

awful

horrible

dreadful

terrible (antonym)

wonderful

marvelous

fantastic

For synonym instruction, assist students with identifying words that mean the same as the target word. Initially, provide a synonym example. Write your example underneath the target word and read the sentence again, replacing the target word with the synonym. Have students identify additional words that they think might mean the same as the target word, add their suggestions to the list, and reread the sentence with the new words inserted. Students may use a dictionary or thesaurus to locate synonyms. The strategy is equally useful for antonym instruction.

SUMMARY

This chapter summarized the 22 narrative-teaching strategies that are useful at different story-presentation stages (i.e., pre-, during-, and poststory) of clinical/classroom work. Examples of each strategy were provided for one storybook, *Gregory the Terrible Eater* (Sharmat, 1980). These 22 strategies are integrated within the narrative-teaching units for 30 different storybooks in the sections that follow. Use the Table of Contents, the Thematic/Topical Index, and the Teaching-Strategies Index when selecting teaching units for students. Moreover, use the 22 strategies with storybooks other than the 30 featured here to create your own magic.

NARRATIVE-TEACHING UNITS

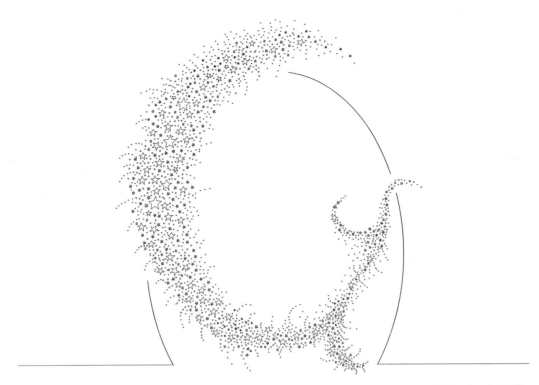

STORIES FOR EARLY-ELEMENTARY GRADES
(Kindergarten and Grades 1 and 2)

Unit 1E
GREAT WHITE BEAR

By Dan Slottje (1994). Greenwich, CT: Armstrong Publishing.
Unit developed by Jill Palmer.

A great white bear lived in the North near a group of Eskimos. The villagers feared him, except for a young girl named Light-Song. A tribal meeting was held to discuss what to do with the bear. Some wanted to kill it, but Light-Song's father disagreed. He said that the bear was protected by the gods, so they should not harm it. One night a great snowstorm fell on the village. Light-Song's mother went to check on her daughter, but she was gone. The bear sensed danger, so he left his den to go out into the storm. He found Light-Song and wrapped himself around her to protect her from the storm. In the morning, the bear carried Light-Song back to her village. The villagers were going to kill the bear until they realized that he had saved Light-Song's life. After that day, the great white bear was never seen again. Many believed that he went back to his "heavenly den." Years later, Light-Song became a leader for her people. (The story is written in rhyme.)

MATERIALS NEEDED

- Make 10 photocopies of the vocabulary card illustration for Unit 1E (see Appendix D), or more or less depending on the number of target words selected (see preparatory set discussion in this unit).

- Obtain a picture book about bears from the library.

- Photocopy a blank, six-category semantic-word map on an overhead transparency (or enlarge the map so all students can see it), or copy enough maps for all students in the group (see Appendix C).

- Photocopy a blank internal-states chart on an overhead transparency (or enlarge the chart so all students can see it), or copy enough charts for all students in the group (see Appendix C).

- Obtain art materials (white construction paper; polar bear ear and paw patterns from Appendix D; black marking pen; cotton balls; glue and scissors for each student).

PRESTORY PRESENTATION

Preparatory Set

See the instructions on page 18 for teaching selected story vocabulary words. Use the following vocabulary words selected for you, or select words appropriate for your specific students.

- sly
- dart
- lair
- deserted
- loyalty

Write each word on a vocabulary card illustration and write the corresponding definition on another card. After all cards have been created, have students match each word to its corresponding definition.

Semantic-Word Map

Obtain some books about bears from your school library. The book titled *Bears* (Jeunesse and Bour, 1989) is an excellent resource for young children. Have the students scan the books to acquire new information. Ask the students to name any words that relate to a bear. List these words where all students can see them, or list them on a semantic-word map. Have the students help organize these words into categories. The following is an example of a semantic-word map for *Great White Bear*.

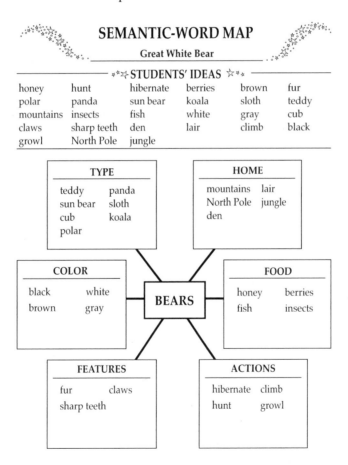

Think Alouds

Point to the cover and say, "I know that this book is about a polar bear that is a good friend to an Eskimo child. How do I know this?"

Read the title and say, "The title of the story is *Great White Bear*." Either model a prediction for the students (e.g., "Because the child is hugging the bear and they are both smiling, I predict the book will be about the friendship between this bear and the child") or ask a prediction question (e.g., "What do you predict this story will be about?").

Scan the illustrations only. Stop at selected points of the story to model a prediction or to ask prediction questions based only on the illustrations.

- What do you think these people in the circle are talking about? Why?

- Why is the mother crying? What has she discovered?

Write down the students' responses for discussion and comparison with actual events after reading the story. Stop the prestory think-aloud activity before the bear finds the child and curls up around her so the ending is not revealed.

DURING-STORY PRESENTATION

Think Alouds

Confusing Information—Read to where the polar bear is looking out at the storm from his den and say, "I don't understand how a polar bear senses danger during a winter storm. This is different than what I would expect. I would expect that the polar bear loves winter storms. What would you expect?"

Mental Picture—Read to where Light-Song's mother is crying and state, "Light-Song is missing and her mother looks really worried. Did you predict that Light-Song was missing when we looked at the pictures? What do you suppose the mother thinks has happened to her child? The idea that I have is that Light-Song is hiding in the corner because she is afraid of the storm. Where do you think Light-Song could be?"

Analogy—Read to where the storm is blowing hard and say, "This storm reminds me of one that scared me when I was a young child. The snow was falling so hard and the wind was blowing so much that I couldn't see very far in front of me. The

cold, strong wind even made some trees blow over. Have you ever seen a storm like this?"

Repair Strategy—Read to where the hunters have the bear cornered and say, "I don't understand why the hunters want to kill the bear. He saved Light-Song's life. I'd better read further to see if Light-Song can change their minds. Do you think she can? What could she say to them to convince them not to kill the bear?"

Extension

After reading the sentence, "The bear sensed danger," use the following extension to clarify *sensed danger:* "Yes, the bear had a feeling that something was very wrong even though he did not know what it was." Provide an example from your own experience: "Once, I sensed danger before an earthquake." Then ask the students, "What were some times when you sensed danger?"

Questioning

See the instructions on pages 23–24 for asking questions about the following figurative-language examples.

- There was *fear in the air.*

- The storm kept attacking with its *icy cold bite.*

- Many think he returned to his *heavenly den.*

POSTSTORY PRESENTATION

Think Alouds

After reading the story, state, "After the bear saved Light-Song's life, he was never seen again. I wonder why the people in the village thought that he died. Where else could he have gone?" Conduct a discussion about think-aloud questions. Compare students' responses before the story was read with the actual story events.

Summarizing

See the instructions on page 24 for summarizing after story reading. Provide the following cloze procedure summary in written form (omitting the answers in parentheses) where all students can see it. Have students follow along as you read it, and then pause for them to fill in the omitted words.

The hunters had him cornered with nowhere to flee.
He might die where he stood, but would fight to be _____ *(free).*

Light-Song ran to him and began stroking his fur.
The fierce, growling bear then started to _____ *(purr).*

The hunters watched the girl, then looked to the sky.
They thanked their gods for not letting her _____ *(die).*

They dropped all their clubs and then let the bear past.
The bear licked the girl, then ran off very _____ *(fast).*

Question-Answer Relationships

See the instructions on page 35 for the question-answer relationships strategy. The following are examples of questions to test students' comprehension of *Great White Bear* (question type is indicated in parentheses after each example):

- Why did the bear wake up the night of the storm? (Right There)

- How did the bear keep Light-Song warm all night? (Right There)

- Why did the villagers fear the bear? (Think and Search)

- Why did Light-Song's father say the gods protect the bear? (Think and Search)

- Why did Light-Song go out into the storm? (Author and You)

- What kept the bear warm all night? (Author and You)

- If a person saved one of your loved ones (e.g., friend, family member), how would you feel toward that person? (On Your Own)

- What do you do for other people when you are their loyal friend? (On Your Own)

Internal-States Chart

See the instructions on pages 32–33 for using the internal-states chart. Engage students in dialogue like the following regarding the characters' feelings:

Educator: How did the villagers feel when they saw the bear?

Students: The villagers were afraid of the bear.

Educator: Why were they afraid?

Students: Because the bear was large and frightening.

The following is an example of an internal-states chart for *Great White Bear*.

INTERNAL-STATES CHART
Great White Bear

CHARACTER(S)	WHEN	FEELING	WHY
Villagers	Saw the bear	Afraid	Bear was large and frightening
Light-Song's father	Tribal meeting	Respect	Felt the gods protected the bear
Bear	Night of the storm	Afraid	Sensed danger
Light-Song's mother	Night of the storm	Worried	Light-Song was missing
Light-Song's mother	After the storm	Relieved	Light-Song was returned
Bear	After the storm	Afraid	Villagers surrounded him
Light-Song	After the storm	Concerned	Villagers wanted to kill bear
Bear	End of story	Thankful	Light-Song saved his life

Art Activity

Art materials needed:

- One sheet of white construction paper, per student
- One set of patterns for the polar bear's ears and paws, per student
- Black marking pens
- Cotton balls
- Glue, scissors

Provide students with a model illustration of a polar bear. Provide materials for students to make their own. Direct students to follow these steps:

1. Trace the outline of your shoe on a sheet of white construction paper for the bear's body.

2. Cut out the patterns of the bear's ears and paws.

3. Draw the bear's eyes, nose, and mouth with a black marking pen.

4. Shred some cotton balls to look like fur. Glue the shredded cotton onto the body, and also onto the ears and paws. Glue the body parts onto the body.

5. Glue on a cotton ball for the bear's tail.

Have students write their names on their bears; tape the bears where all students can see them for the remainder of the unit.

Story Retelling

After listening to the story several times, have students retell the story and tape-record their retellings. Have students listen to their retellings. Have an aide or older peer help them with transcribing their retellings and with reading their own retellings.

Journals

Have the students draw a picture of their most loyal friend. If the students can write, have them write what they like about their friend. If the students do not write, have them dictate their descriptions and write for them in their journals next to their drawings.

Unit 2E
GREGORY, THE TERRIBLE EATER

By Mitchell Sharmat (1980). New York: Scholastic.
Unit developed by Carol J. Strong and Kelly Hoggan North.

Gregory the goat is a terrible eater. He won't eat healthy goat food (e.g., paper, cardboard), but he will eat human food (e.g., fruits, vegetables). His worried parents take Dr. Ram's advice and give him one new healthy goat food each day. The strategy works too well—Gregory eats all the healthy goat food in sight. His parents solve the problem by bringing him a huge pile of junk goat food from the town dump. Gregory eats it all at one time and gets a stomachache. From then on, Gregory eats healthy goat food, but he eats it in moderation.

MATERIALS NEEDED

- Make six photocopies of the vocabulary card illustration for Unit 2E (see Appendix D), or more or less depending on the number of target words selected (see preparatory set discussion in this unit).

- Obtain a picture book about goats from the library.

- Photocopy a blank, four-category semantic-word map on an overhead transparency (or enlarge the map so all students can see it), or copy enough maps for all students in the group (see Appendix C).

- Photocopy a blank internal-states chart on an overhead transparency (or enlarge the chart so all students can see it), or copy enough charts for all students in the group (see Appendix C).

- Photocopy a blank, three-episode map on an overhead transparency (or enlarge the map so all students can see it), or copy enough maps for all students in the group (see Appendix C).

- Obtain art materials (one sheet of white construction paper per student and colored markers).

PRESTORY PRESENTATION

Preparatory Set

Ask students questions such as "What are your favorite foods?" "What are some foods that you hate?" "What are the names of some junk foods?" and "Can you name some healthy foods?" Make lists of students' responses. Because more than one student will likely love a specific food, count the number of students who love each food and convert those numbers into a simple bar chart. Students can then visually compare the responses and learn about graphing and organizing information as well.

See the instructions on page 18 for teaching selected story vocabulary words. Use the following vocabulary words selected for you, or select words appropriate for your specific students.

- average
- revolting
- hamper

Write each word on a vocabulary card illustration and write the corresponding definition on another card. After all cards have been created, have students match each word to its corresponding definition.

Semantic-Word Map

Obtain a picture book about goats or farm animals from your school library. Have students scan the picture book and identify characteristics of goats. Write these

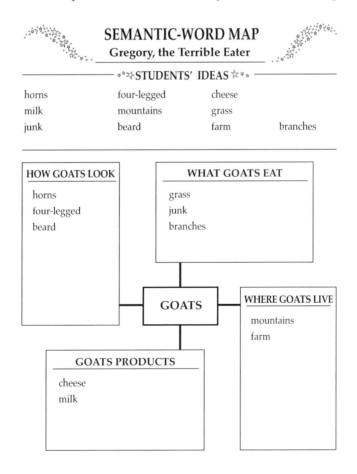

SEMANTIC-WORD MAP
Gregory, the Terrible Eater

STUDENTS' IDEAS

horns	four-legged	cheese	
milk	mountains	grass	
junk	beard	farm	branches

HOW GOATS LOOK
horns
four-legged
beard

WHAT GOATS EAT
grass
junk
branches

GOATS

WHERE GOATS LIVE
mountains
farm

GOATS PRODUCTS
cheese
milk

characteristics in a list as they are identified. Then help students organize their list of ideas by labeling the categories on a blank, four-category semantic-word map (see Appendix C) and sorting their ideas by category. An example of a semantic-word map for *Gregory, the Terrible Eater* is provided on the previous page.

Think Alouds

Show the cover and say, "From the cover, I know that this book is about a goat who is thinking about some "people" foods, not "goat" foods. How do I know he is thinking?"

Point to the title and state, "The title of this story is *Gregory, the Terrible Eater.*" Either model a prediction for the students (e.g., "The goat is surrounded by junk, but he is thinking about people foods. I predict that this book is about a goat who is not eating what goats usually eat"), or ask a question (e.g., "What do you predict this story is about?" or "What do goats usually eat?"). Or, after showing the cover and reading the title, you might simply ask, "What do you think the book is about?"

Scan the illustrations only. Stop at selected points of the story to model a prediction or to ask the students prediction questions.

- Why do you think Gregory is covering his mouth?

- What do you think Gregory's parents are talking to the doctor about?

- What do you think Gregory is eating now? Do you think he likes this kind of food?

- What is he eating now? Do you think his parents are happy that he's eating these things?

Write down the students' responses for discussion and comparison with actual events after reading the story. Stop the prestory think-aloud strategy where Gregory becomes sick so the end of the story will not be revealed.

DURING-STORY PRESENTATION

Directed Reading/Thinking Activity

If you did not provide think-aloud models and prediction questions for the book's cover, begin with the cover.

- Show the cover and say, "This goat is surrounded by junk, which goats sometimes like to eat. He has a big smile on his face and he's thinking about something. What do you think this book will be about?"

- Read to where Father and Mother Goat take Gregory to Dr. Ram. Ask, "What do you think Dr. Ram will do to get Gregory to eat right? Why do you think so?"

- Read to where Mother and Father Goat are at the town dump. Ask, "What do you think his parents will do to stop Gregory from eating too much? Why do you think so? What evidence or proof do you have?"

After the story is complete, have the students determine which of their predictions were correct.

Extension

After reading Dr. Ram's statement, "I've treated picky eaters before…. They have to develop a taste for good food slowly," use the following extension to clarify *develop a taste:* "Dr. Ram says Gregory should try one new goat food each day—maybe he will develop a taste for goat food." Provide an example from your own experience: "When I was little, I hated cheese. I developed a taste for cheese by trying little bites of cheese once in awhile. Then ask the students, "Can you think of something you had to develop a taste for?"

Questioning

See the instructions on pages 23–24 for asking questions about the following figurative-language examples:

- I think this is a meal *fit for a goat*.

- It's all right to eat like a goat, but you shouldn't *eat like a pig*.

POSTSTORY PRESENTATION

Think Alouds

After reading the story, use the think-aloud strategy for problem solving. For example, say, "Gregory was eating everything in sight—clothes, the furniture. I wonder why Gregory's parents decided to bring him more junk to eat." Conduct a discussion about think-aloud questions. Compare students' responses before the story was read with the actual story events.

Question-Answer Relationships

See the instructions on page 35 for the question-answer relationships strategy. The following are examples of questions to test students' comprehension of *Gregory, the Terrible Eater* (question type is indicated in parentheses after each example):

- What is the name of one food that Gregory's parents ate? (Right There)

- What type of food did Gregory like to eat? (Right There)

- Why did Gregory's parents think he was a fussy eater? (Think and Search)

- What are two things Gregory's parents did to help him eat like a goat? (Think and Search)

- Why did Gregory get a stomachache? (Author and You)

- Was Gregory an average goat by the end of the story? Why or why not? (Author and You)

- Why is candy called junk food? (On Your Own)

- Why should you try to eat less junk food and more healthy food? (On Your Own)

Internal-States Chart

See the instructions on pages 32–33 for using the internal-states chart. Engage students in dialogue like the following regarding the characters' feelings:

Educator:	At the beginning of the story, how did Gregory feel when his parents offered him tin cans and boxes to eat?
Students:	He didn't like that kind of food.
Educator:	Why didn't he like it?
Students:	Because he liked eggs, fruits, and vegetables.

The following is an example of an internal-states chart for *Gregory, the Terrible Eater*.

INTERNAL-STATES CHART
Gregory, the Terrible Eater

CHARACTER(S)	WHEN	FEELING	WHY
Gregory	Parents offered him tin cans and boxes	Unhappy	Wanted fruits and vegetables
Mother and Father Goat	Gregory wouldn't eat goat food	Worried	Thought something was wrong
Mother and Father Goat	Gregory ate everything in house	Worried	Gregory eating like a pig
Gregory	He ate the pile of junk from the dump	Sick	Had eaten too much food

Word Substitution

See the instructions on pages 40–41 for word-substitution exercises. The following is an example sentence with its target word emphasized, followed by lists of synonyms and antonyms:

Gregory was a *terrible* eater.

terrible (synonym)	*terrible* (antonym)
awful	wonderful
horrible	marvelous
dreadful	fantastic

Episode Map

See the instructions on pages 29–30 for developing an episode map. For students who do not read, provide stick-figure drawings for the characters and for each of the episodes. The following is an example of an episode map for *Gregory, the Terrible Eater*.

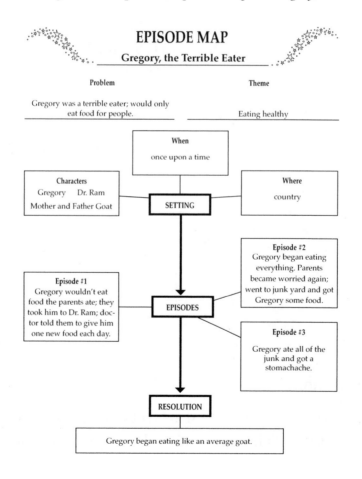

EPISODE MAP

Gregory, the Terrible Eater

Problem

Gregory was a terrible eater; would only eat food for people.

Theme

Eating healthy

When

once upon a time

Characters

Gregory   Dr. Ram

Mother and Father Goat

SETTING

Where

country

Episode #2

Gregory began eating everything. Parents became worried again; went to junk yard and got Gregory some food.

Episode #1

Gregory wouldn't eat food the parents ate; they took him to Dr. Ram; doctor told them to give him one new food each day.

EPISODES

Episode #3

Gregory ate all of the junk and got a stomachache.

RESOLUTION

Gregory began eating like an average goat.

Story Retelling

Model story retelling for the students using the episode map. Then, provide support for a group retelling by using a cloze procedure. That is, say part of a sentence, pause and look expectantly, and then have students complete the sentence. The procedure could go as follows:

Mother and Father Goat thought that Gregory was a terrible _____ (eater). All Gregory ate was _____ (fruits, vegetables, etc.). His parents thought he should be eating _____ (newspaper, boxes, etc.). So his parents took Gregory to Doctor _____ (Ram). Dr. Ram told them to give Gregory one new _____ (food) every day until he eats _____ (everything).

So, that's what Gregory's parents did, and Gregory began eating goat _____ (food). But his parents had a new problem. Now Gregory was eating everything in the _____ (house).

So, Gregory's parents went to the town _____ (dump) and got him a huge pile of _____ (junk). Gregory ate it all up at one time and got a _____ (stomachache). He learned his lesson and started eating like an average _____ (goat), and he didn't _____ (overeat).

Then have students retell the story individually using the episode map. Tape-record their retellings and let them listen to their retellings.

Journals

Provide a writing or drawing prompt for each journal-writing episode. Some prompts for reading/response journals follow:

- What did you like or dislike about *Gregory, the Terrible Eater?*

- Do you think Dr. Ram's advice was good? Why?

- Should Gregory's parents have brought him all the junk from the town dump to eat? Why?

Some dialogue-journal topic examples follow:

- Favorite junk foods

- Recycling junk

- Strange foods that my pet likes

Direct students who do not write to explain their pictures. Write their responses next to their drawings.

Art Activity

Art materials needed:

- One sheet of white construction paper per student
- Colored marking pens

Provide the students with art supplies for making drawings. Have them think of one food that children like and one food that Gregory developed a taste for and draw each of these. When completed, have students label their pictures, show them to the group, and describe them. Display all drawings by category (food for people versus food for goats) so that students can compare the two.

Story Generation

Have students create a story about a person who ate too much of one type of food. Provide scaffolds for their stories in the following manner:

- Draw a story line for *Gregory, the Terrible Eater* where all students can see it. As a group, recount what happened in the story. Draw or write on the story line, moving from left to right:

Gregory won't eat goat food	Parents take him to Dr. Ram	Tries one new goat food per day	Gregory eats everything		
1	2	3	4	5	6

- Model a brief story of your own (two to three episodes) about a person (or animal) who ate too much of one type of food.

- Draw a story line for your model story where all students can see it.

- As a way to prepare students for writing and to generate ideas, have students think of their favorite junk foods. List their favorite foods underneath their names where everyone can see them. Have them select/identify the one junk food they like best and allow them to say why.

- As further preparation for writing, have each student list words on a sheet of paper related to the selected junk food; help students cluster their ideas (taste, size, cost, why the food is a favorite) on their papers. A semantic-word map can be used for clustering the ideas.

- Have students draw their own story lines on sheets of paper and use these lines to plan their own brief stories (i.e., only two or three events).

- Using their story lines, have students work in pairs and tell their stories to their partners before they start to write.

- Have students write their brief stories (or dictate their stories to an older student or aide).

- Have students read their stories aloud to their partners, edit, and revise. Then have students read their stories to the group.

- As students become more independent with generating stories, reduce the use of scaffolds.

Unit 3E
SAM IS MY HALF BROTHER

By Lizi Boyd (1990). New York: Viking Penguin.
Unit developed by Shwu-Jiuan Wang and Carol J. Strong.

Hessie's father and stepmother called from the hospital to tell her that she had a new baby brother named Sam. Hessie was afraid that Sam would get all the attention and love. When summer vacation began, Hessie went to the lake house and lived with her father, stepmother, and Sam. During this time she was unhappy and jealous of Sam. Her father discovered her fears and reassured her. She learned that having a half brother didn't mean she was not a whole daughter.

MATERIALS NEEDED

- Make 10 photocopies of the vocabulary card illustration for Unit 3E (see Appendix D), or more or less depending on the number of target words selected (see preparatory set discussion in this unit).

- Photocopy a blank story map on an overhead transparency (or enlarge the map so all students can see it), or copy enough story maps for all students in the group (see Appendix C).

- Photocopy a blank internal-states chart on an overhead transparency (or enlarge the chart so all students can see it), or copy enough charts for all students in the group (see Appendix C).

PRESTORY PRESENTATION

Semantic-Word Map

Draw two family trees where all students can see them. Draw one as your own family tree, and discuss the various branches with students. Explain to them what each branch represents. Then draw a fictional family tree depicting half brothers and half sisters. Tell the students that we all have different family trees with branches that represent all of the people in our families. Encourage the students to draw their own family trees with help from their parent(s) or caregiver at home. Have them bring the family trees back to school to share with the group.

Preparatory Set

Talk about the concept of *half*. Show an object and divide it into two parts. For example, cut an apple into two parts or tear a piece of paper into two pieces. Have the students provide some examples of *half*. Point out the title of the book. Ask students to guess the meaning of *half brother*.

See the instructions on page 18 for teaching selected story vocabulary words. Use the following vocabulary words selected for you, or select words appropriate for your specific students.

- disappointed
- sneak
- peek

- shriek
- discover

Write each word on a vocabulary card illustration and write the corresponding definition on another card. After all cards have been created, have students match each word to its corresponding definition.

Think Alouds

Show the cover and say, "From the cover, I know that this book is about a girl who enjoys playing with a baby. How do you think I know this?"

Point to the title and state, "The title of the story is *Sam Is My Half Brother*." Either model a prediction for the students (e.g., "I predict that this story will be about a girl who takes care of her half brother") or ask a prediction question (e.g., "What do you think the story will be about?").

Scan the illustrations only. Stop at selected points of the story to model a prediction or to ask prediction questions.

- Who do you think that man is calling? What could he be saying to the person he is talking to?

- Why is the little girl crying? What do you think her daddy will say to her to make her feel better?

Write down the students' responses for discussion and comparison with actual events after reading the story. Stop the prestory think-aloud strategy where Hessie is sitting on Daddy's lap in the forest so the end of the story will not be revealed.

DURING-STORY PRESENTATION

Think Alouds

Analogy—Read to where Hessie is having a hard time sleeping because Sam is crying and state, "This reminds me of a time I couldn't sleep because the neighbors were playing loud music. I was very tired, but the noise was so loud that I couldn't fall asleep. It made me really mad. Has something like this ever happened to you?"

Confusing Information—Read to where Hessie wishes she was still an only child and say, "I don't understand why Hessie still wishes she was an only child. This is different than what I would expect. I would expect her to be excited about having a new baby brother. Why do you think she wants to be the only child?"

Repair Strategy—Read to where Hessie thinks that Daddy and Molly like her only half as much as Sam and state, "I don't understand why Hessie thinks that Daddy and Molly don't like her. I think they like her just as much as they like Sam because she is their daughter. I'd better keep reading to find out what Daddy will say to make Hessie feel better. What do you think he will tell her?"

Mental Picture—Read to where Hessie decides to be "the best big sister." Show the picture and say, "Hessie is imagining some things that she can do to be a good big sister to Sam. The idea that I have is that she is really going to like doing things for her brother. Can you think of some other things Hessie may do to be a good big sister to Sam?"

Extension

After reading the sentence, "Next summer, I'll take you to my secret place in the woods," use the following extension to clarify *secret place:* "Yes, Hessie's secret place was a quiet place where she could think and play. No one knew where her secret place was." Provide an example from your own experience: "My secret place is in the back corner of my basement behind some big boxes. I go there to think, read, or just be alone. But now

69

I've told you where it is, so it's not a secret anymore." Then ask the students, "Do you have a secret place to take a special friend?" Explain that if they tell where it is, the place will no longer be secret.

Questioning

See the instructions on pages 23–24 for asking questions about the following figurative-language example:

- Sam's ears are *new to this world.*

POSTSTORY PRESENTATION

Think Alouds

After reading the story, state, "At first, Hessie didn't like Sam because he got all of Molly and Daddy's attention. Hessie didn't tell Daddy how she was feeling. She just ran to the woods and cried. What should Hessie have said to Daddy so he would understand her feelings?" Conduct a discussion about think-aloud questions. Compare students' responses before the story was read with the actual story events.

Summarizing

See the instructions on page 24 for summarizing after story reading. Use an oral cloze procedure like the following with students.

Hessie ran to the _____ (woods). She sat on her big _____ (rock) and sulked. "Babies, babies, babies! There are too many _____ (rules). You can't _____ (shout). You can't wake them _____ (up). They wiggle and _____ (squirm) when you hold them. And everything is baby this and baby _____ (that)! You're always waiting for the _____ (baby)! I want to go _____ (home)."

Ask, "What does Hessie mean when she says, 'I want to go home'?"

Story Map

See the instructions on page 38 for developing a story map. For students who do not read, provide stick-figure drawings for the characters and for each episode. The following is an example of a story map for *Sam Is My Half Brother*.

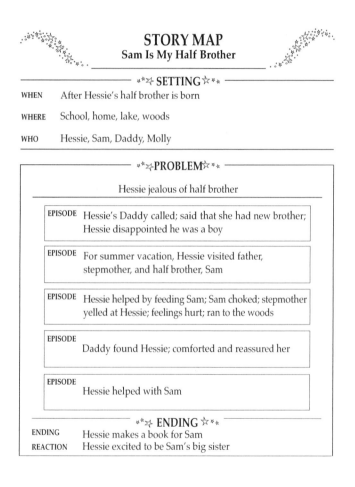

STORY MAP
Sam Is My Half Brother

✳ SETTING ☆ ✳

WHEN	After Hessie's half brother is born
WHERE	School, home, lake, woods
WHO	Hessie, Sam, Daddy, Molly

✳ PROBLEM ☆ ✳

Hessie jealous of half brother

EPISODE	Hessie's Daddy called; said that she had new brother; Hessie disappointed he was a boy
EPISODE	For summer vacation, Hessie visited father, stepmother, and half brother, Sam
EPISODE	Hessie helped by feeding Sam; Sam choked; stepmother yelled at Hessie; feelings hurt; ran to the woods
EPISODE	Daddy found Hessie; comforted and reassured her
EPISODE	Hessie helped with Sam

✳ ENDING ☆ ✳

ENDING	Hessie makes a book for Sam
REACTION	Hessie excited to be Sam's big sister

Word Substitution

See the instructions on pages 40–41 for the word-substitution strategy. The following is an example sentence with its target word emphasized, followed by a list of synonyms:

"But I don't want to WAIT!" Hessie *whined*.

whined

griped

whimpered

cried

complained

Question-Answer Relationships

See the instructions on page 35 for the question-answer relationships strategy. The following are examples of questions to test students' comprehension of *Sam Is My Half Brother* (question type is indicated in parentheses after each example):

- Who is Hessie's half brother? (Right There)

- What's the meaning of *stepmother?* (Author and You)

- Why does Hessie feel jealous of Sam? (Think and Search)

- Why does Sam always cry? (Author and You)

- What did Hessie make for Sam? (Right There)

- How does Hessie feel about Sam? (Think and Search)

- What does *half brother* mean? (On Your Own)

- What can big brothers and sisters do to help when there is a new baby in the house? (On Your Own)

Dramatic Play

Reenact the story using guided dramatic play. See the instructions on pages 27–29.

Internal-States Chart

See the instructions on pages 32–33 for using the internal-states chart. Engage the students in dialogue like the following regarding the characters' feelings:

Educator: How did Hessie feel when Sam was born?

Students: Hessie felt disappointed.

Educator: Why was she disappointed?

Students: Because she wanted a sister.

The following is an example of an internal-states chart for *Sam Is My Half Brother*.

INTERNAL-STATES CHART
Sam Is My Half Brother

CHARACTER(S)	WHEN	FEELING	WHY
Hessie	Sam born	Disappointed	Wanted a sister
Hessie	Got to see Sam	Curious	Never seen Sam before
Hessie	Sam spit up	Disgusted	He was a mess
Hessie	Had to work in garden	Whiny	Wanted to go swimming
Hessie	Shouted at ducks	Upset	Scolded for shouting and had hurt feelings
Hessie	Fed bread to Sam	Sad	Scolded for trying to feed the baby
Hessie	Daddy found her in the woods	Happy	Daddy still loved her; she could be Sam's big sister

Unit 4E   "STAND BACK," SAID THE ELEPHANT, "I'M GOING TO SNEEZE!"

By Patricia Thomas (1990). New York: Lothrop, Lee & Shepard.
Unit developed by Kelly Hoggan North.

An elephant warned his jungle friends that he needed to sneeze. The animals tried to convince the elephant not to sneeze; they reminded him of the chaos that occurred when he last sneezed. The elephant explained that he must sneeze. Then, when he was on the verge of sneezing, a mouse jumped from behind a rock and frightened the elephant so badly that he forgot to sneeze. When the mouse reminded the elephant that he forgot to sneeze, the elephant began to laugh. His loud laugh caused the same chaos in the jungle that would have occurred had he sneezed. The mouse, who fell into a puddle as a result of the laugh, told the elephant to laugh softly next time. (The story is written in rhyme.)

MATERIALS NEEDED

- Make 10 photocopies of the vocabulary card illustration for Unit 4E (see Appendix D), or more or less depending on the number of target words selected (see preparatory set discussion in this unit).

- Obtain pictures or books about elephants from the library.

- Photocopy a blank, five-category semantic-word map on an overhead transparency (or enlarge the map so all students can see it), or copy enough maps for all students in the group (see Appendix C).

- Photocopy a blank internal-states chart on an overhead transparency (or enlarge the chart so all students can see it), or copy enough charts for all students in the group (see Appendix C).

- Photocopy a blank flow chart on an overhead transparency (or enlarge the chart so all students can see it), or copy enough charts for all students in the group (see Appendix C).

- Obtain art materials for the journal/art activity, each student's journal and one pencil per student; for the dramatic play/art activity, materials to create props (e.g., construction paper, colored pencils, scissors, glue, masking tape).

PRESTORY PRESENTATION

Preparatory Set

Conduct a discussion about sneezing. Ask the students the following questions:

- What is a sneeze?

- What causes a sneeze?

- Do animals sneeze?

- What do sneezes feel like?

- When do people sneeze?

The questions can be answered in unison or individually, or the children may act out some of the answers.

See the instructions on page 18 for teaching selected story vocabulary words. Use the following vocabulary words selected for you, or select words appropriate for your specific students.

- hurricane
- shriek
- confusing
- scale
- quiver

Write each word on a vocabulary card illustration and write the corresponding definition on another card. After all cards have been created, have students match each word to its corresponding definition.

Semantic-Word Map

Conduct a discussion about elephants. Ask the students to think of every word they can related to elephants. Look at pictures, magazines, and books about elephants to obtain information. Help the students organize the words into categories. An example of a semantic-word map for *"Stand Back," Said the Elephant, "I'm Going to Sneeze!"* is provided on the following page.

Think Alouds

Show the cover and say, "From the cover, I know that this book is about an elephant who is going to do something to make all the jungle animals run away from him. How do you think I know this?"

Point to the title and state, "The title of the story is *'Stand Back,' Said the Elephant, 'I'm Going to Sneeze!'*" Either model a prediction (e.g., "I predict that this story will be about an elephant who sneezes so hard that it frightens all the jungle animals away") or ask a prediction question (e.g., "What do you think the story will be about?").

Scan the illustrations only. Stop at selected points of the story to model a prediction or to ask prediction questions.

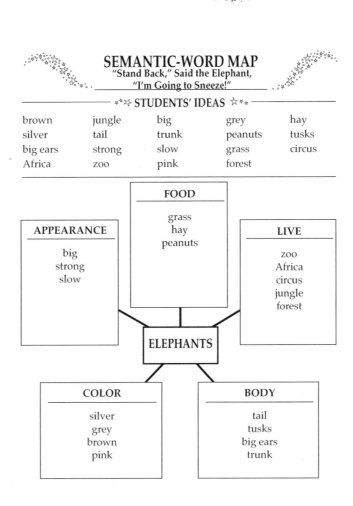

SEMANTIC-WORD MAP
"Stand Back," Said the Elephant,
"I'm Going to Sneeze!"

— *✶ STUDENTS' IDEAS ✶* —

brown	jungle	big	grey	hay
silver	tail	trunk	peanuts	tusks
big ears	strong	slow	grass	circus
Africa	zoo	pink	forest	

FOOD

grass
hay
peanuts

APPEARANCE

big
strong
slow

LIVE

zoo
Africa
circus
jungle
forest

ELEPHANTS

COLOR

silver
grey
brown
pink

BODY

tail
tusks
big ears
trunk

- What do you think the elephant is doing with his trunk wrapped around that tree?

- What happened to make the bear drop his honey? What do you think he is afraid of?

Write down the students' responses for discussion and comparison with actual events after reading the story. Stop the prestory think-aloud strategy before the mouse jumps out to scare the elephant so the ending of the story will not be revealed.

DURING-STORY PRESENTATION

Directed Reading/Thinking Activity

Read to where the elephant is just about to sneeze. Have the students predict whether he will actually sneeze and what could possibly happen to keep him from sneezing. Write these predictions where all students can see them. (After the story is complete, have the students determine if their predictions were correct.)

Extension

After reading the sentence, "It was very confusing and not too amusing," use the following extension to clarify *not too amusing:* "Yes, it was not too amusing. The whales had peacock tails and the wings of the cockatoo were stuck on the kangaroo." Provide an example from your own experience: "It was not too amusing when I tripped on a branch and landed right in a mud puddle." Then ask the students, "Can you think of something not too amusing?"

Questioning

See the instructions on pages 23–24 for asking questions about the following figurative-language examples:

- Nothing's so bad as a *bear that is bare.*

- Your sneeze is a *gale…or a hurricane!*

- Every parakeet was *bare as a sheet* from his head to his feet.

POSTSTORY PRESENTATION

Think Alouds

After reading the story, state, "I know of some ways to prevent a sneeze. Can you think of some things you have tried to prevent a sneeze? Do you think there is anything

else the mouse could have done to stop the elephant from sneezing besides scaring him?" Conduct a discussion about think-aloud questions. Compare students' responses before the story was read with the actual story events.

Question-Answer Relationships

See the instructions on page 35 for the question-answer relationships strategy. The following are examples of questions to test students' comprehension of *"Stand Back," Said the Elephant, "I'm Going to Sneeze!"* (question type is indicated in parentheses after each example):

- Where were the wings of the cockatoo stuck? (Right There)

- What did the bees use for stingers? (Right There)

- What made the elephant forget that he needed to sneeze? (Think and Search)

- Why did the mouse shout "BOO"? (Think and Search)

- Why did the elephant begin to giggle after he forgot to sneeze? (Author and You)

- How would an elephant's sneeze be different from a human's sneeze? (Author and You)

- Why do you think this elephant was afraid of mice? (On Your Own)

- What can you do when you're going to sneeze? (On Your Own)

Internal-States Chart

See the instruction on pages 32–33 for using the internal-states chart. Engage the students in dialogue like the following regarding the characters' feelings:

Educator: How did the elephant feel when he needed to sneeze?

Students: The elephant felt sorry.

Educator: Why did he feel sorry?

Students: Because the last time he sneezed, he hurt his friends.

The following is an example of an internal-states chart for *"Stand Back," Said the Elephant, "I'm Going to Sneeze!"*

INTERNAL-STATES CHART
"Stand Back," Said the Elephant, "I'm Going to Sneeze!"

CHARACTER(S)	WHEN	FEELING	WHY
Elephant	Had to sneeze	Sorry	Wanted to protect his friends
Jungle animals	Tried to get elephant not to sneeze	Scared	Afraid they would be hurt
Mouse	Scared elephant	Mischievous	Wanted to give elephant a scare

Flow Chart

See the instructions on pages 31–32 for using a flow chart. An example of a flow chart for *"Stand Back," Said the Elephant, "I'm Going to Sneeze!"* is provided on the following page.

Story Retelling

Retell the story to the students (using the flow chart as a guide) to provide a model of connected speech. Then help students produce the story in extended language units by using a cloze procedure. An example of a retelling using the cloze procedure is provided here:

> *An elephant warned his jungle friends that he needed to _____ (sneeze). The animals tried to convince the elephant not to _____ (sneeze); they reminded him of what happened the last time he _____ (sneezed). The*

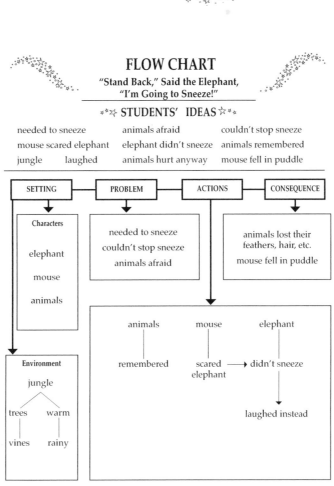

FLOW CHART
"Stand Back," Said the Elephant,
"I'm Going to Sneeze!"

☆ STUDENTS' IDEAS ☆

needed to sneeze	animals afraid	couldn't stop sneeze
mouse scared elephant	elephant didn't sneeze	animals remembered
jungle laughed	animals hurt anyway	mouse fell in puddle

elephant explained that he must _____ (sneeze). When he was just about to sneeze, a mouse jumped from behind a rock and _____ (scared) him. The elephant was so scared that he forgot to _____ (sneeze). When the mouse reminded the elephant that he forgot to sneeze, the elephant began to _____ (laugh). His laugh was very _____ (loud), which caused his jungle friends to lose all of their _____ (fur) and _____ (feathers). And the mouse fell into a _____ (puddle). The mouse told the elephant to laugh _____ (softly) next time.

Then have each student retell the story to a partner. Finally, have each student retell the story into a tape recorder. Let them listen to their stories.

Journals/Art Activity

Art materials needed:

- Each student's journal
- Pencils

Ask the students to draw pictures in their journals of their favorite part of the story and then explain their drawings. Have students label their drawings and write a brief description on the journal page. For students who do not read or write, write down their dictated explanations on the journal page and read their explanations for them.

Dramatic Play/Art Activity

Examples of art materials needed to create props:

- Construction paper
- Colored pencils or marking pens
- Scissors
- Glue
- Masking tape

See the instructions on pages 27–29 for guided dramatic play. After students have volunteered for roles, discuss the necessary props for each animal in *"Stand Back," Said the Elephant, "I'm Going to Sneeze!"* Then have students make their props for the reenactment. For example, direct the student who will play the zebra to cut out some black stripes and tape them to his or her body. When the elephant begins to laugh, have the student tear the stripes off. Direct the student playing a bird to make some feathers and to tear them off during the laughing scene.

Unit 5E
STREGA NONA

By Tommie de Paola (1975). New York: Scholastic.
Unit developed by Kari A. Fabrizio.

An old woman named Strega Nona hired Big Anthony to help clean her house and tend her garden. She instructed Big Anthony never to touch her magic pasta pot because it was very valuable. Big Anthony saw Strega Nona sing a song to the magic pot, which caused the pot to make pasta. After the pasta was made, she sang another song and blew three kisses to make the pasta stop. The next time Strega Nona left the house, Big Anthony took the pot and sang the song to make pasta for the entire village. When they were finished eating, Anthony sang the other song but did not know that he should blow the three kisses. The pasta overflowed and began to cover the village. When Strega Nona returned, she stopped the pasta and saved the village. She punished Anthony by making him eat all the pasta.

MATERIALS NEEDED

- Obtain different kinds of pasta and pictures of pasta dishes.

- Photocopy a blank, five-category semantic-word map on an overhead transparency (or enlarge the map so all students can see it), or copy enough maps for all students in the group (see Appendix C).

- Make 10 photocopies of the vocabulary card illustration for Unit 5E (see Appendix D), or more or less depending on the number of target words selected (see preparatory set discussion in this unit).

- For the internal-states map, obtain a large sheet of white construction paper or a blank transparency, or work where there is a chalkboard (see the internal-states chart discussion in this unit).

- Obtain art materials (different types of uncooked pasta, string or elastic, scissors, construction paper, and glue; five, enlarged photocopies of the vocabulary card illustration [see the story retelling/art activity discussion in this unit]).

- Photocopy a blank discussion web on an overhead transparency (or enlarge the web on paper so all students can see it), or copy enough webs for all students in the group (see Appendix C).

PRESTORY PRESENTATION

Semantic-Word Map

Conduct a discussion about spaghetti. Ask, "Have you ever eaten spaghetti? Have you eaten anything else that looks like spaghetti? Have you heard the word *pasta?*" Explain that *pasta* is another word for noodles. Bring different types of pasta and pictures of pasta dishes. Discuss toppings that can be put on pasta. Have students recall the kinds of pasta (names, shapes, sizes) they have seen. Also have them name some kinds of toppings for pasta and some names of different pasta dishes that they have eaten. Organize

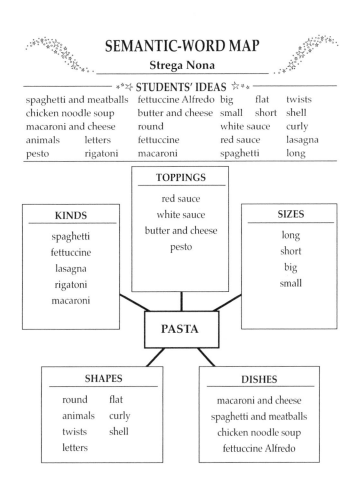

SEMANTIC-WORD MAP
Strega Nona

STUDENTS' IDEAS

spaghetti and meatballs fettuccine Alfredo big flat twists
chicken noodle soup butter and cheese small short shell
macaroni and cheese round white sauce curly
animals letters fettuccine red sauce lasagna
pesto rigatoni macaroni spaghetti long

TOPPINGS

red sauce
white sauce
butter and cheese
pesto

KINDS

spaghetti
fettuccine
lasagna
rigatoni
macaroni

SIZES

long
short
big
small

PASTA

SHAPES

round flat
animals curly
twists shell
letters

DISHES

macaroni and cheese
spaghetti and meatballs
chicken noodle soup
fettuccine Alfredo

their suggestions on a semantic-word map by category. An example of a semantic-word map for *Strega Nona* is provided above.

Preparatory Set

Discuss the importance of obeying parents and teachers. Have students recall when parents or teachers have told them not to touch something. Ask students what happened when they didn't obey.

See the instructions on page 18 for teaching selected story vocabulary words. Use the following vocabulary words selected for you, or select words appropriate for your specific students.

• valuable   • potion   • barricade   • convent   • compliment

Write each word on a vocabulary card illustration and write the corresponding definition on another card. After all cards have been created, have students match each word to its corresponding definition.

Think Alouds

Show the cover and say, "From the cover, I know that this book is about an old lady who likes to cook using a big black pot. What types of things do you suppose she cooks in her pot?"

Point to the title and state, "The title of this story is *Strega Nona*." Model a prediction for the students (e.g., "I predict that the story will be about a dish that the old woman makes called 'Strega Nona.'") or ask a question (e.g., "What do you think *Strega Nona* means?").

Scan the illustrations only. Stop at selected points of the story to model a prediction or to ask the students prediction questions.

- The old woman is pointing to her pot as she is speaking to the boy. What could she be saying to the boy about the pot?

- It looks like the pot is overflowing with pasta. What do you think the boy did to make the pot overflow? What can he do to stop it?

Write down the students' responses for discussion and comparison with actual events after reading the story. Stop the prestory think-aloud activity before Strega Nona gives a fork to Anthony so the ending of the story will not be revealed.

DURING-STORY PRESENTATION

Think Alouds

Confusing Information—Read to where all the people in town talked about Strega Nona in whispers and say, "I don't understand why all of the people in the town whisper about Strega Nona. She looks very nice and pleasant. This is different

than what I would expect. I would expect that all of the townspeople would like her and say only good things about her. What would you expect? Why do you think everyone talks about her in whispers?"

Repair Strategy—Read to where everyone at the town square laughed at Big Anthony because he told them about Strega Nona's pot and say, "I don't understand why the townspeople are laughing at Big Anthony. They all know that Strega Nona is magical. I'd better read on to see how Big Anthony convinces them that the pot can really make magic. What do you think he will do?"

Mental Picture—Read to where Big Anthony does not blow three kisses to stop the pot from making pasta and say, "The pasta pot is overflowing because Anthony does not know the magic spell. The idea that I have is that he will stop the pot from cooking by finding Strega Nona's magic book. He will look up the magic words and stop the pasta pot from cooking anymore pasta. How do you think he will get the pasta pot to stop?"

Analogy—Read to where the pasta is filling the town and the people are making a barricade to hold it back and say, "This reminds me of the time it rained so hard that our town flooded. There were sandbags lining the streets to barricade the water, but it didn't help. All of the stores and some of the houses flooded. Have you ever seen a flood or had to make a barricade to hold something back?"

Extension

After reading the sentence, "The punishment must fit the crime," use the following extension to clarify *punishment must fit the crime:* "Yes, Big Anthony's punishment was to eat all of the pasta. That will surely teach him to follow Strega Nona's rules." Provide an example from your own experience: "I was once punished for speeding by having to pay a ticket. That punishment fit my crime." Then ask the students, "What punishment would fit the crime of taking someone's toy without asking and accidentally breaking it?"

POSTSTORY PRESENTATION

Think Alouds

After reading the story, state, "Big Anthony had to eat all of the pasta for his punishment. What other punishments could have been given to him for disobeying Strega Nona?" Conduct a discussion about think-aloud questions. Compare students' responses before the story was read with the actual story events.

Question-Answer Relationships

See the instructions on page 35 for the question-answer relationships strategy. The following are examples of questions to test students' comprehension of *Strega Nona* (question type is indicated in parentheses after each example).

- What chores did Big Anthony have to do for Strega Nona? (Right There)

- When Strega Nona left, what did she tell Big Anthony he could eat? (Right There)

- What things did Big Anthony and the townspeople do to try and stop the pasta? (Think and Search)

- How many days passed from the time Big Anthony heard the magic song to when he used the pot to make pasta? (Think and Search)

- Why did Big Anthony touch the pasta pot when he was told not to? (Author and You)

- Why did the men of the town want to "string Big Anthony up"? (Author and You)

- Why is it important to obey parents and teachers when they tell you not to do something? (On Your Own)

- What should the punishment be for throwing your trash on the ground instead of in a trash can? (On Your Own)

Internal-States Chart

Adapt the internal-states chart to form an internal-states map for *Strega Nona* (the following is an example). Draw the map where all students can see it. Supply the information about Big Anthony's feelings and omit the information regarding why he felt that way and when he felt it. Have students recall from memory to complete the map, or have them read or look through the book to locate the specific information omitted. Ask a why question (e.g., "Why does Big Anthony feel thankful and happy?"). Write the students' responses on the map. Follow-up with a when question (e.g., "When did he feel that way?").

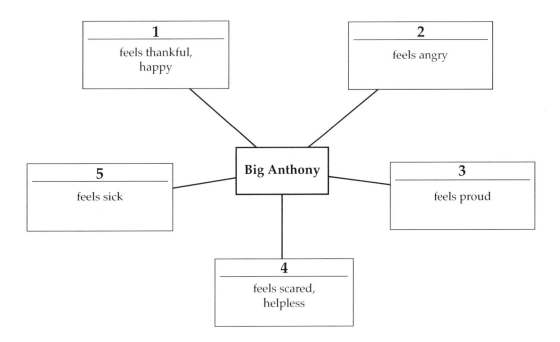

Art Activities

1. Art materials needed:

   - Different types of uncooked pasta that have holes (e.g., macaroni, rigatoni, penne, mostaccioli)
   - String or elastic
   - Scissors

Direct students to make a pasta bracelet or belt. Show students a model of a bracelet or belt that you have made. Direct students to measure the amount of string needed and cut the appropriate length. Have students select the types of pasta they wish to use and to string these on their bracelets or belts. Assist students with tying their string ends. Have students display their bracelets or belts and describe the types of pasta used and the sequences they used in their designs.

2. Art materials needed:

- different shapes and sizes of uncooked pasta
- a sheet of construction paper for each student
- glue

Allow students to make a pasta picture. Direct them to glue the pasta onto construction paper to make a picture. Have them label their pictures and describe them to the group.

Story Retelling/Art Activities

Paste key words from the setting and each of the episodes of *Strega Nona* onto separate cut-out pasta pots. (Enlarge the pasta pot illustration if necessary.) Give each student one of the pasta pots representing either the setting or one of the four episodes:

- *Setting:* Strega Nona hires Big Anthony; tells him not to touch the pasta pot.

- *Episode 1:* Big Anthony sees Strega Nona sing magic song and make pasta; he tells the townspeople; they think he's lying.

- *Episode 2:* Strega Nona leaves; Big Anthony disobeys; makes pasta for all villagers.

- *Episode 3:* Big Anthony does not know all magic actions; he can't stop the pot from making pasta; pasta covers village.

- *Episode 4:* Strega Nona returns and stops the pasta pot; Big Anthony is punished.

Have students arrange the pots in chronological order. Have each student retell part of the story, using the cues from the pasta pots.

Discussion Web

See the instructions on pages 26–27 for the discussion-web strategy. The following is an example of a discussion web for *Strega Nona*.

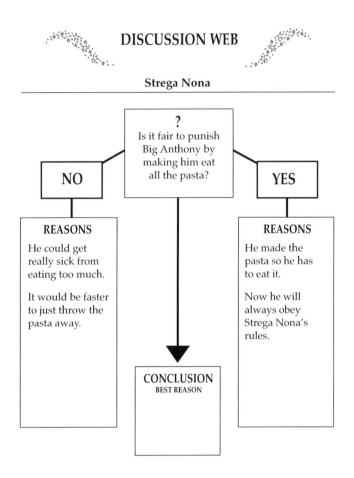

DISCUSSION WEB

Strega Nona

?
Is it fair to punish Big Anthony by making him eat all the pasta?

NO

YES

REASONS

He could get really sick from eating too much.

It would be faster to just throw the pasta away.

REASONS

He made the pasta so he has to eat it.

Now he will always obey Strega Nona's rules.

CONCLUSION
BEST REASON

Unit 6E
THE BIGGEST BEAR

By Lynd Ward (1952). Boston: Houghton Mifflin.
Unit developed by Curtis G. Thomas and Rod Bullock.

Johnny Orchard wanted a bear rug. Because his father and grandfather didn't hunt bears, Johnny went hunting on his own to find a bear. While hunting, Johnny found a bear cub and took it home. The cub had an enormous appetite and grew to be very large. Johnny's father told him to find the bear a new home. Johnny took the bear into the woods to set it free, but the bear returned. After repeated attempts to return the bear to the woods, Johnny's father told him to shoot the bear. On the last trip, Johnny and the bear were trapped by men who captured animals for a zoo. The men took the bear to the zoo, and Johnny was able to visit him there.

MATERIALS NEEDED

- Obtain a picture book about bears from the library.

- Photocopy a blank, five-category semantic-word map on an overhead transparency (or enlarge the map so all students can see it), or copy enough maps for all students in the group (see Appendix C).

- Make 10 photocopies of the vocabulary card illustration for Unit 6E (see Appendix D), or more or less depending on the number of target words selected (see preparatory set discussion in this unit).

- Photocopy a blank flow chart on an overhead transparency (or enlarge the chart so all students can see it), or copy enough charts for all students in the group (see Appendix C).

- Obtain a stuffed teddy bear (see story retelling discussion in this unit).

PRESTORY PRESENTATION

Semantic-Word Map

Locate pictures of different kinds of bears from books and magazines. A particularly good book is *Bears* (Jeunesse and Bour, 1989). After looking at the pictures, ask students to name everything that comes to mind when they think of bears. List their responses where all students can see them. Help students identify ways to categorize their ideas. An example of a semantic-word map for *The Biggest Bear* is provided on the following page.

Preparatory Set

See the instructions on page 18 for teaching selected story vocabulary words. Use the following vocabulary words selected for you, or select words appropriate for your specific students.

- timber
- humiliated
- delighted
- trial
- bait

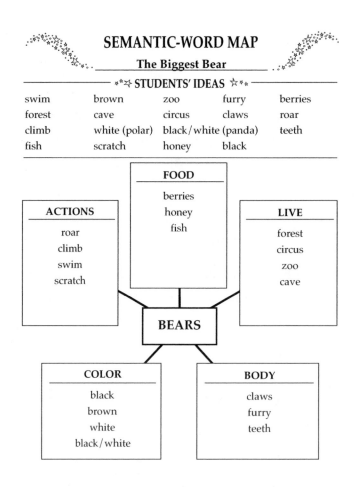

SEMANTIC-WORD MAP
The Biggest Bear

STUDENTS' IDEAS

swim	brown	zoo	furry	berries
forest	cave	circus	claws	roar
climb	white (polar)	black/white (panda)	teeth	
fish	scratch	honey	black	

FOOD
berries
honey
fish

ACTIONS
roar
climb
swim
scratch

LIVE
forest
circus
zoo
cave

BEARS

COLOR
black
brown
white
black/white

BODY
claws
furry
teeth

Write each word on a vocabulary card illustration and write the corresponding definition on another card. After all cards have been created, have students match each word to its corresponding definition.

Think Alouds

Show the cover and model a prediction such as, "From the cover, I think that this book is about a boy who has a pet bear." Or, ask a question such as, "Why do you suppose the boy has a gun?"

Point to the title and state, "The title of this story is *The Biggest Bear.*" Then, either model a prediction (e.g., "I predict that this story will be about a bear that is bigger than

all the other bears in the forest"), or ask a prediction question (e.g., "What do you think the story will be about?").

Scan the illustrations only. Stop at selected points to model predictions or to ask prediction questions.

- What do you think the boy is going to do in the forest?

- What could these men be saying about the bear? Why?

Write down the students' responses for discussion and comparison with actual events after reading the story. Stop the prestory think-aloud activity where Johnny takes the bear into the forest to shoot him so that the ending of the story is not revealed.

DURING-STORY PRESENTATION

Direct Reading/Thinking Activity

Read to where Johnny and his father decide that there is only one thing to do with the bear. Have the students predict what Johnny will do with the bear. Write these predictions where all students can see them.

Read to where Johnny and the bear are trapped in the cage. Have the students predict who has set the trap and for what purpose. Write these predictions where all students can see them. After the story is complete, have the students determine which of their predictions were correct.

Questioning

See the instructions on pages 23–24 for asking questions about the following figurative-language examples:

- Better a bear in the orchard than an *Orchard in the bear.*

- If I ever see a bear I'll shoot him *so fast he won't know what hit him.*

- He was a *trial and tribulation* to the whole valley.

Extension

After reading the sentence, "There was hardly anything he didn't like, and Johnny's mother got pretty upset when he started looking for things on the kitchen shelf," use the following extension to clarify *pretty upset:* "Yes, she was very upset when the bear tore apart her kitchen in search of something to eat." Provide an example from your own experience: "I was pretty upset when I wrecked my car." Then ask the students, "What are some things that make you pretty upset?"

POSTSTORY PRESENTATION

Think Alouds

After reading the story, state, "Johnny tried to take the bear back to the forest three times and it didn't work. The bear always found his way back to Johnny. Can you think of something else Johnny could have done to make the bear stay in the forest?" Conduct a discussion about think-aloud questions. Compare students' responses before the story was read with the actual story events.

Question-Answer Relationships

See the instructions on page 35 for the question-answer relationships strategy. The following are examples of questions to test students' comprehension of *The Biggest Bear* (question type is indicated in parentheses after each example):

- Why did Johnny go bear hunting? (Right There)

- How did Johnny's parents respond when they saw the bear? (Right There)

- What things did the bear do to upset the neighbors? (Think and Search)

- How much time passed while Johnny had the bear? (Think and Search)

- Why did the bear keep returning to Johnny? (Author and You)

- Why was Johnny going to shoot the bear? (Author and You)

- Why are animals in the zoo? (On Your Own)

- What should you do if you see a bear in the wild? (On Your Own)

Flow Chart

See the instructions on pages 31–32 for creating a flow chart. For students who do not read, use stick figures for the characters and for the actions. The following is an example of a flow chart for *The Biggest Bear*.

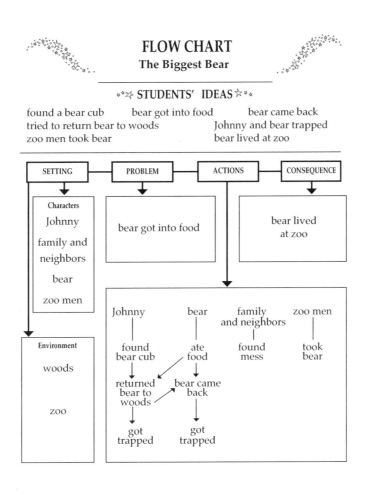

Music

Teach students the song "The Bear Went Over the Mountain" (unknown origin). Write the words where all students can see them. Have students read along as they sing.

The bear went over the mountain,
The bear went over the mountain,
The bear went over the mountain,
To see what he could see.

And all that he could see,
And all that he could see,
Was the other side of the mountain,
The other side of the mountain,
The other side of the mountain,
Was all that he could see.

Story Retelling/Summarizing

Retell the story first to provide a model for story retelling. Then, retell the story with the students using a cloze-summary procedure, filling in the blanks (see summarizing strategy on page 24).

There once was a boy named Johnny _____ (Orchard). Johnny wanted a bear _____ (rug). But his father and grandfather didn't hunt bears, so Johnny went hunting on his own to find a _____ (bear). When he was hunting, he found a bear _____ (cub) and took it _____ (home). The cub liked to eat a lot, and it grew to be very _____ (large). Johnny's father told him to find the bear a new _____ (home). Johnny took the bear into the _____ (woods) to set it _____ (free), but the bear _____ (came back). Johnny tried again and again to take the bear to the _____ (woods). Finally, Johnny's father told him to _____ (shoot) the bear. On the last trip, some men from a _____ (zoo) trapped Johnny and the _____ (bear). The men took the bear to the _____ (zoo), and Johnny got to go to the zoo to _____ (visit) the _____ (bear).

Obtain a stuffed teddy bear and have the students retell the story by playing "Pass the Bear." As each student gets the bear, direct him or her to add another event to the story. Allow students to use the flow chart as a guide if necessary.

Story Generation

See the instructions on pages 35–37 for story generation. Provide students with a prompt. For example, make up a story about a pet you found and wanted to keep.

Unit 7E
THE PROUD AND FEARLESS LION

By Ann and Reg Cartwright (1986). Woodbury, NY: Barron's Educational Series.
Unit developed by Cathy Nuttall.

A lion roared loudly at the same time every morning to scare all the animals. One night, while all the other animals took shelter during a storm, the lion stayed outside to prove how fearless he was. The next morning the lion did not roar, so the animals went to find him and discovered he was sick. The animals agreed to help him if he would agree not to scare them anymore. When the lion recovered, he looked for his friends and could not find them. A mouse told the lion that two hunters had captured the animals and were taking them to a circus. The lion and mouse rescued the animals and chased the two hunters out of the jungle forever. The lion kept his promise never to scare the animals again.

MATERIALS NEEDED

- Make 10 photocopies of the vocabulary card illustration for Unit 7E (see Appendix D), or more or less depending on the number of target words selected (see preparatory set discussion in this unit).

- Obtain a picture book about jungle animals from the library.

- Photocopy a blank, four-category semantic-word map on an overhead transparency (or enlarge the map so all students can see it), or copy enough maps for all students in the group (see Appendix C).

- Obtain art materials (a large sheet of white butcher paper or newsprint, one sheet of white construction paper per student, pencils and crayons, scissors, and tape).

- Photocopy a blank story map on an overhead transparency (or enlarge the map so all students can see it), or copy enough maps for all students in the group (see Appendix C).

PRESTORY PRESENTATION

Preparatory Set

Discuss the title and ask the students what *proud* and *fearless* mean. Have them predict what they think the lion will be like. Discuss the attributes of the animals that are shown on the book's cover—what they might sound like, look like, and where they might live. Ask students whether they have seen animals like these before.

See the instructions on page 18 for teaching selected story vocabulary words. Use the following vocabulary words selected for you, or select words appropriate for your specific students.

- fearless
- proud
- shelter
- attack
- scurrying

Write each word on a vocabulary card illustration and write the corresponding definition on another card. After all cards have been created, have students match each word to its corresponding definition.

Semantic-Word Map

Provide books, magazines, and pictures of jungle animals or jungles. Ask students to think about what lives and grows in a jungle and what jungles are like. List their ideas where all students can see them. Then assist students with categorizing their ideas. The following is an example of a semantic-word map for *The Proud and Fearless Lion*.

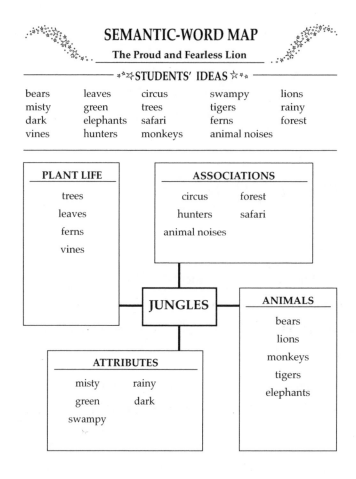

Art Activity

Art materials needed:

- A large sheet of white butcher paper or newsprint for the mural
- One sheet of white construction paper per student
- Pencils and crayons
- Scissors
- Tape

Provide a mural on a bulletin board of a jungle scene that includes trees, bushes, and swamps. Have each student draw, color, and cut out an animal that lives in the jungle. Have them tape their pictures on the mural and name and describe their animals for the group.

Think Alouds

Point to the cover and say, "I know that this book is about a group of jungle animals that are friends. How do I know this?"

Read the title and say, "The title of the story is *The Proud and Fearless Lion*." Then, either model a prediction (e.g., "I predict that this story will be about the lion and how he saves his jungle friends") or ask a prediction question (e.g., "What do you think this story will be about?").

Scan the illustrations only. Stop at selected points of the story to model a prediction or to ask prediction questions.

- Why do you think the lion is sleeping outside in the rainstorm?

- How is the lion feeling in this picture? What could the mouse be saying to him?

Write down the students' responses for discussion and comparison with actual events after story reading. Stop the prestory think-aloud activity where the hunters are having breakfast next to the animals in the cage so the ending of the story is not revealed.

DURING-STORY PRESENTATION

Think Alouds

Confusing Information—Read to where the lion sleeps through the rainstorm and say, "I don't understand how the lion could sleep outside during that storm. This is different than what I would expect. I would expect that he would be too cold and wet to sleep well. What would you expect?"

Mental Picture—Read to where the jungle animals discover that the lion is missing and say, "The lion is missing and the mouse wants to find out what has happened to him. What could be the cause of his disappearance? The idea that I have is that the lion is still sleeping on the hill. What do you think has happened to him?"

Analogy—Read to where the lion could only squeak and nod his head because he was so sick and say, "This reminds me of a time when I got so sick that I lost my voice. I couldn't speak for three days. I couldn't even go to school. Have you ever been this sick?"

Repair Strategy—Read to where the mouse and lion fall asleep while thinking of a plan to rescue their friends and say, "I don't understand why they didn't try to rescue their friends in the dark. I'd better keep reading so I can find out what plan they use to rescue the animals. What do you think their plan will be? Do you think they will be successful at rescuing the animals from the hunters?"

Extension

After reading the sentence, "The next morning the rain had stopped and the jungle was unusually quiet," use the following extension to clarify *unusually quiet:* "Yes it was unusually quiet. The animals were not as noisy as usual, and the jungle seemed very still." Provide an example from your own experience: "It was unusually quiet in the school lunchroom today because the principal was eating there." Then ask the students, "Can you think of a time or place when it was unusually quiet?"

Questioning

See the instructions on pages 23–24 for asking questions about the following figurative-language examples.

- Once there was a *proud and fearless lion.*

- *A little rain never hurt anyone.*

- I think you have a bad attack of *soricus throaticus.*

- While you were sleeping, two hunters came and *drove the animals* into a cage.

POSTSTORY PRESENTATION

Think Alouds

After reading the story, state, "After the lion and the mouse saved their friends, they charged the hunters and chased them out of the jungle because they wanted to teach them a lesson. Is there another way the animals could have taught the hunters a lesson?" Conduct a discussion about think-aloud questions. Compare students' responses before the story was read with the actual story events.

Summarizing

See the instructions on page 24 for summarizing after story reading. Use an oral cloze procedure like the following with students.

Once upon a time, there was a proud and fearless _____ (lion). Every morning, the lion would roar and scare the other_____(animals). One night, the lion stayed outside in a _____ (storm). The next morning, he was sick and he couldn't _____ (roar). The other animals found him and took care of him. The lion promised _____ (not to scare them anymore). When the lion got better, he looked for the _____ (animals), but he couldn't find them. A mouse told him they were all captured by some _____ (hunters). The lion and the mouse found the animals and tried to

think of a _____ (plan) for saving them. The lion scared the hunters away by _____ (roaring). The mouse found the key and unlocked the _____ (cage). The animals chased the hunters out of the _____ (jungle). The lion kept his promise that he would never _____ (scare the animals again).

Story Map

See the instructions on page 38 for developing a story map. For students who do not read, draw stick figures for the characters and for each episode. The following is an example of a story map for *The Proud and Fearless Lion*.

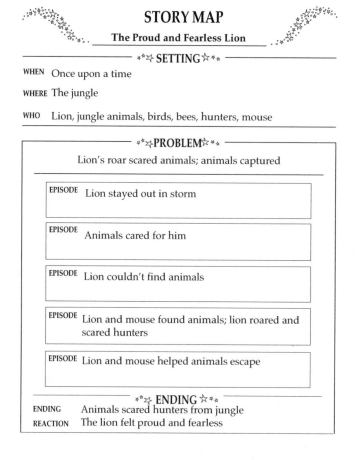

STORY MAP

The Proud and Fearless Lion

SETTING

WHEN   Once upon a time

WHERE The jungle

WHO   Lion, jungle animals, birds, bees, hunters, mouse

PROBLEM

Lion's roar scared animals; animals captured

EPISODE   Lion stayed out in storm

EPISODE   Animals cared for him

EPISODE   Lion couldn't find animals

EPISODE   Lion and mouse found animals; lion roared and scared hunters

EPISODE   Lion and mouse helped animals escape

ENDING

ENDING   Animals scared hunters from jungle
REACTION   The lion felt proud and fearless

Question-Answer Relationships

See the instructions on page 35 for the question-answer relationships strategy. The following are examples of questions to test students' comprehension of *The Proud and Fearless Lion* (question type is indicated in parentheses after each example):

- What would the lion do every morning to scare the other jungle animals? (Right There)

- Why did the lion stay out in the rain all night? (Right There)

- When the rain stopped, why didn't the lion roar? (Think and Search)

- How did the hunters drive the animals into the cage? (Author and You)

- What was the lion and mouse's plan to get the animals out of the cage? (Think and Search)

- How would the animals feel about being taken from the jungle and put in a circus? (Author and You)

- How do you take care of someone who has a bad cold? (On Your Own)

- When animals live in a zoo, what kinds of care do they need? (On Your Own)

Dramatic Play

Reenact the story using guided dramatic play. See the instructions on pages 27–29.

Story Generation

See the instructions on pages 35–37 for story generation. Use the following writing prompt: The hunters sneaked back into the jungle with 10 more hunters to help them recapture the animals. Think of new ways for the animals to get rid of all the hunters, decide on the best approach, and retell the story adding your new ending.

Unit 8E
THE PUPPY WHO WANTED A BOY

By Jane Thayer (1988). New York: William Morrow.
Unit developed by Janell Frost.

Petey, a puppy, asked his mother for a boy for Christmas. Because boys were in short supply, she told him that maybe he could find another dog that wanted to give his boy away. Petey looked, but the dogs that he found did not want to give their boys away. Then the tired puppy came to a sign that read "Home for Boys." Petey's wish came true in a big way, for he found 50 boys and a new home.

MATERIALS NEEDED

- Make 10 photocopies of the vocabulary card illustration for Unit 8E (see Appendix D), or more or less depending on the number of target words selected (see preparatory set discussion in this unit).

- Photocopy a blank story map on an overhead transparency (or enlarge the map so all students can see it), or copy enough maps for all students in the group (see Appendix C).

- Photocopy a blank internal-states chart on an overhead transparency (or enlarge the chart so all students can see it), or copy enough charts for all students in the group (see Appendix C).

- Obtain art materials (one popsicle stick and one paper plate per student; glue; scissors; different types of macaroni, beans, seeds, and buttons; yarn; string; cotton balls; construction paper; and marking pens).

- Photocopy a discussion web on an overhead transparency (or enlarge the web so all students can see it), or copy enough webs for all students in the group (see Appendix C).

PRESTORY PRESENTATION

Preparatory Set

Talk about dogs and puppies and ask:

- Who has a dog or puppy for a pet?

- How big are dogs? How big are puppies?

- What do puppies like to do?

- What care do you need to provide for a puppy?

See the instructions on page 18 for teaching selected vocabulary words. Use the following vocabulary words selected for you, or select words appropriate for your specific students.

- dreadful • terrifying • trotting • politely • lonely

Write each word on a vocabulary card illustration and write the corresponding definition on another card. After all cards have been created, have students match each word to its corresponding definition.

Think Alouds

Show the cover and say, "From the cover, I know that this book is about a dog who is playing outside in the winter. How do I know this?"

Point to the title and state, "The title of this story is *The Puppy Who Wanted a Boy.*" Then either model a prediction for the students (e.g., "I predict that this story will be about a puppy who tries to find a boy to be his owner") or ask a prediction question (e.g., "What do you think this story will be about?").

Scan the illustrations only. Stop at selected points of the story to model a prediction or to ask questions.

- What do you think the puppy is saying to the big dog? Who do you think that big dog is? How is the puppy feeling? Why?

- What do you think the puppy is looking at through the window? How is he feeling? How can you tell he is feeling that way?

Write down students' responses for discussion and comparison with actual events after reading the story. Stop the prestory think-aloud activity where Petey is looking in the window at the home for boys so the ending of the story will not be revealed.

Music

The song "B-I-N-G-O" is easily learned and remembered. After learning the original version, sing the song substituting the name of the puppy in the book (P-E-T-E-Y).

Finally, invite the children to use the names of their own dogs or to choose a dog's name to sing about (e.g., T-U-F-F-Y). Following are the song lyrics using a substituted dog's name.

> *There was a dog who had a boy*
> *and Petey was his name-o*
> *P-E-T-E-Y*
> *P-E-T-E-Y*
> *P-E-T-E-Y and Petey was his name-o.*

To add variation, repeat the song and insert a clap instead of the P in P-E-T-E-Y. Continue until the children insert a clap for each letter instead of P-E-T-E-Y.

DURING-STORY PRESENTATION

Directed Reading/Thinking Activity

Read to where Petey decides to ask the setter politely if he wants to give his boy away. Have the students predict what the setter will say to Petey. Write these predictions where all students can see them.

Read to where the lady at the home for boys discovers the little boy and Petey on the stairs. Have the students predict whether she will let the boy keep Petey. Write these predictions where all students can see them. After the story is complete, have the students determine if their predictions were correct.

Extension

After reading the sentence, "They're terribly short of boys this year," use the following extension to clarify *terribly short:* "Yes, there is a big shortage of boys. Almost all of the pets already have boys." Provide an example from your own experience: "At school, we are terribly short of computers. There aren't enough to go around." Then ask the students, "What are some other things that we are terribly short of?"

Questioning

See the instructions on pages 23–24 for asking questions about the following figurative-language examples:

- Petey *trembled with joy.*

- He *padded slowly* up the walk of the home.

- He *frisked about* and licked every one of the boys.

POSTSTORY PRESENTATION

Think Alouds

After reading the story, state, "Petey asked four dogs if they wanted to give their boys away, and they all said no. Do you think all dogs feel the same way about their boys? What would you do if you had a dog to make sure he didn't want to give you away?" Conduct a discussion about think-aloud questions. Compare students' responses before the story was read with the actual story events.

Question-Answer Relationships

See the instructions on page 35 for the question-answer relationships strategy. The following are examples of questions to test students' comprehension of *The Puppy Who Wanted a Boy* (question type is indicated in parentheses after example):

- What did the puppy want for Christmas? (Right There)

- Did his mom find him a boy? Why? (Right There)

- Why did the puppy want a boy? (Author and You)

- What kinds of dogs did the puppy find? (Think and Search)

- How did the dogs treat Petey when he asked if he could have their boys? (Think and Search)

- Why didn't the other dogs want to give their boys away? (Author and You)

- How does a puppy usually find a home? (On Your Own)

- How do boys and girls usually find their pets? (On Your Own)

Story Map

See the instructions on page 38 for developing a story map. For students who do not read, draw stick figures for the characters and episodes. The following is an example of a story map for *The Puppy Who Wanted a Boy.*

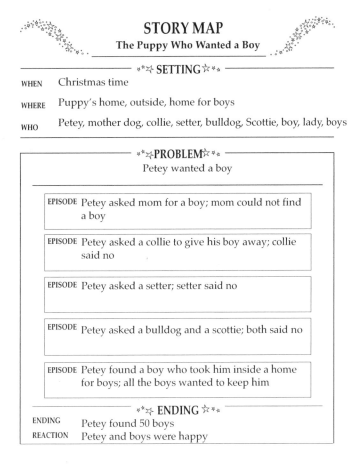

STORY MAP
The Puppy Who Wanted a Boy

SETTING

WHEN	Christmas time
WHERE	Puppy's home, outside, home for boys
WHO	Petey, mother dog, collie, setter, bulldog, Scottie, boy, lady, boys

PROBLEM
Petey wanted a boy

EPISODE Petey asked mom for a boy; mom could not find a boy

EPISODE Petey asked a collie to give his boy away; collie said no

EPISODE Petey asked a setter; setter said no

EPISODE Petey asked a bulldog and a scottie; both said no

EPISODE Petey found a boy who took him inside a home for boys; all the boys wanted to keep him

ENDING

ENDING	Petey found 50 boys
REACTION	Petey and boys were happy

Word Substitution

See the instructions on pages 40–41 for the word-substitution strategy. The following are example sentences with their target words emphasized, followed by lists of synonyms:

- I'll ask the collie *politely* if he'll give his boy away.

  politely

  nicely

  gently

  kindly

- He remembered how *cross* the collie and the setter and the bulldog had been.

  cross

  mad

  mean

  angry

Internal-States Chart

See the instructions on pages 32–33 for the internal-states strategy. Engage the students in dialogue like the following regarding the characters' feelings:

Educator:	How did Petey feel when he told his mother that he wanted a boy for Christmas?
Students:	Petey was excited!
Educator:	Why was he excited?
Students:	Because he felt grown-up enough to leave his mother and find a boy to love.

An example of an internal-states chart for *The Puppy Who Wanted a Boy* is provided on the following page.

INTERNAL-STATES CHART
The Puppy Who Wanted a Boy

CHARACTER(S)	WHEN	FEELING	WHY
Petey	Told mother Christmas wish	Excited	Wanted a boy
Mother dog	Could not find a boy for Petey	Sad	Wanted a boy for Petey
Petey	Dogs wouldn't give their boys away	Sad	Wanted boy; tired from looking
Boys	They saw Petey	Happy; excited	Wanted a puppy

Dramatic Play/Art Activity

Art materials needed:

- One popsicle stick and one paper plate per student
- Glue
- Scissors
- Different types of macaroni, beans, seeds, buttons
- Yarn, string, cotton balls
- Construction paper
- Marking pens

Provide a model of a paper-plate puppet for the students. Direct the students to make puppets of the characters in the story using the available materials. Let students use their completed puppets as props in dramatic play when reenacting the story sequence.

Reenact the story using guided dramatic play. See the instructions on pages 27–29.

Discussion Web

See the instructions on pages 26–27 for the discussion-web strategy. The following is an example of a discussion web for *The Puppy Who Wanted a Boy*.

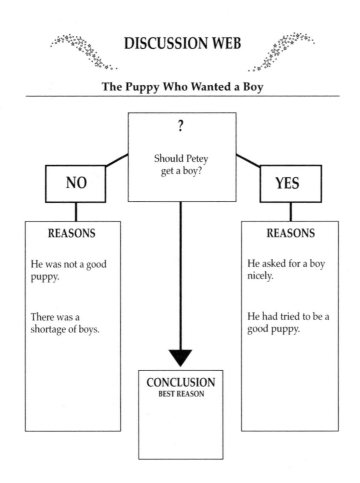

DISCUSSION WEB

The Puppy Who Wanted a Boy

? Should Petey get a boy?

NO

YES

REASONS

He was not a good puppy.

There was a shortage of boys.

REASONS

He asked for a boy nicely.

He had tried to be a good puppy.

CONCLUSION
BEST REASON

Unit 9E
THE RAINBOW FISH

By M. Pfister (1992). New York: North-South Books.
Unit developed by Kelly Hoggan North.

A beautiful rainbow-colored fish was envied by all the other fish in the ocean. The other fish wanted Rainbow Fish to share his beautiful scales with them, but he was too proud to share. He eventually alienated all of the fish until he had no friends. After following the advice of the starfish, Rainbow Fish sought out the wise octopus. The octopus told Rainbow Fish that if he wanted to be happy, he should give each fish a glittering scale. Rainbow Fish had a difficult time following the advice at first, but found that for each glittering scale he shared, he gained a new friend as well as happiness.

MATERIALS NEEDED

- Make eight photocopies of the vocabulary card illustration for Unit 9E (see Appendix D), or more or less depending on the number of target words selected (see preparatory set discussion in this unit).

- Obtain books about fish and ocean life from the library.

- Photocopy a blank, four-category semantic-word map on an overhead transparency (or enlarge the map so all students can see it), or copy enough maps for all students in the group (see Appendix C).

- Photocopy a blank three-episode map on an overhead transparency (or enlarge the map so all students can see it), or copy enough maps for all students in the group (see Appendix C).

- Obtain art materials (a large sheet of white butcher paper or newsprint; and for each student, a fish-scale and fish pattern from Appendix D, pencils, several sheets of colored construction paper, aluminum foil, glue, glitter, scissors, and tape).

PRESTORY PRESENTATION

Preparatory Set

Talk about sharing. Ask students to tell of an experience when they shared and how they felt when they did it. Discuss why it is sometimes difficult to share things and what we can do to help someone who doesn't want to share.

See the instructions on page 18 for teaching selected story vocabulary words. Use the following vocabulary words selected for you, or select words appropriate for your specific students.

- emerge
- scales
- admire
- ocean

Write each word on a vocabulary card illustration and write the corresponding definition on another card. After all cards have been created, have students match each word to its corresponding definition.

Semantic-Word Map

Obtain some books on fish and ocean life. Have students scan the books and call out any words that are related to ocean life. Organize the information into categories of things found in the ocean. The following is an example of a semantic-word map for *The Rainbow Fish*.

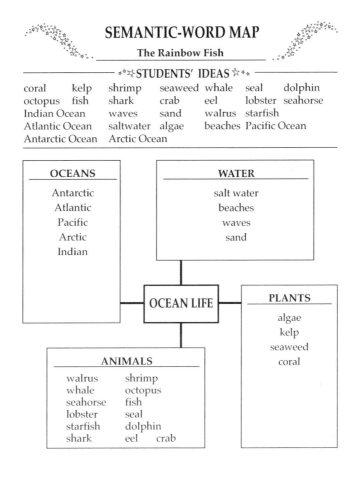

SEMANTIC-WORD MAP

The Rainbow Fish

STUDENTS' IDEAS

coral	kelp	shrimp	seaweed	whale	seal	dolphin
octopus	fish	shark	crab	eel	lobster	seahorse
Indian Ocean		waves	sand	walrus	starfish	
Atlantic Ocean		saltwater	algae		beaches	Pacific Ocean
Antarctic Ocean		Arctic Ocean				

OCEANS
Antarctic
Atlantic
Pacific
Arctic
Indian

WATER
salt water
beaches
waves
sand

OCEAN LIFE

PLANTS
algae
kelp
seaweed
coral

ANIMALS

walrus	shrimp
whale	octopus
seahorse	fish
lobster	seal
starfish	dolphin
shark	eel crab

Think Alouds

Tell the students that this book was first written in Switzerland under the title *Der Regenbogenfish*. Ask them to figure out what that title means. Point out the translator and ask what that person contributed to the story.

Point to the cover and say, "I know that this book is about a fish with pretty rainbow-colored scales. How do I know this?"

Read the title and say, "The title of the story is *The Rainbow Fish*." Either model a prediction for the students (e.g., "Because this fish is swimming along in rainbow-colored water, I predict the book will be about how much he likes rainbows") or ask a prediction question (e.g., "What do you predict this story will be about?").

Scan the illustrations only. Stop at selected points of the story to model a prediction or ask prediction questions.

- What do you think the other fish in the ocean are looking at? Why? What might they be thinking?

- Why does the fish look so sad? What will he do to make himself feel better?

Write down their responses for discussion and comparison with actual events after reading the story. Stop the prestory think-aloud activity before the fish shares his scales with the other fish in the ocean so the ending is not revealed.

Music

Play the song "Under the Sea" from the movie *The Little Mermaid*. Ask the students to sing along with the words or to listen. Ask the students what they think it would be like to live in the ocean.

DURING-STORY PRESENTATION

Think Alouds

Confusing Information—Read to where Rainbow Fish is invited to play with the other fish, but he just glides past and ignores them and say, "I don't understand

why Rainbow Fish doesn't want to play with the other fish. This is different than what I would expect. I would expect that Rainbow Fish would like to play with his ocean friends. What would you expect? Can you think of some reasons why he won't play with them?"

Mental Picture—Read to where Rainbow Fish finds the cave where the octopus lives and state, "That cave looks very scary. It is dark and all that Rainbow Fish can see are two glaring eyes. What do you suppose Rainbow Fish is feeling? The idea that I have is that he is scared and he wants to swim back to lighter water. How do you think he is feeling?"

Analogy—Read to where Rainbow Fish decides that he likes sharing his scales with the other fish and say, "This reminds me of the time I shared my toys with my brother and we had a good time playing together. It made me happy to do something nice. Have you ever shared something with another person and felt good about doing it?"

Repair Strategy—Read to where Rainbow Fish says that he would never be happy without his scales and that he can't possibly share them and say, "I don't understand why Rainbow Fish thinks that he won't be happy without his scales. I'd better read further to see if he will change his mind and decide to share with the other fish. Do you think he will decide to share? What do you suppose will change his mind?"

Extension

After reading the sentence, "A rather peculiar feeling came over the Rainbow Fish," use the following extension to clarify *peculiar feeling:* "Yes, when the Rainbow Fish started to share his scales, he started feeling weird. He actually liked the feeling of sharing." Provide an example from your own experience: "I had a peculiar feeling when I wore eyeglasses for the first time." Then ask the students, "Can you think of a time when you have had a peculiar feeling?"

Questioning

See the instructions on pages 23–24 for asking questions about the following figurative-language examples.

- One day he *poured out his troubles* on the starfish.

- The waves have *told me your story.*

- The octopus *disappeared into a dark cloud of ink.*

- *Happy as a splash.*

POSTSTORY PRESENTATION

Think Alouds

After reading the story, state, "What could Rainbow Fish have said to the blue fish the first time he asked for a scale so he didn't sound so rude? Can you think of some ways to tell a person 'no' politely?" Conduct a discussion about think-aloud questions. Compare students' responses before the story was read with the actual story events.

Question-Answer Relationships

See the instructions on page 35 for the question-answer relationships strategy. The following are examples of questions to test students' comprehension of *The Rainbow Fish* (question type is indicated in parentheses after each example):

- How did the fish in the ocean feel when Rainbow Fish wouldn't share his scales? Why? (Think and Search)

- Who gave Rainbow Fish advice? (Right There)

- If you were the wise octopus, what would you tell Rainbow Fish to do? Why? (Author and You)

- To whom did Rainbow Fish give his first scale? (Right There)

- How did Rainbow Fish feel when he shared his scales? (Think and Search)

- If you were Rainbow Fish and you gave away all your scales, how would you feel? Why? (Author and You)

- What are some things that are hard for you to share? (On Your Own)

- How do you feel when someone shares with you? (On Your Own)

Word Substitution

See the instructions on pages 40–41 for the word-substitution strategy. The following is an example sentence with its target word emphasized, followed by lists of synonyms and antonyms:

The *wise* old octopus may be able to help you.

wise (synonym)	*wise* (antonym)
smart	dumb
knowing	stupid
learned	foolish

Dramatic Play

Reenact the story using guided dramatic play. See the instructions on pages 27–29.

Episode Map

See the instructions on pages 29–30 for developing an episode map. For students who do not read, draw stick figures for the characters and for each episode. An example of an episode map for *The Rainbow Fish* is provided on the following page.

Art Activity

Art materials needed:

- A large sheet of white butcher paper or newsprint for a mural
- A fish pattern and fish-scale pattern for each student

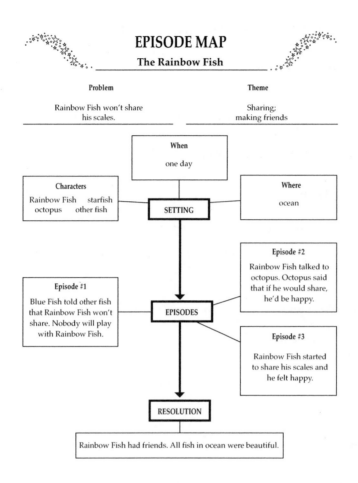

EPISODE MAP
The Rainbow Fish

Problem

Rainbow Fish won't share his scales.

Theme

Sharing; making friends

When
one day

Characters
Rainbow Fish   starfish
octopus   other fish

SETTING

Where
ocean

Episode #2
Rainbow Fish talked to octopus. Octopus said that if he would share, he'd be happy.

Episode #1
Blue Fish told other fish that Rainbow Fish won't share. Nobody will play with Rainbow Fish.

EPISODES

Episode #3
Rainbow Fish started to share his scales and he felt happy.

RESOLUTION

Rainbow Fish had friends. All fish in ocean were beautiful.

- Pencils
- Several sheets of colored construction paper
- Aluminum foil
- Glue
- Glitter
- Tape

To create a mural, draw a model of the ocean on a large sheet of butcher paper or newsprint and pin it to a bulletin board or tape it to a wall. Label and discuss plant and animal life in the ocean. Refer to the semantic-word map developed in this unit.

Provide students with a completed model illustration of a rainbow-colored fish, the patterns, and materials to make their own. Direct students to follow these steps:

- Trace the fish pattern on a sheet of colored construction paper for the fish's body and then cut out the fish.

- Using the fish-scale pattern, cut out scales of different colors and of aluminum foil.

- Glue the scales on the fish body.

- Dab some glue on the scales and fish and sprinkle all with glitter. Let dry.

- Tape the fish to the mural on the bulletin board.

As students are constructing their fish, discuss colors of the rainbow and how to select those colors for the fish scales. Instruct students how to alternate the different colored scales with aluminum foil scales to make a rainbow pattern on their fish. When students tape their fish to the mural, have them tell why they put their fish in each specific location (e.g., "I'm putting my fish by this plant because it might eat it").

Unit 10E
THE SHOW-AND-TELL FROG

By Joanne Oppenheim (1992). New York: Bantam Books.
Unit developed by Dawn Gummersall.

Allie found a frog for show-and-tell, but he disappeared before she could take him to school. She looked everywhere but she couldn't find him, so she left for school empty-handed. Unbeknown to Allie, the frog hopped along with her as she met her classmates on the way to school. In class, Allie watched and listened to the other students' show-and-tell presentations. All of a sudden, out jumped her frog, which created chaos in the classroom. Finally, she caught and introduced her lost-and-found, show-and-tell frog.

MATERIALS NEEDED

- Obtain books, magazines, or pictures about frogs from the library.

- Photocopy a blank, four-category semantic-word map on an overhead transparency (or enlarge the map so all students can see it), or copy enough maps for all students in the group (see Appendix C).

- Make 10 photocopies of the vocabulary card illustration for Unit 10E (see Appendix D), or more or less depending on the number of target words selected (see preparatory set discussion in this unit); two shoe boxes.

- Photocopy a blank discussion web on an overhead transparency (or enlarge the web so all students can see it), or copy enough webs for all students in the group (see Appendix C).

- Photocopy a blank story map on an overhead transparency (or enlarge the map so all students can see it), or copy enough maps for all students in the group (see Appendix C).

- Obtain art materials (several sheets of white construction paper per student, pencils, crayons, and a stapler).

PRESTORY PRESENTATION

Semantic-Word Map

Obtain some books, magazines, or pictures about frogs. An excellent book is *Frog* (Savage, 1995). Scan the materials with the students and ask them to think of words that are related to frogs. Then help the students organize the words into categories. An example of a semantic-word map for *The Show-and-Tell Frog* is provided on the following page.

Preparatory Set

Show the cover of the book and read the title. Talk about show-and-tell. Ask the students what types of things are good to bring for show-and-tell, or let students name

SEMANTIC-WORD MAP

The Show-and-Tell Frog

— ✩ STUDENTS' IDEAS ✩ —

green	brown	spots	pond	lake
lilypad	(eats) flies	(eats) bugs	croaks	jumps
hop	ribbit	long tongue	quick	fast
little				

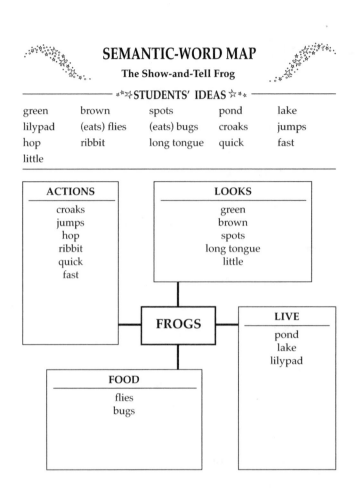

some items that they have shared during show-and-tell. Make a list and categorize the items into a semantic map.

Ask students to share an object that they may have with them or to show something that they are wearing. Have each child *show* the item and *tell* about it (e.g., what it is called, what it looks like, what it does, where it came from, etc.).

See the instructions on page 18 for teaching selected story vocabulary words. Use the following vocabulary words selected for you, or select words appropriate for your specific students.

- inside/outside
- on/off
- behind/in front
- under/over
- between/beside

Play a game called "Frog and Box." Provide two shoe boxes for a small group of four to six students (the boxes must be six-sided with a top and a bottom). Use the 10 vocabulary cards created for the prepositions listed above.

- Divide the 10 vocabulary cards among the students in the group. Explain that the cards will be called "frogs" for this activity.

- Have the students place their frogs inside a box, under a box, behind a box, etc., so they match the words printed on them. For "between," use both boxes and have a student put the frog between them.

- As students place the frogs in the specified locations, state the relationship (e.g., "Yes, that frog is inside of the box"). Encourage the students to help each other name the locations.

Music

Teach the following song using visual cues and cloze techniques. Use hand motions for numbers, sitting on the log, and jumping into the pool.

Five green and speckled frogs, sat on a speckled log,
Eating some most delicious bugs. (yum, yum)
One jumped into the pool, where it was nice and cool,
Then there were four green speckled frogs. (gllb, gllb)

Model a cloze technique with:

Four green and speckled ___ (frogs),
sat on a speckled ____ (log),
Eating some most delicious _____ (bugs). (yum, yum)
etc.

Repeat the cloze technique with the remaining numbers:

Three …
Two …
One …

Think Alouds

Show the cover and say, "From the cover, I know that this book is about a frog that causes some problems at school. How do I know this?"

Point to the title and state, "The title of this story is *The Show-and-Tell Frog.*" Then either model a prediction for the students (e.g., "I predict that this story will be about a girl who takes her frog to school for show-and-tell") or ask a prediction question (e.g., "What do you think the story will be about?").

Scan the illustrations only. Stop at selected points of the story to model a prediction or to ask prediction questions.

- What do you think has happened to the frog? What should the girl do about it?

- How do you think the frog can keep from being spotted by all the children?

Write down students' responses for discussion and comparison with actual events after reading the story. Stop the prestory think-aloud activity where Lisa is showing the picture of her baby brother so that the ending of the story will not be revealed.

DURING-STORY PRESENTATION

Directed Reading/Thinking Activity

Read to where Lisa is showing the other students a picture of her baby brother. Have the students predict what the frog will do to get Allie's attention. Write these predictions where all students can see them.

Read to where Allie and Christopher are chasing the frog around the classroom. Have the students predict how Allie will actually catch the frog and whether she will get to show her frog to the class. Write these predictions where all students can see them. After the story is complete, have the students determine if their predictions were correct.

Extension

After reading the sentence, "This is a show-and-taste," use the following extension to clarify *show-and-taste*. "Yes, instead of Annie telling her classmates about the strawberries, they will get to taste them." Provide an example from your own experience: "I brought some homemade apple pie for show-and-taste once." Then ask, "Can you think of a show-and-taste that you or someone else has shared?"

Help clarify the play on words by helping students create similar phrase changes:

- What could we say if Annie had brought perfume? ("Show-and-smell") (Repeat for show-and-hear, show-and-feel.)

POSTSTORY PRESENTATION

Think Alouds

After reading the story, state, "When Allie finds her frog, she says that it is her lost-and-found, show-and-tell frog. What could Allie have done to prevent her frog from ever getting lost?" Conduct a discussion about think-aloud questions. Compare students' responses before the story was read with the actual story events.

Word Substitution

See the instructions on pages 40–41 for the word-substitution strategy. The following are example sentences with their target words emphasized, followed by lists of synonyms:

- She *bumped* into her friend Annie.

  bumped
  ran
  knocked
  crashed
  slammed
  stumbled

- She felt something *strange* brush against her leg.

  strange

  weird

  different

  funny

  surprising

  freaky

Question-Answer Relationships

See the instructions on page 35 for the question-answer relationships strategy. The following are examples of questions to test students' comprehension of *The Show-and-Tell Frog* (question type is indicated in parentheses after each example):

- How did Allie know her frog was missing? (Right There)

- When did the frog get out of the box? (Think and Search)

- Where did Allie look for her frog? (Right There)

- Why didn't Allie tell her mom about the frog? (Author and You)

- At the bus stop, what was Christopher carrying? (Right There)

- Where did Christopher find his shells? (Right There)

- When the frog was loose in the classroom, some of the students were afraid and some wanted to catch it. What would you do if a frog was loose in your classroom? (On Your Own)

- When Lisa showed a picture of her baby brother, Allie thought it would be fun to have a baby brother. Do you think it would be fun to have a baby brother? (On Your Own)

Discussion Web

See the instructions on pages 26–27 for the discussion-web strategy. The following is an example of a discussion web for *The Show-and-Tell Frog*.

DISCUSSION WEB

The Show-and-Tell Frog

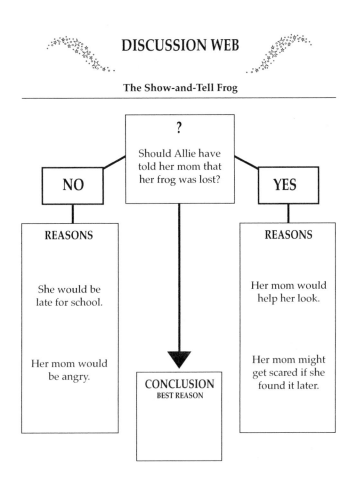

Story Map

See the instructions on page 38 for developing a story map. An example of a story map for *The Show-and-Tell Frog* is provided on the following page.

Story Retelling/Summarizing

Retell the story to the students to provide a story-retelling model. Then, using a cloze procedure, help the students retell the story.

Once upon a time, there was a girl named _____ (Allie). Allie found a _____ (frog) for show-and-tell, but he disappeared before she could take him to _____ (school). She looked everywhere but she couldn't find him, so she left for school

STORY MAP
The Show-and-Tell Frog

————— *⋆⊰ SETTING ⊱⋆* —————

WHEN Sunday and Monday

WHERE Allie's room, school

WHO Allie and frog, Christopher, Jenny, Annie, Benji, Lisa, teacher

—————— *⋆⊰ PROBLEM ⊱⋆* ——————

Allie lost show-and-tell frog

EPISODE	Allie looked; couldn't find frog; had to leave for school; didn't know frog was in backpack
EPISODE	Went to bus stop; saw Christopher's shells; frog got into Christopher's bag
EPISODE	Got on the school bus; saw Jenny's ring
EPISODE	Bumped into Annie getting off bus; spilled strawberries; frog got into Annie's bag
EPISODE	Had show and tell; frog jumped out; students yelled; tried to catch it

—————— *⋆⊰ ENDING ⊱⋆* ——————

ENDING Caught frog; took turn to show-and-tell

REACTION Allie happy because she found her frog

without the _____ (frog). However, the frog was not _____ (lost). He hopped along with her as she met her _____ (classmates) on the way to _____ (school). In class, Allie watched and listened to the other students do their _____ (show-and-tell) presentations. All of a sudden, out jumped her _____ (frog), which caused a lot of trouble in the _____ (classroom). Finally, she caught and introduced her _____ (lost-and-found), show-and-tell _____ (frog).

Next, assign each of the students a story episode and have them retell the story in a round. Finally, pretend that it is show-and-tell day. Have each student retell the story for his or her show-and-tell.

Dramatic Play/Art Activity

Art materials needed:

- Several sheets of white construction paper per student
- Pencils and crayons
- Stapler

Assign students to bring something from home for the next session. Send a note to parents or phone parents explaining that each child should bring something for show-and-tell. (Provide something for students who do not bring an object.)

In the session, discuss each item. Write down what each child wants to say about his or her show-and-tell item. Put each sentence on a separate page of paper, and let the student draw a picture to go with each sentence. Staple the pages so that they form a book. Let each student practice his or her show-and-tell presentation using the book as a prompt.

Then conduct a practice show-and-tell session in a small group. Have each child stand in front of the group and tell about his or her item. Follow with participation in a show-and-tell activity in the front of the entire class.

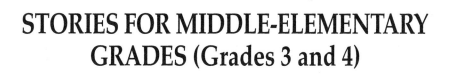

STORIES FOR MIDDLE-ELEMENTARY GRADES (Grades 3 and 4)

Unit 1M
AMAZING GRACE

By Mary Hoffman (1991). New York: Dial Books for Young Readers.
Unit developed by Kevin Costa, Kelly Hoggan North, and Carol J. Strong.

Grace loved to hear stories and to act out the most exciting parts. At school, her teacher told the students that they would be doing the play *Peter Pan*. Grace wanted to play the role of Peter Pan, but her friends told her that she couldn't, because Peter Pan wasn't a girl and he wasn't black. Grace told her mother and grandmother what her friends had said. Her mother was angry, but Nana knew that Grace could be anything she wanted to be. Nana took Grace to a ballet where the role of Juliet was danced by a black ballerina. Grace tried out for and won the role of Peter Pan, and the play was a big success.

MATERIALS NEEDED

- Obtain video clips of a cartoon version of *Peter Pan* and of the movie *Hook.*

- Make 12 photocopies of the vocabulary card illustration for Unit 1M (see Appendix D), or more or less depending on the number of target words selected (see preparatory set discussion in this unit).

- Construct a compare/contrast chart where all students can see it (see compare/contrast chart discussion in this unit).

- Photocopy a blank internal-states chart on an overhead transparency (or enlarge the chart so all students can see it), or copy enough charts for all students in the group (see Appendix C).

- Photocopy a blank three-episode map on an overhead transparency (or enlarge the map so all students can see it), or copy enough maps for all students in the group (see Appendix C).

- Obtain art materials (a large sheet of white construction paper, several sheets of colored construction paper, colored marking pens, scissors, and tape).

PRESTORY PRESENTATION

Preparatory Set

Discuss acting. Ask the students to name their favorite actors and actresses and to explain why they like them.

Discuss popular children's movies. Ask students to name a movie they would like to be in. Have students explain why they would like to play a particular part. Discuss the actions, character attributes, props, and costumes needed to play roles that they like.

Discuss the difference between a cartoon actor or actress and a real-life actor or actress. To demonstrate the differences and similarities, show video clips from a cartoon production of *Peter Pan* and the movie *Hook.*

See the instructions on page 18 for teaching selected story vocabulary words. Use the following vocabulary words selected for you, or select words appropriate for your specific students.

- amazing
- tutu
- audition
- imaginary
- stunning
- success

Write each word on a copy of the vocabulary card illustration and write the corresponding definition on another card. After all cards have been created, have students match each word to its corresponding definition.

Think Alouds

Point to the cover and say, "I know that this book is about an African-American girl who is happy. How do I know this?"

Read the title and say, "The title of this story is *Amazing Grace*. I predict that this story will be about a girl named Grace who has an amazing talent. What do you suppose that talent might be?"

Scan the illustrations only. Stop at selected points of the story to model a prediction or to ask prediction questions based only on the illustrations:

- Who is that woman talking to Grace? How does Grace feel about her? How can you tell? What could the woman be saying?

- Why do you think the children are all raising their hands? What do you think the teacher asked them?

Write down the students' responses for discussion and comparison with actual events after reading the story. Stop the prestory think-aloud strategy where Grace is dancing in her imaginary tutu so the end of the story will not be revealed.

Compare/Contrast Chart

Develop a compare/contrast chart for the moral of the story: "You can be anything you want, Grace, if you put your mind to it." The following is an example of such a chart.

Imaginary	Real—what you can do if you put your mind to it
Fly like Peter Pan	Learn to fly a plane
Bend steel with your bare hands	Exercise and lift weights to become strong
Fairy godmother turns your old clothes into beautiful ones	Learn to sew and make your own beautiful clothes
Swim deep in the ocean like the Little Mermaid	Take swimming and scuba diving lessons; learn to use an oxygen tank and wear a wet suit

DURING-STORY PRESENTATION

Directed Reading/Thinking Activity

Read to where Nana tells Grace that Grace can be anything she wants if she will put her mind to it. Have the students predict what Nana will do to help Grace believe that she can be Peter Pan in the school play. Write these predictions where all students can see them.

Read to where the class meets for auditions to choose who will be Peter Pan. Have the students predict whether Grace will try out for the part and why.

Questioning

See the instructions on pages 23–24 for asking questions about the following figurative-language examples:

- …and *wove a wicked web* as Anansi the Spider.

- Then she was Doctor Grace and *their lives were in her hands.*

- …she *had been Peter Pan* all weekend.

Extension

After reading the sentence, "After the ballet Grace played the part of Juliet, dancing around her room in her imaginary tutu," use the following extension to clarify *played the part*: "Yes, she practiced and imagined how Peter Pan would be and acted like she really was Peter Pan." Provide an example from your own experience: "At Halloween, I once played the part of Darth Vadar from *Star Wars*. I wore a Darth Vadar mask and a long black cape, and I pretended to be very scary and mysterious." Then ask the students, "Can you think of a time you've played the part of someone else?"

POSTSTORY PRESENTATION

Think Alouds

After reading the story, state, "Grace was discouraged when her friends told her that she could not be Peter Pan because she was a girl and because she was black. She told her mother and Nana and they helped her solve the problem. What could she have done on her own to solve this problem?" Conduct a discussion about think-aloud questions. Compare students' responses before the story was read with the actual story events.

Question-Answer Relationships

See the instructions on page 35 for the question-answer relationships strategy. The following are examples of questions to test students' comprehension of *Amazing Grace* (question type is indicated in parentheses after each example):

- What did Grace love to hear from Nana? (Right There)

- What did Grace do during and after hearing a story? (Right There)

- What part did Grace want in the school play? (Think and Search)

- Why did the other students think that Grace couldn't play Peter Pan? Name two reasons. (Think and Search)

- Why did Nana take Grace to see the ballet *Romeo and Juliet*? (Author and You)

- Why did Grace say, "I feel as if I could fly all the way home!" after the play was over? (Author and You)

- If you were trying out for Peter Pan, what part would you want to play? Why? (On Your Own)

- What is something you could do if you put your mind to it? (On Your Own)

Internal-States Chart

See the instructions on pages 32–33 for developing an internal-states chart. Engage the students in dialogue like the following regarding the characters' feelings:

Educator: How did Grace feel when her friends told her that she couldn't play the part of Peter Pan?

Students: Grace felt sad.

Educator: Why did she feel sad?

Students: Because she thought it wouldn't matter if Peter Pan was a boy or a girl.

The following is an example of an internal-states chart for *Amazing Grace*.

INTERNAL-STATES CHART
Amazing Grace

CHARACTER(S)	WHEN	FEELING	WHY
Grace	Friends told her she couldn't be Peter	Sad	She thought it shouldn't matter that she was a girl and that she was black
Ma	Natalie told Grace that she couldn't be Peter Pan because Peter wasn't black	Angry	Skin color shouldn't make a difference
Nana	Took Grace to ballet	Determined	Grace could be anything she wanted to be if she put her mind to it
Grace	Played Peter Pan	Happy	Play was a big success

Episode Map

See the instructions on pages 29–30 for using an episode map. The following is an example of an episode map for *Amazing Grace*.

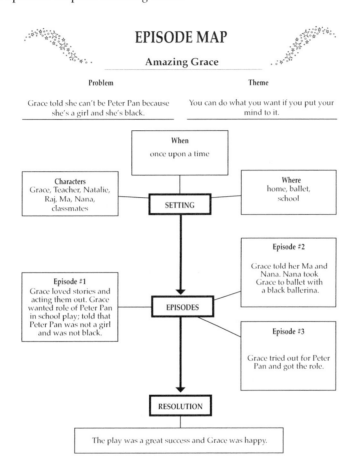

Art Activity

Art materials needed:

- A large sheet of white construction paper
- Several sheets of colored construction paper
- Colored marking pens
- Scissors
- Tape

Have students make a billboard that reads, "Stunning New Peter Pan," and tape the billboard to the wall for display. Using the colored construction paper, help them make theater tickets, writing only the most important words on the tickets (e.g., *Peter Pan*, Admit One), and theater programs, listing the characters and the actors and actresses.

Dramatic Play

Discuss the actions, props, and dialogue of the characters in the video clip shown previously from the movie *Peter Pan*. Have students pick the role they would like to play; encourage students to audition for a part regardless of their gender or race. Hold tryouts. Videotape each student auditioning for his or her part. Watch the videotape and discuss the similarities and differences observed between the movie and the students' auditions.

Practice and then perform one scene from the play for a small audience (use the billboard, theater tickets, and theater programs made during the art activity). Videotape the performance for later review.

Story Retelling/Summarizing

Retell the story. Then have students help you retell it using a cloze procedure.

Grace was a little girl who loved to hear _____ (stories), and she loved to act out the most exciting _____ (parts). At school, her teacher told the students that they would be doing the play called _____ (Peter Pan). Grace wanted to play the role of _____ (Peter), but Raj told her she couldn't because Peter Pan wasn't a _____ (girl), and Natalie told her she couldn't because Peter Pan wasn't _____ (black). When Grace told her mother what her friends had said, her mother was _____ (angry). Grace's grandmother told her that she could be anything she wanted to be if she _____ (put her mind to it). Nana took Grace to see a _____ (ballet) where the role of Juliet was danced by a black _____ (ballerina). Grace decided to practice for the play. She tried out and won the role of _____ (Peter Pan). The play was a big

_____ (success). Grace knew in the end that she could be anything she
wanted to be if she _____ (put her mind to it).

Next, have each student retell the story using the episode map for cues. Finally,
have students tell the story individually and tape-record their accounts.

Unit 2M
EYES OF THE DRAGON

By Margaret Leaf (1987). New York: Lothrop, Lee & Shepard.
Unit developed by Kelly Hoggan North and Tobey Fields.

In a village in China, the people were afraid of wild beasts and men that lived nearby, so the magistrate persuaded the people to build a great wall around their village. Because the wall was plain, the magistrate hired an artist to paint a dragon on it. The artist agreed to paint the wall if he could paint it in his own manner. When the painting was complete, the magistrate noticed that the dragon had no eyes. He ordered the artist to complete the painting before being paid for his work. The artist reluctantly painted the eyes, collected his money, and left the village. As the villagers admired the dragon's fiery eyes, it screamed and shook and broke free from the wall, leaving the wall to crumble into pieces. The dragon disappeared into a black cloud.

MATERIALS NEEDED

- Make 12 photocopies of the vocabulary card illustration for Unit 2M (see Appendix D), or more or less depending on the number of target words selected (see preparatory set discussion in this unit).

- Obtain pictures of dragons from books or magazines.

- Photocopy a blank, three-category semantic-word map on an overhead transparency (or enlarge the map so all students can see it), or copy enough maps for all students in the group (see Appendix C).

- Photocopy a blank four-episode map on an overhead transparency (or enlarge the map so all students can see it), or copy enough maps for all students in the group (see Appendix C).

- Photocopy a blank discussion web on an overhead transparency (or enlarge the web so all students can see it), or copy enough webs for all students in the group (see Appendix C).

- Photocopy a blank story-grammar cue chart on an overhead transparency (or enlarge the chart so all students can see it), or copy enough charts for all students in the group (see Appendix C).

PRESTORY PRESENTATION

Preparatory Set

Talk about decision-making and the consequences of making a poor decision. Discuss how we can't always predict the consequences of our decisions and that we need to listen to people who have experience. Have students think of a poor decision they have made and the consequences of that decision. Discuss lessons learned the hard way.

See the instructions on page 18 for teaching selected story vocabulary words. Use the following vocabulary words selected for you, or select words appropriate for your specific students.

- clever
- magistrate
- stern
- Confucius
- inspection
- consequences

Write each word on a copy of the vocabulary card illustration and write the corresponding definition on another card. After all cards have been created, have students match each word to its corresponding definition.

Semantic-Word Map

Obtain some books and pictures about dragons. Have students scan the books and call out words and ideas that are related to dragons. Organize the information into categories of dragon characteristics on a semantic-word map. The following is an example of a semantic-word map for *Eyes of the Dragon*.

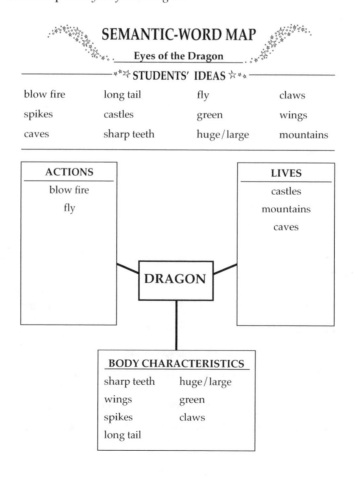

SEMANTIC-WORD MAP

Eyes of the Dragon

STUDENTS' IDEAS

blow fire	long tail	fly	claws
spikes	castles	green	wings
caves	sharp teeth	huge/large	mountains

ACTIONS
blow fire
fly

LIVES
castles
mountains
caves

DRAGON

BODY CHARACTERISTICS
sharp teeth   huge/large
wings   green
spikes   claws
long tail

Think Alouds

Point to the cover and say, "I know that this book is about a frightening dragon. How do I know this?"

Read the title and say, "The title of this story is *Eyes of the Dragon*." Either model a prediction for the students (e.g., "I predict that this story will be about a dragon who has evil, fiery eyes") or ask a prediction question (e.g., "What do you think this story will be about?").

Scan the illustrations only. Stop at selected points of the story to model a prediction or to ask prediction questions based only on the illustrations:

- Where do you think this story takes place? How can you tell?

- What could this man be painting? Why are people gathering to watch him paint? Do you think his painting is really important? Why?

Write down the students' responses for discussion and comparison with actual events after reading the story. Stop the prestory think-aloud activity before the dragon comes to life so the ending of the story will not be revealed.

DURING-STORY PRESENTATION

Directed Reading/Thinking Activity

Read to where the elders have suggested that the magistrate listen to the artist. Have the students predict what they think the magistrate will do. Also, have the students predict what might happen to the dragon if its eyes are painted. Write these predictions where all students can see them.

Questioning

See the instructions on pages 23–24 for asking questions about the following figurative-language examples:

- The children *scattered like a flock of frightened chickens.*

- The scales along his back *looked like a row of mountains.*

POSTSTORY PRESENTATION

Think Alouds

After reading the story, state, "The magistrate acted foolishly by demanding that the artist paint the dragon's eyes. Do you think the artist should have painted them? What could the artist have said to the magistrate to change his mind?" Conduct a discussion about think-aloud questions. Compare students' responses before the story was read with the actual story events.

Question-Answer Relationships

See the instructions on page 35 for the question-answer relationships strategy. The following are examples of questions to test students' comprehension of *Eyes of the Dragon* (question type is indicated in parentheses after each example):

- Why did the people in the little village build the wall? (Right There)

- Who gave the magistrate the idea to have the wall painted? (Right There)

- What did the elders think about the magistrate's idea to paint the wall? (Think and Search)

- Did the magistrate think about and consider the conditions that the artist set? How do you know? (Think and Search)

- If you were the artist, would you have painted in the eyes of the dragon? (Author and You)

- Why do you think the magistrate acted like he did? (Author and You)

- How can making a poor decision harm others? (On Your Own)

- Think of a situation when you did not consider the consequences of your actions. What happened? (On Your Own)

Episode Map

See the instructions on pages 29–30 for developing an episode map. The following is an example of an episode map for *Eyes of the Dragon*.

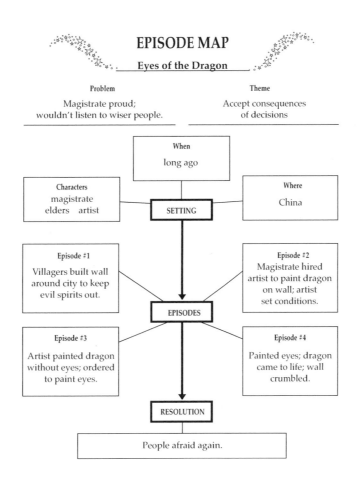

Word Substitution

See the instructions on pages 40–41 for the word-substitution strategy. The following is an example sentence with its target word emphasized, followed by lists of synonyms and antonyms:

The dragon was so *grand* and beautiful that no one made a sound.

grand (synonym)	*grand* (antonym)
great	small
immense	common
magnificent	humble
majestic	

Discussion Web

See the instructions on pages 26–27 for the discussion-web strategy. The following is an example of a discussion web for *Eyes of the Dragon*.

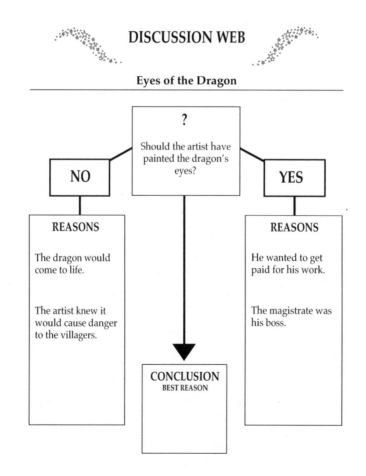

DISCUSSION WEB

Eyes of the Dragon

?
Should the artist have painted the dragon's eyes?

NO

YES

REASONS

The dragon would come to life.

The artist knew it would cause danger to the villagers.

REASONS

He wanted to get paid for his work.

The magistrate was his boss.

CONCLUSION
BEST REASON

Story-Grammar Cue Chart

See the instructions on page 37 for using the story-grammar cue chart. The following is an example of a story-grammar cue chart for *Eyes of the Dragon*.

STORY-GRAMMAR CUE CHART
Eyes of the Dragon

STORY GRAMMAR	STORY	CHECK-OFF
Setting: When: Where: Who:	Long ago A little village in China Magistrate, elders, artist	☐
Problem:	Magistrate proud and would not listen to wise people	☐
Episode #1:	Villagers afraid of evil spirits; magistrate had villagers build wall; wall protected city	☐
Internal Response:	Safe from evil, satisfied	
Episode #2:	Magistrate thought wall too plain; hired artist; artist set conditions	☐
Internal Response:	Excited, anticipating beautiful wall	
Episode #3:	Magistrate inspected wall; dragon painted without eyes	☐
Internal Response:	Anger, disappointment	
Episode #4:	Magistrate ordered artist to paint eyes; artist painted eyes; dragon came to life	☐
Internal Response:	Fear, shock, horror	
Ending:	Dragon jumped off wall; wall crumbled	☐
Reaction:	People afraid again	

Journals

Tell students to write their reactions to the story. Suggest writing prompts such as how students felt about the story, what the characters were like, or the consequences of the magistrate's foolishness.

Story Retelling

Provide the students with a completed episode map to follow as you model story retelling for them. Next, assign an episode to each student in the group and have students retell the story in a round-robin fashion. Then, have each student retell the story individually to a partner. Finally, have the students retell it to the entire group. If desired, tape-record each retelling and let the students listen to their work.

Story Generation

See the instructions on pages 35–37 for the story-generation strategy. Have students rewrite the ending of the story with the artist refusing to paint the dragon's eyes.

Unit 3M
HECKEDY PEG

By Audrey Wood (1987). San Diego, CA: Harcourt Brace.
Unit developed by Kelly Hoggan North.

A mother went to the market to buy her children some gifts. While she was gone, Heckedy Peg, a witch, came to the house and turned the children into food. She loaded the children into her cart and took them to her hut. When the mother returned, she found the children missing. A blackbird showed the mother to the witch's hut. The witch told the mother to guess which child had been turned into which food. The mother guessed the children correctly by placing each gift next to the food that went with it. The children turned back into themselves and they chased the witch to a bridge, where she jumped into the water and was never heard from again.

MATERIALS NEEDED

- Make 16 photocopies of the vocabulary card illustration for Unit 3M (see Appendix D), or more or less depending on the number of target words selected (see preparatory set discussion in this unit).

- Obtain pictures of witches from books, magazines, or coloring books.

- Photocopy a blank, four-category semantic-word map on an overhead transparency (or enlarge the map so all students can see it), or copy enough maps for all students in the group (see Appendix C).

- Construct a compare/contrast chart where all students can see it (see compare/contrast chart discussion in this unit).

- Obtain art materials (white construction paper, pencils, and crayons).

- Photocopy a blank story map on an overhead transparency (or enlarge the map so all students can see it), or copy enough maps for all students in the group (see Appendix C).

PRESTORY PRESENTATION

Preparatory Set

Have students recall stories or movies that include witches (e.g., *Wizard of Oz, Sleeping Beauty, Snow White, Hansel and Gretel)*. Ask them to describe the actions and attributes of the witches in those stories.

Talk about what a stranger is and what parents and teachers teach us about strangers. Ask hypothetical questions about what students would do if a stranger came to the door and wanted to be let in.

See the instructions on page 18 for teaching selected story vocabulary words. Use the following vocabulary words selected for you, or select words appropriate for your specific students.

- stranger
- windowsill
- pity
- despair
- hearth
- rapped
- overjoyed
- hobbled

Write each word on a copy of the vocabulary card illustration and write the corresponding definition on another card. After all cards have been created, have students match each word to its corresponding definition.

Semantic-Word Map

Locate several pictures of witches from books, magazines, or coloring books. Have the students identify attributes and actions of witches. Categorize student contributions using a semantic-word map. The following is an example of a semantic-word map for *Heckedy Peg*.

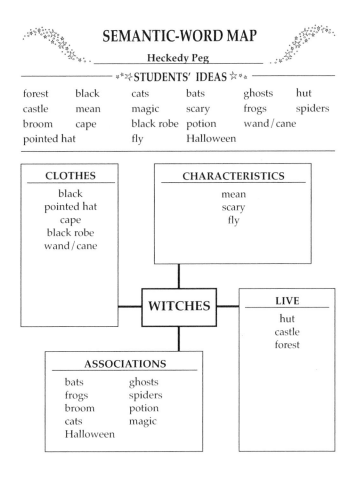

SEMANTIC-WORD MAP

Heckedy Peg

STUDENTS' IDEAS

forest	black	cats	bats	ghosts	hut
castle	mean	magic	scary	frogs	spiders
broom	cape	black robe	potion	wand/cane	
pointed hat		fly	Halloween		

CLOTHES
black
pointed hat
cape
black robe
wand/cane

CHARACTERISTICS
mean
scary
fly

WITCHES

LIVE
hut
castle
forest

ASSOCIATIONS
bats   ghosts
frogs   spiders
broom   potion
cats   magic
Halloween

159

Think Alouds

Point to the cover and say, "I know that this story is about several children who are playing together and having a good time. How do I know this?"

Read the title and say, "The title of this story is *Heckedy Peg*." Either model a prediction for the students (e.g., "I predict that this story will be about a game that the children play called 'Heckedy Peg'") or ask a prediction question (e.g., "What do you think 'Heckedy Peg' means?").

Scan the illustrations only. Stop at selected points of the story to model a prediction or to ask prediction questions based only on the illustrations:

- What do you think the mother is saying to the children in this picture? Could the children be in trouble? Why?

- Who is that old woman at the window? What do you think she wants?

- What do you think the mother is looking for near all of those black, thick trees?

Write down the students' responses for discussion and comparison with actual events after reading the story. Stop the prestory think-aloud activity before the witch's food is changed back to the children so the ending of the story will not be revealed.

DURING-STORY PRESENTATION

Directed Reading/Thinking Activity

Read to where the witch won't let the mother in the house because the mother's feet are dirty and the mother tells the witch that she will cut off her own feet. Have the students predict whether the mother will really cut off her feet and how she will trick the witch to get into the hut. Write these predictions where all students can see them.

Read to where the mother is full of despair because she doesn't know who her children are. Have the students predict how she will figure out which child is which. Write these predictions where all students can see them.

Extension

After reading the sentence, "A blackbird who had seen everything took pity on the mother and hopped down to the windowsill," use the following extension to clarify *took pity*: "Yes, the blackbird felt sorry for the mother and decided to help her." Provide an example from your own experience: "When I was young, I found a bird with a broken wing. I took pity on the bird and nursed it back to health. I felt sorry for it because it couldn't fly, so I helped it heal." Then ask the students, "Have you ever taken pity on someone or something?"

Questioning

See the instructions on pages 23–24 for asking questions about the following figurative-language examples:

- Come now, *sweet chickens.*

- *My supper grows cold.*

- *Quick as a wink,* the children turned back into themselves.

POSTSTORY PRESENTATION

Think Alouds

After reading the story, state, "The children did not obey their mother when she told them not to play with fire and not to let a stranger in. Consequently, a witch kidnapped them, turned them into food, and almost ate them. What other things could have happened to the children because of their disobedience?" Conduct a discussion about think-aloud questions. Compare students' responses before the story was read with the actual story events.

Question-Answer Relationships

See the instructions on page 35 for the question-answer relationships strategy.

The following are examples of questions to test students' comprehension of *Heckedy Peg* (question type is indicated in parentheses after each example):

- What did the mother tell the children to do? (Right There)

- What did the witch want the children to do? (Right There)

- Why did the children finally let the witch in? (Think and Search)

- Why did the bird help the mother find her children? (Author and You)

- Why do you think the witch wouldn't let the mother in? (Author and You)

- How did the mother know who her children were? (Think and Search)

- What would you do if a stranger came to your door? (On Your Own)

- What would you do if your brother or sister played with fire? (On Your Own)

Word Substitution

See the instructions on pages 40–41 for the word-substitution strategy. The following are example sentences with their target words emphasized, followed by lists of synonyms:

- Because you are such good children, you may ask for anything you want and I will bring it home from the *market*.

    market
    store
    shop
    business

- The witch took the children deep into the woods to her *hut*.

    hut
    hide-out
    shed
    cabin
    shack

Compare/Contrast Chart

Using a compare/contrast chart, have the students describe the attributes of the seven children, what they wanted from the market, and what the witch turned them into. The following is an example of a compare/contrast chart for *Heckedy Peg*.

Name	Age	Sex	Eye	Hr	Clothes	Wanted	Turned Into
Monday	13	G	BL	BR	Vest	Butter	Bread
Tuesday	11	B	BR	BR	Jacket	Knife	Pie
Wednesday	9	G	BR	BR	BL Dress	Pitcher	Milk
Thursday	8	B	H	BR	Vest	Honey	Porridge
Friday	6	G	BL	BR	P Shirt	Salt	Fish
Saturday	5	B	BL	BR	Y Shirt	Crackers	Cheese
Sunday	4	B	BL	BL	Vest	Egg Pudding	Roast Rib

Art Activity

Art materials needed:

- One piece of white construction paper per student
- Pencils and crayons

Instruct students to draw and color pictures of the children after they were turned into food, and pictures of the gifts that were brought to them by their mother. Tell them to label the foods and the gifts. Discuss how the mother knew which child was which.

Story Map

See the instructions on page 38 for developing a story map. The following is an example of a story map for *Heckedy Peg*.

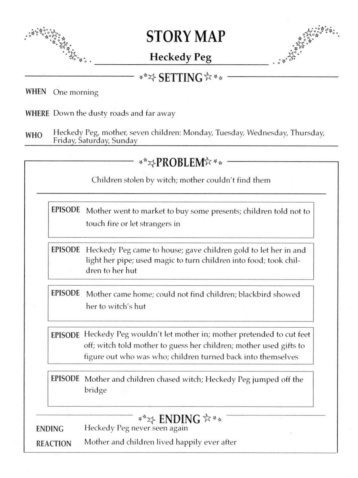

STORY MAP

Heckedy Peg

— *SETTING* —

WHEN One morning

WHERE Down the dusty roads and far away

WHO Heckedy Peg, mother, seven children: Monday, Tuesday, Wednesday, Thursday, Friday, Saturday, Sunday

PROBLEM

Children stolen by witch; mother couldn't find them

EPISODE Mother went to market to buy some presents; children told not to touch fire or let strangers in

EPISODE Heckedy Peg came to house; gave children gold to let her in and light her pipe; used magic to turn children into food; took children to her hut

EPISODE Mother came home; could not find children; blackbird showed her to witch's hut

EPISODE Heckedy Peg wouldn't let mother in; mother pretended to cut feet off; witch told mother to guess her children; mother used gifts to figure out who was who; children turned back into themselves

EPISODE Mother and children chased witch; Heckedy Peg jumped off the bridge

ENDING

ENDING Heckedy Peg never seen again

REACTION Mother and children lived happily ever after

Story Retelling/Summarizing

Provide each student with a completed story map. First, model a story retelling for the group. Then retell it using a cloze procedure like the one following, with the students completing phrases or sentences. Finally have each student retell it using the story map for cues. Tape-record their retellings, if desired.

Once upon a time, there was a mother and her seven _____ (children). The mother went to the market to buy her children some _____ (gifts). A witch named _____ (Heckedy Peg) came to the house while the mother was gone and turned the children into _____ (food). Heckedy Peg loaded the children into her _____ (cart) and took them to her ____ (hut). When the mother returned, she found out that her children were _____ (gone). A bird told her where they were. The witch told the mother to guess which child was which _____ (food). The mother guessed correctly by putting each gift next to the _____ (food) that it went with. The children turned back into _____ (themselves). They chased the witch to a _____ (bridge). She jumped into the _____ (water). The witch was never _____ (seen again). The mother and children lived happily _____ (ever after).

Story Generation

See the instructions on pages 35–37 for the story-generation strategy. Have students generate stories about a witch who came to their homes and turned them into animals. First, have them list their favorite animals. Then, have each student select one animal from his or her list to be turned into. Have them write some words that describe their animals. Proceed with the instructions for story generation described in Chapter 2.

Unit 4M
RUDE GIANTS

By Audrey Wood (1993). San Diego, CA: Harcourt Brace.

Unit developed by Jillyn Abel and Shelly Anderson.

Beatrix, the butter maid, and her best friend, Gerda the cow, lived in a peaceful village. Two rude giants moved into the village and caused chaos for the villagers. Beatrix and Gerda went about their daily activities in spite of the giants' behavior. However, one day Gerda was taken by the giantess. Beatrix saved Gerda by tricking the giants into learning good manners. The villagers and the giants then became friends. When the giants' first baby was born, it behaved rudely. They knew exactly who to send him to: Beatrix and Gerda, the finest teachers in the land.

MATERIALS NEEDED

- Make 18 photocopies of the vocabulary card illustration for Unit 4M (see Appendix D), or more or less depending on the number of target words selected (see preparatory set discussion in this unit).

- Photocopy a blank, three-category semantic-word map on an overhead transparency (or enlarge the map so all students can see it), or copy enough maps for all students in the group (see Appendix C).

- Photocopy a blank internal-states chart on an overhead transparency (or enlarge the chart so all students can see it), or copy enough charts for all students in the group (see Appendix C).

- Photocopy a blank story-grammar cue chart on an overhead transparency (or enlarge the chart so all students can see it), or copy enough charts for all students in the group (see Appendix C).

- Obtain necessary art materials (one sheet of white construction paper and a pencil per student; one large sheet of butcher paper, one sheet of 8½" x 11" paper, and one pencil per student; one sheet of white construction paper per student, pencils and crayons, one cardboard box, and tape); and tape recorder.

PRESTORY PRESENTATION

Preparatory Set/Art Activity

Conduct a discussion about rude behavior. Ask the students to explain what it means to be rude. Ask them to think of some examples of rude behavior and write these where all students can see them. Ask students to recall some things they have done that were rude.

Art materials needed:

- One sheet of white construction paper per student
- One pencil per student

Have the students draw pictures of a giant and of themselves standing next to the giant. Talk about an athlete who is extremely tall (e.g., Michael Jordan); ask whether the athlete is a giant. Discuss the fact that a giant is not real. Discuss the difference between a giantess and a giant.

See the instructions on page 18 for teaching selected story vocabulary words. Use the following vocabulary words selected for you, or select words appropriate for your specific students.

- cozy
- cottage
- butter maid

- clumsy
- quarreled
- glistening

- scooped
- bellowed
- slurp

Write each word on a copy of the vocabulary card illustration and write the corresponding definition on another card. After all cards have been created, have students match each word to its corresponding definition.

Think Alouds

Point to the cover and say, "I know that this book is about two mean giants. How do I know this?"

Read the title and say, "The title of this story is *Rude Giants*." Either model a prediction for the students (e.g., "I predict that this story will be about these two giants and all of the rude things they do to the girl and the cow") or ask a prediction question (e.g., "What do you think the story will be about?").

Scan the illustrations only. Stop at selected points of the story to model a prediction or to ask prediction questions based only on the illustrations:

- The villagers are looking toward the castle. How do you think they feel about the giants?

- The giants are looking into the mirror, and they look surprised. Why do you suppose they look that way?

Write down the students' responses for discussion and comparison with actual events after reading the story. Stop the prestory think-aloud activity where all of the villagers are heading toward the giants' castle so the ending of the story is not revealed.

Semantic-Word Map

Refer to the list of rude behaviors developed earlier in this unit. Now ask students to think of examples of polite behaviors. List their ideas where everyone can see them and categorize them into manners used at the table, manners used at school, and manners used at home with friends and family. Use these ideas to create a semantic-word map. The following is an example of a semantic-word map for *Rude Giants*. (Note: Three of the manners listed in students' ideas appear twice on the semantic-word map.)

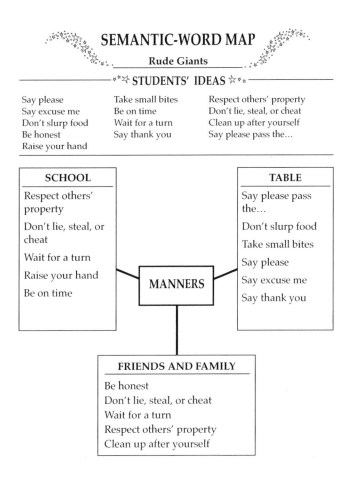

SEMANTIC-WORD MAP

Rude Giants

STUDENTS' IDEAS

Say please
Say excuse me
Don't slurp food
Be honest
Raise your hand

Take small bites
Be on time
Wait for a turn
Say thank you

Respect others' property
Don't lie, steal, or cheat
Clean up after yourself
Say please pass the…

SCHOOL

Respect others' property

Don't lie, steal, or cheat

Wait for a turn

Raise your hand

Be on time

TABLE

Say please pass the…

Don't slurp food

Take small bites

Say please

Say excuse me

Say thank you

MANNERS

FRIENDS AND FAMILY

Be honest
Don't lie, steal, or cheat
Wait for a turn
Respect others' property
Clean up after yourself

DURING-STORY PRESENTATION

Think Alouds

Mental Picture—Read to where the villagers wonder what the rude giants will do next and say, "The villagers are getting sick of the giants and are wondering what they will do next. I wonder what they will do. The idea that I have is that they are so angry with the giants that they will think of a plan to get the giants to leave. I think they will have a town council meeting and kick the giants out of their village. What is your idea about how they will get rid of the giants?"

Analogy—Read to where the giants are stealing from the villagers and say, "This reminds me of a time when a rude classmate stole my colored pencils. The classmate lied and said that somebody else took them. Has a person ever stolen something from you? How did it make you feel? What did you do about it?"

Confusing Information—Read to where Beatrix goes to the village and all the townspeople gather together and say, "I don't understand why Beatrix left Gerda at the castle while she went to town to meet with the villagers. This is different than what I would expect. I would expect that she would take Gerda and run to get away from the hungry giants. What would you expect?"

Repair Strategy—Read to where Beatrix runs to the village and say, "Beatrix left Gerda at the castle all alone with the hungry giants. I wonder why she did that. I'd better read on to find out whether she will save Gerda and help the giants. What do you think she will do to help them? What will the villagers do to help the giants?"

Extension

After reading the sentence, "The giants' stomachs rumbled like thunder beyond the mountains," use the following extension to clarify *rumbled like thunder*: "Yes, they were so hungry that when their stomachs growled, it sounded like thunder." Provide an example from your own experience: "The train that goes through town everyday at noon is so

loud that it rumbles like thunder." Then ask the students, "What are some things you can think of that rumble like thunder?"

POSTSTORY PRESENTATION

Think Alouds

After reading the story, state, "Beatrix taught the giants to be polite and clean. When the giants had a rude baby, they had to send it to Gerda and Beatrix to learn polite manners. Why didn't the giants teach their baby how to be polite? What else could they have done on their own to teach the baby polite manners?" Conduct a discussion about think-aloud questions. Compare students' responses before the story was read with the actual story events.

Art Activity

Art materials needed:

- One large sheet of butcher paper per student
- One sheet of 8½" x 11" paper per student
- Pencils

Have students work in pairs to make outline drawings of themselves on large pieces of butcher paper. Then have students draw a picture of a person on a regular 8½" x 11" piece of paper. Label each students' outline on the butcher paper as a giant and each smaller picture as a villager. Conduct a discussion and have students compare the two pictures (e.g., size, amount of food each would eat, size of home and furnishings needed, etc.).

Word Substitution

See the instructions on pages 40–41 for the word-substitution strategy. The following are example sentences with their target words emphasized, followed by lists of synonyms:

- They *trampled* the flowers.

    trampled

    squashed

    walked on

    smashed

    crushed

- "Why, just look at this messy place," Beatrix *scolded*.

    scolded

    yelled

    nagged

    hollered

    urged

Question-Answer Relationships

See the instructions on page 35 for the question-answer relationships strategy. The following are examples of questions to test students' comprehension of *Rude Giants* (question type is indicated in parentheses after each example):

- What did Gerda give Beatrix every morning? (Right There)

- Why were Beatrix and Gerda going to the market? (Right There)

- What did Beatrix do when the giantess took Gerda? (Think and Search)

- What is one way Beatrix tricked the giants into not eating Gerda? (Think and Search)

- Why were the villagers so upset when the giants came into their village? (Author and You)

- What would have happened to Gerda if Beatrix had not gone to the castle? (Author and You)

- How does using polite manners help us to get along better with people? (On Your Own)

- How do you teach a new baby to have polite manners? (On Your Own)

Internal-States Chart

See the instructions on pages 32–33 for developing an internal-states chart. Engage the students in dialogue like the following regarding the characters' feelings:

Educator: How did Gerda and Beatrix feel about their lives before the giants moved into their village?

Students: Gerda and Beatrix felt carefree.

Educator: Why did they feel carefree?

Students: Because life was going well for them.

The following is an example of an internal-states chart for *Rude Giants*.

INTERNAL-STATES CHART
Rude Giants

CHARACTER(S)	WHEN	FEELING	WHY
Gerda, Beatrix	Before giants	Carefree	Life was good
Villagers	Giants arrived	Scared	Giants big, rude
Gerda	After stolen	Scared	Giant might eat her
Giants	Learn manners	Happy	Felt polite
Giants	After bath	Shocked	Were beautiful
Everyone	At dinner	Happy	Were friends

Story-Grammar Cue Chart

See the instructions on page 37 for developing a story-grammar cue chart. The following is an example of a story-grammar cue chart for *Rude Giants*.

STORY-GRAMMAR CUE CHART
Rude Giants

STORY GRAMMAR	STORY	CHECK-OFF
Setting:		☐
When:	Long ago	
Where:	Cozy cottage, happy valley	
Who:	Gerda the cow, Beatrix the butter maid	
Problem:	Giants moved in; trampled, quarreled, stole	☐
Episode #1:	Beatrix and Gerda went to market; giantess took Gerda; Beatrix jumped on giant's shoe	☐
Internal Response:	Scared	
Episode #2:	Giants started to eat Gerda; Beatrix said had to clean castle; giants cleaned castle	☐
Internal Response:	Giants hungrier than ever	
Episode #3:	Giants started to eat Gerda; Beatrix said had to learn manners; giants learned manners; Beatrix said must be beautiful; giants became beautiful	☐
Internal Response:	Still hungry	
Episode #4:	Giants hungry; didn't know what to do; Beatrix called villagers; people took food to giants	☐
Internal Response:	Happy, full	
Ending:	Beatrix and Gerda taught giants' rude child polite manners; had party every week with villagers	☐
Reaction:	Everybody was happy	

Story Retelling/Art Activity

Art materials needed:

- One sheet of construction paper per student
- Pencils and crayons
- Tape
- One cardboard box

Assign the setting, each episode, and the ending to different students. Ask each to draw the designated story part. After the students have drawn their pictures, have them arrange the pictures in the correct sequence. Next, have the students tape the pictures together into one long picture. Roll the picture up to make a scroll. Have a box already cut out to look like a television. Place the scroll in the box. While scrolling each picture across the cut-out television screen, ask the student responsible for the drawing to retell that story frame. Tape-record the story and let the students listen to their story as the pictures are scrolled across the screen again.

Journals

Have the students describe times when they have observed others being rude. Have students describe how they felt about these people and how they were treated when they were being rude.

Unit 5M
SAM, BANGS & MOONSHINE

By Evaline Ness (1966). Austin, TX: Holt, Rinehart & Winston.
Unit developed by Jill S. Turnier.

A little girl named Sam was told by her father to talk *real*, not *moonshine*. Sam was known for lying and telling stories; she told people that she had a mermaid mother and a baby kangaroo. She sent Thomas, her friend, to visit her mermaid mother and to find her baby kangaroo near a large sea rock. A storm developed, and Bangs, Sam's wise cat, followed Thomas, who had ridden his bicycle to the sea rock. When Sam's father came home from work, she told him that Thomas and Bangs were out on the sea rock. Sam's father searched and found Thomas, but not Bangs. Sam was sent to bed. During the night, Bangs came home. In the morning, Sam decided that *moonshine* was not *real* and that lying was wrong. She decided to give her baby kangaroo (a gerbil) to Thomas.

MATERIALS NEEDED

- Make 16 photocopies of the vocabulary card illustration for Unit 5M (see Appendix D), or more or less depending on the number of target words selected (see preparatory set discussion in this unit).

- Construct a compare/contrast chart where all students can see it (see compare/contrast chart discussion in this unit).

- Photocopy a blank internal-states chart on an overhead transparency (or enlarge the chart so all students can see it), or copy enough charts for all students in the group (see Appendix C).

- Photocopy a blank story map on an overhead transparency (or enlarge the map so all students can see it), or copy enough maps for all students in the group (see Appendix C); and have a tape recorder available.

PRESTORY PRESENTATION

Preparatory Set

Read the title and discuss the word *moonshine*. Use the word *moonshine* in the following sentences to help the students guess its meaning. Discuss the meaning of the word further after reviewing the sentences.

- I don't believe my brother when he talks moonshine.

- I talked moonshine when I told my mom that dogs could fly.

- I talk moonshine when I'm not telling the truth.

- My sister loves to tell moonshine stories that are hard to believe.

Talk about what lying (i.e., moonshine) is and how it can affect people. Discuss the difference between pretending and lying and provide examples of each.

Read the following sentences. Have the students tell you whether each sentence is moonshine or real.

- My mother is 10 feet tall.

- Birds build nests in the trees.

- I have a pet dinosaur in my backyard.

- All girls have blond hair.

- Cats are mammals.

- Fish swim in the ocean, rivers, and lakes.

- At night, alligators hide under my bed.

Ask the students to write one moonshine and one real sentence to read aloud. Allow classmates to guess which sentences are moonshine and which are real.

See the instructions on page 18 for teaching selected story vocabulary words. Use the following vocabulary words selected for you, or select words appropriate for your specific students.

- sodden
- scoured
- diminishing
- curious

- stalked
- flummadiddle
- laryngitis
- torrents

Write each word on a copy of the vocabulary card illustration and write the corresponding definition on another card. After all cards have been created, have students match each word to its corresponding definition.

Think Alouds

Point to the cover and say, "I know that this book is about a black cat that lives near the ocean. How do I know this?"

Read the title and say, "The title of this story is *Sam, Bangs & Moonshine*." Either model a prediction for the students (e.g., "I predict that this story will be about a mischievous cat that talks moonshine") or ask a prediction question (e.g., "What do you think this story will be about?").

Scan the illustrations only. Stop at selected points of the story to model a prediction or to ask prediction questions based only on the illustrations:

- Why do you think this girl is lying on that rug? What could she be thinking about? How is the cat feeling?

- The girl sitting in the chair looks sad. What do you think has caused her to feel that way?

- The cat is lying on the rock next to the lighthouse. What do you think has happened? Is it still alive? Is it sleeping?

Write down the students' responses for discussion and comparison with actual events after reading the story. Stop the prestory think-aloud activity where Sam gives her gerbil to Thomas so the ending of the story will not be revealed.

DURING-STORY PRESENTATION

Directed Reading/Thinking Activity

Read to where Sam peers through the window at the rain as she wonders where Thomas and Bangs are. Have the students predict how they think Sam is feeling. Ask them what they think will happen to Thomas and Bangs. Write these predictions where all students can see them. After the story is complete, have the students determine which of their predictions were correct.

Extension

After reading the sentence, "Moonshine is flummadiddle," use the following extension to clarify *flummadiddle*: "Yes, *flummadiddle* is a make-believe word that Bangs made up for the words *pretend* or *make-believe.*" Provide an example from your own experience: "When I was a child, I had a pretend friend. It was flummadiddle." Then ask the students, "Have ever done anything that was flummadiddle?"

Questioning

See the instructions on pages 23–24 for asking questions about the following figurative-language examples:

- The ragged old rug on the doorstep was a *chariot drawn by dragons.*

- Moonshine *spells trouble.*

- When the sun *made a golden star* on the cracked window…

- She was almost knocked off the doorstep when a sudden gust of wind *drove torrents of rain* against her face.

- She could see nothing through the *gray ribbed curtain of rain.*

- She listened to the rain *hammer on the tin roof.*

POSTSTORY PRESENTATION

Think Alouds

After reading the story, state, "Sam sent Thomas to look for her kangaroo in a dangerous place. How could she have saved Thomas if her father hadn't come home when he did?" Conduct a discussion about think-aloud questions. Compare students' responses before the story was read with the actual story events.

Summarizing

See the instructions on page 24 for summarizing after story reading. Help students retell the story using a cloze procedure like the following, with the students completing phrases or sentences.

On an island lived a girl named _____ (Samantha), who had the habit of _____ (lying). Sam had a cat named _____ (Bangs) and a friend named _____ (Thomas). Thomas always did what Sam told him to do. One day, Sam told Thomas to look for her baby _____ (kangaroo) in a cave behind _____ (Blue Rock).

Continue summarizing in the same manner through to the end of the story.

Compare/Contrast Chart

Use a compare/contrast chart to clarify the real and imaginary statements in the story. Have the students list all Sam's *moonshine* statements on one side of the chart and all of the corresponding *real* events on the other side. The following is an example of a compare/contrast chart for *Sam, Bangs & Moonshine*.

Moonshine	Real
Mermaid mother	Mother died
Fierce lion at home	Bangs (cat) at home
Pet baby kangaroo	Gerbil
Bangs can talk	Cats cannot talk
Chariot drawn by dragons	Dragons do not exist
Sam visits the moon	Sam can't visit the moon

Question-Answer Relationships

See the instructions on page 35 for the question-answer relationships strategy. The following are examples of questions to test students' comprehension of *Sam, Bangs & Moonshine* (question type is indicated in parentheses after each example):

- What did Thomas beg to see every day? (Right There)

- Where did Sam send Thomas to search for her baby kangaroo? (Right There)

- Did Thomas believe everything that Sam said? Why? (Think and Search)

- Why couldn't Thomas's bike be found? (Author and You)

- Why did Bangs follow Thomas? (Author and You)

- Why did Sam give Thomas her gerbil? (Author and You)

- Why is it important to be honest with your friends? (On Your Own)

• How would you feel if a family member was hurt because of a lie you told? (On Your Own)

Internal-States Chart

See the instructions on pages 32–33 for using an internal-states chart. Engage the students in dialogue like the following regarding the characters' feelings:

Educator: How did Thomas feel when he rode his bike to Blue Rock?

Students: He felt curious.

Educator: Why did he feel curious?

Students: Because he wanted to find a kangaroo and mermaid.

The following is an example of an internal-states chart for *Sam, Bangs & Moonshine*.

INTERNAL-STATES CHART
Sam, Bangs, & Moonshine

CHARACTER(S)	WHEN	FEELING	WHY
Thomas	Rode bike to Blue Rock	Curious; eager	Wanted to find kangaroo and mermaid
Bangs	Followed Thomas	Concerned	Warned Thomas of the rising tide
Sam	Cried and looked out window	Worried	Wanted Thomas, Bangs to return
Father	Left house to search for Bangs and Thomas	Angry; worried	Stormy weather; Bangs and Thomas not back
Sam	Gave her gerbil to Thomas	Guilty	To ask forgiveness from Thomas

Journals

Have the students write in their journals about a personal experience. Use the following writing prompts:

- Have you ever talked "moonshine" before? Describe the experience and whether you were punished, and whether someone got hurt. (As a model, share a personal experience of your own with the students.)

- Pretend that you are Sam. What would you have done to help save Thomas and Bangs? (E.g., Would you have gone out in the rain and looked for them?)

Story Map

See the instructions on page 38 for developing a story map. Create the setting for the story by drawing a map where all students can see it showing Thomas's house, the harbor, Blue Rock, and Sam's house. Draw the route that Thomas took while searching for the "baby kangaroo." Sketch the four main characters.

Write the story's episodes near the map. Then draw a line from each episode to where the episode occurred on the map. An example of the episodes from a story map for *Sam, Bangs & Moonshine* is provided on the following page.

Story Retelling

See the instructions on pages 39–40 for story retelling. Using the story map for support, have the students tell the story in round-robin fashion, each providing one episode.

Transfer the story map to 8½" x 11" paper. Duplicate one story map for each student. Direct them to take their maps home for story-retelling practice. Have the students retell the story to a familiar person (teacher, parent, sibling) who does not know the story.

Have students tape-record their versions of the story (while using the story map). Assist the students in writing their stories from the tape recordings. Have them read their stories to the group.

STORY MAP

Sam, Bangs & Moonshine

———————— **☆ SETTING ☆** ————————

WHEN Once upon a time

WHERE Thomas's house, harbor, Blue Rock, Sam's house

WHO Sam, Bangs, Thomas, Sam's father

———————— **☆PROBLEM☆** ————————

Sam didn't know the difference between what's
false and what's real

| EPISODE | Sam's father left for work; reminded Sam to talk *real*, not *moonshine* |

| EPISODE | Sam told Thomas to find baby kangaroo at Blue Rock; Thomas left on bike; Bangs followed |

| EPISODE | It began to rain; Sam worried about Bangs and Thomas; Sam's father searched at Blue Rock |

| EPISODE | Sam's father found Thomas, but not Bangs; Sam decided that moonshine was bad |

| EPISODE | Bangs appeared at Sam's window; Sam went to Thomas's house and gave him her gerbil |

———————— **☆ ENDING ☆** ————————

ENDING
REACTION

Sam learned that telling false stories (moonshine) could hurt
people; decided to stop talking moonshine
**

** None provided in story. Ask students to tell how Sam
and Thomas felt when Sam gave Thomas the gerbil.

Unit 6M
STELLALUNA

By Janell Cannon (1993). San Diego, CA: Harcourt Brace.
Unit developed by Janet Jensen with assistance from her son, Jeff.

After a newborn bat named Stellaluna was separated from her mother, she fell head first into a nest of birds and was adopted by them. She adapted to her new surroundings by learning the rules and habits of the bird family. She also shared some of her own survival skills with the birds but had little success. Eventually, Stellaluna reunited with her mother, but she still kept and valued her friendship with the birds.

MATERIALS NEEDED

- Obtain books about bats and birds from the library, then construct a compare/contrast chart on an overhead transparency or where all students can see it.

- Make 16 photocopies of the vocabulary card illustration for Unit 6M (see Appendix D), or more or less depending on the number of target words selected (see preparatory set discussion in this unit).

- Photocopy a blank discussion web on an overhead transparency (or enlarge the web so all students can see it), or copy enough webs for all students in the group (see Appendix C).

- Obtain art materials (two identical sets of the following pictures: a tree, two bats, a moon, a nest, two birds; a barrier to place on a table between two students). Patterns for the bats, moon, nest, and birds are provided in Appendix D.

- Photocopy a blank story map on an overhead transparency (or enlarge the map so all students can see it), or copy enough maps for all students in the group (see Appendix C).

- Photocopy the picture-story maps and obtain a die and pawns from a board game (see story-mapping discussion in this unit).

- Obtain an audio- or videotape recorder (see dramatic play discussion in this unit).

PRESTORY PRESENTATION

Compare/Contrast Chart

Locate some books from the library about bats and birds. Two excellent resources are *Bats* (Shebar, 1990) and *Birds* (Jeunesse, Delafosse, and Mettler, 1993). Have the students scan the books. Develop a compare/contrast chart for birds and bats. An example compare/contrast chart for *Stellaluna* is provided on the following page.

	BIRDS	BATS
Homes:	trees, nests	caves
Sleep habits:	night, right-side up, in nest	day, hang upside down in tree or cave
Foods:	worms, insects	fruits, mother's milk
Harm to us:	eat crops	can carry rabies
Vision:	excellent	poor, better at night
Body covering:	feathers	fur
Noises they make:	chirp, sing, some talk	squeak
Species:	bird	mammal

Preparatory Set

See the instructions on page 18 for teaching selected vocabulary words. Use the following vocabulary words selected for you, or select words appropriate for your specific students.

- clambered
- babble
- perch
- scent
- sultry
- limp
- stuttered
- mango

Write each word on a vocabulary card illustration and write the corresponding definition on another card. After all cards have been created, have students match each word to its corresponding definition.

Have students list their five least favorite foods and place stars by the three they dislike the most. Have them report these three to a student recorder or you. Make a bar chart of most disliked foods, with number of students on the vertical axis and specific foods on the horizontal axis. Following is an example of a bar chart.

FOODS WE DISLIKE

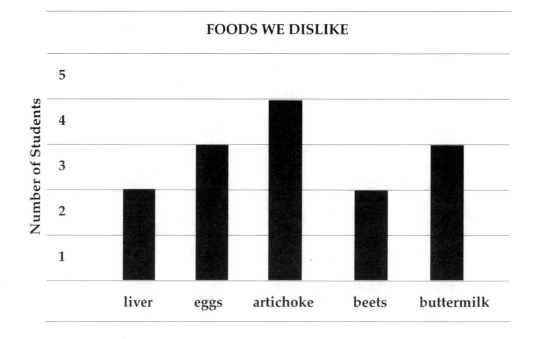

Think Alouds

Point to the cover and say, "I know that this book is about a bat who is having a hard time landing on a branch. How do you think I know this?"

Read the title and say, "The title of this story is *Stellaluna*. 'Luna' is Spanish for 'moon.'" Then, either model a prediction for the students (e.g., "I predict that this story will be about a bat who loves to fly by the light of the moon") or ask a prediction question (e.g., "What do you think this story will be about?").

Scan the illustrations only. Stop at selected points of the story to model a prediction or to ask prediction questions based only on the illustrations:

- The owl looks scary. What do you think he has done to the bat? Where do you think the bat will land?

- Why do you think the birds and bat are hanging over the side of the nest? How do you think the mother bird feels about this behavior?

Write down the students' responses for discussion and comparison with actual events after reading the story. Stop the prestory think-aloud strategy where Stellaluna is hanging right-side up from a branch so the end of the story will not be revealed.

DURING-STORY PRESENTATION

Think Alouds

Mental Picture—Read to where Stellaluna has just been dropped by her mother and is calling out for her and say, "Stellaluna looks scared and her mother won't answer her when she calls. I wonder what happened to the mother. The idea that I have is that mother bat was eaten by the owl. What do you think has happened to Stellaluna's mother?"

Analogy—Read to where Stellaluna promises to obey all the rules of the house and say, "This reminds me of a time when I stayed with my cousins for two weeks. One day we ate all of my aunt's chocolate cake. I got in trouble because I didn't follow the rules of the house. One rule was to ask before you eat. Do you have to follow any rules of the house in your home? What are some of them? How do you feel about following rules that you don't like?"

Confusing Information—Read to where Stellaluna is unsuccessful at landing on the branch as gracefully as her bird friends and say, "Stellaluna can't seem to get the hang of landing as well as her bird friends. She failed all five times. This is different than what I would expect. I would expect that Stellaluna would be the best at flying and landing. What would you expect? Do you think she has problems with landing because she is a bat or because she is clumsy? Why?"

Repair Strategy—Read to where another bat informs Stellaluna that she is hanging upside down and say, "I don't understand why that other bat is trying to tell Stellaluna she is upside down, especially after Stellaluna promised Mother Bird to never hang upside down. I'd better read on to see if Stellaluna will continue to hang by her thumbs. What do you think the other bat will say to her to make her turn around?"

Extension

After reading the sentence, "One night, as Mother Bat followed the heavy scent of ripe fruit, an owl spied her," use the following extension to clarify *heavy scent:* "Yes, the smell of ripe fruit was very strong. She could smell it from a distance." Provide an example from your own experience: "The heavy scent of the skunk gave me a headache," or "I knew my mother had been in the house from the heavy scent of her perfume." Then ask the students, "What other things can have a heavy scent?"

POSTSTORY PRESENTATION

Think Alouds

After reading the story, state, "Stellaluna tried to help her bird friends learn her bat life style by teaching them to hang upside down, eat fruit, and fly at night. What other differences have you noticed between bat and bird life styles?" Conduct a discussion about think-aloud questions. Compare students' responses before the story was read with the actual story events.

Journals

Discuss how attributes are often assigned to animals (e.g., *busy as a bee, mad as a wet hen, quiet as a mouse*). Have students list as many phrases as they can. Which are positive and which are negative?

Use students' journals as an opportunity for them to expand their awareness of figurative language related to birds and bats. Discuss the phrases listed below. What does each mean? What is the origin of each phrase? (Reference books from your school library can be used to answer the latter question.) Have students write about one of these in their journals:

- bats in the belfry
- she's an old bat
- birdbrain
- empty nest

- he drives me batty
- bird's-eye view
- dingbat
- try your wings

- blind as a bat
- eats like a bird
- birds of a feather flock together

Discussion Web

See the instructions on pages 26–27 for the discussion-web strategy. The following is an example of a discussion web for *Stellaluna*.

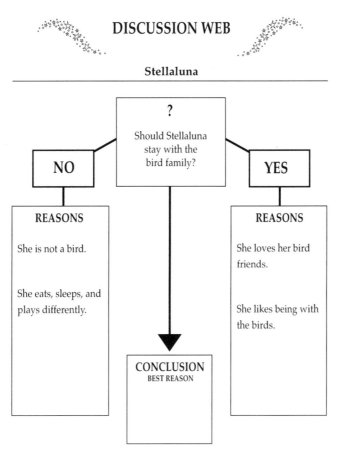

DISCUSSION WEB

Stellaluna

?
Should Stellaluna stay with the bird family?

NO

YES

REASONS

She is not a bird.

She eats, sleeps, and plays differently.

REASONS

She loves her bird friends.

She likes being with the birds.

CONCLUSION
BEST REASON

Art Activity

Art materials needed:

- Two identical sets of the following pictures: a tree, two bats, a moon, a nest, two birds
- A barrier to place on a table between two students

Divide the group in half. Provide each group with a picture set. Have one student in each group participate in a barrier game. The other students can be silent observers of

191

their teammates. Place a barrier on the table between the two students. Direct one student to make a scene with his or her picture set and to describe the scene to the student on the opposite side; direct the listening student to place the pictures as described. Remove the barrier and compare the two scenes. Then start over with the original listening student directing the actions of a new student from the opposite team.

Story Map

See the instructions on page 38 for developing a story map. The following is an example of a story map for *Stellaluna.* Also, use the picture-story map provided on the following page to reinforce and enhance understanding of the story sequence. Provide one die. Have students each take a turn rolling the die, moving a token or pawn (from a board game), and saying the episodes that they pass over and land on. (If desired, divide students into groups and provide each group with necessary materials.)

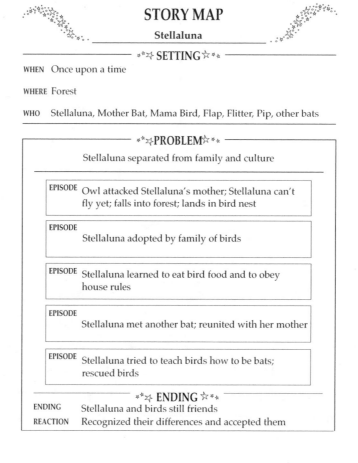

STORY MAP

Stellaluna

SETTING

WHEN Once upon a time

WHERE Forest

WHO Stellaluna, Mother Bat, Mama Bird, Flap, Flitter, Pip, other bats

PROBLEM

Stellaluna separated from family and culture

EPISODE Owl attacked Stellaluna's mother; Stellaluna can't fly yet; falls into forest; lands in bird nest

EPISODE Stellaluna adopted by family of birds

EPISODE Stellaluna learned to eat bird food and to obey house rules

EPISODE Stellaluna met another bat; reunited with her mother

EPISODE Stellaluna tried to teach birds how to be bats; rescued birds

ENDING

ENDING Stellaluna and birds still friends

REACTION Recognized their differences and accepted them

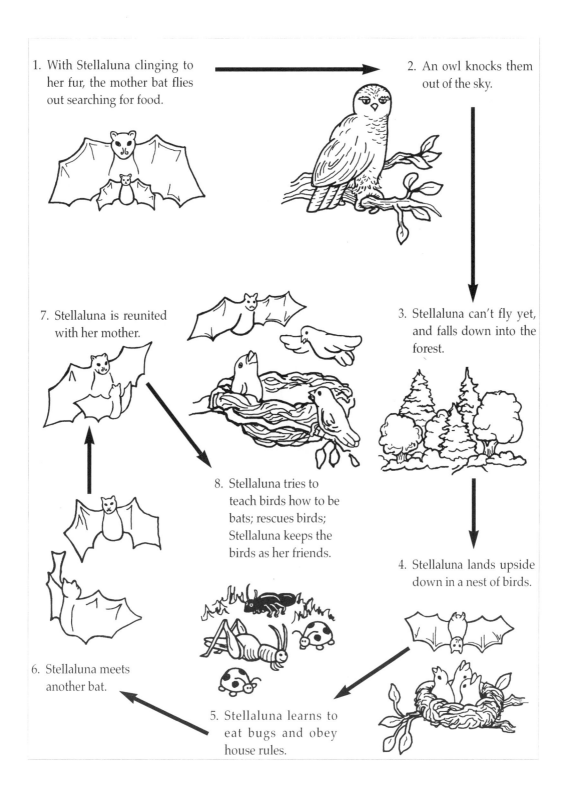

1. With Stellaluna clinging to her fur, the mother bat flies out searching for food.

2. An owl knocks them out of the sky.

3. Stellaluna can't fly yet, and falls down into the forest.

4. Stellaluna lands upside down in a nest of birds.

5. Stellaluna learns to eat bugs and obey house rules.

6. Stellaluna meets another bat.

7. Stellaluna is reunited with her mother.

8. Stellaluna tries to teach birds how to be bats; rescues birds; Stellaluna keeps the birds as her friends.

Dramatic Play

Assign students to play the roles of news reporters and the various characters in *Stellaluna*. Then, instruct the students playing reporters to interview characters and write a news story. If desired, provide students with simple costumes (e.g., press passes, camera, and wings). Direct students to interview Stellaluna about her experiences and to interview other characters as well. Have students tape-record or videotape the interviews. Have students switch roles as desired. The following are some possible interview questions:

- For Stellaluna: How did you feel as you were falling out of the tree? Did you think you would ever see your mother again? How do bugs taste? Why did you decide to stay with the birds? What did they teach you? Do you plan to visit your adoptive bird family? What do you have in common with the birds?

- For Mother Bird: Why did you adopt Stellaluna? What are your house rules?

- For baby birds: What did you think when this strange creature suddenly crashed headfirst into your nest? Why did you try to sleep outside your nest, hanging upside down?

- For Mother Bat: How did you search for Stellaluna? How did you know Stellaluna was really your baby? What will you do if you become separated again?

- For the bat who found Stellaluna: Tell us how you found Stellaluna. Can you describe what she was doing when you first saw her? What was your reaction?

Story Generation

Using the story map created earlier in this unit, outline with the students the basic plot (main character separated from his or her family, adopted by another, learned new habits, and reunited with his or her family). Have students write their own story, substituting other animals or people for characters and changing the setting. For example, they might choose to write about a farm animal adopted by a wild animal, or aliens from outer space adopted by a family in their home town.

Unit 7M
SYLVESTER AND THE MAGIC PEBBLE

By William Steig (1969). New York: Simon and Schuster.
Unit developed by Susan Bartholomew.

Sylvester Duncan, a donkey, found a magic pebble. While on his way home to share his good fortune with his parents, he was startled by a hungry lion. Sylvester panicked and wished that he was a rock. Through the magical powers of the pebble, his wish was granted. Later, because he was no longer touching the magic pebble, he was unable to return to being a donkey. While Sylvester sat hopeless and helpless as a rock, his parents searched everywhere but were unable to find him. A year passed, and his parents resigned themselves to life without Sylvester. One day Mr. and Mrs. Duncan went on a picnic. They spread their lunch on a large rock, Sylvester. Mr. Duncan found the magic pebble and placed it on the rock. As the parents talked about him, Sylvester wished he was a donkey again. He turned back into a donkey and the family was reunited.

MATERIALS NEEDED

- Make eight photocopies of the vocabulary card illustration for Unit 7M (see Appendix D), or more or less depending on the number of target words selected (see preparatory set discussion in this unit).

- Photocopy a blank, six-category semantic-word map on an overhead transparency (or enlarge the map so all students can see it), or copy enough maps for all students in the group (see Appendix C).

- Photocopy a blank story map on an overhead transparency (or enlarge the map so all students can see it), or copy enough maps for all students in the group (see Appendix C).

- Photocopy a blank internal-states chart on an overhead transparency (or enlarge the chart so all students can see it), or copy enough charts for all students in the group (see Appendix C).

- Obtain art materials (one rock for each student, one or two sets of tempera paints, one paintbrush per student).

PRESTORY PRESENTATION

Preparatory Set

Give each student a rock. Ask the students to think of some fun things they can do with their rocks. Ask them if there was no one else to play with, what types of things they could do with their rocks.

See the instructions on page 18 for teaching selected story vocabulary words. Use the following vocabulary words selected for you, or select words appropriate for your specific students.

- flaming
- mysterious
- bewildered
- inquiring
- remarkable
- perplexed
- gradually
- ceased

Write each word on one half of a vocabulary card. Write the corresponding definition on the other half of the card. (Note: Usually the word and definition for each word are written on separate cards. In this unit, the word and definition share a card.)

Play a matching game with the vocabulary cards:

- Cut each illustration in half using jigsaw-type cutting. Tape the vocabulary card illustration halves randomly where all students can see them.

- Have students take turns matching vocabulary words with their definitions. As matches are made, place completed illustrations in a pile. More skilled students can also use the words correctly in a sentence before placing a matched pair of cards on the pile.

Think Alouds

Point to the cover and say, "I know that this book is about some donkeys and other farm animals. The donkeys are talking to the other animals to obtain some information. What do you think they could be asking?"

Read the title and say, "The title of this story is *Sylvester and the Magic Pebble.*" Then, model a prediction for the students (e.g., "I predict that this story will be about a donkey named Sylvester who finds a magic pebble and uses it to play tricks on his parents and friends") or ask a prediction question (e.g., "What do you think this story will be about?").

Scan the illustrations only. Stop at selected points of the story to model a prediction or ask prediction questions based only on the illustrations:

- What do you think the donkey has discovered about the pebble that he found? How do you think it works?

- Why does the lion look so puzzled? What could have happened to the donkey?

- Why do you suppose there are dogs all over the field? What could they be looking for?

197

Write down the students' responses for discussion and comparison with actual events after reading the story. Stop the prestory think-aloud activity when Sylvester's father finds the magic pebble and puts it on the large rock so the ending of the story will not be revealed.

Semantic-Word Map

Ask students to name everything that comes to mind when they think of the word *rock*. List ideas where all students can see them and organize the information into categories using a semantic-word map. The following is an example of a semantic-word map for *Sylvester and the Magic Pebble*.

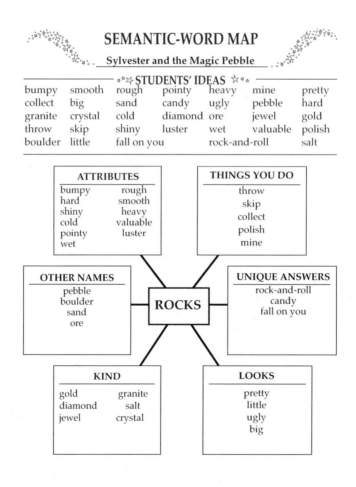

SEMANTIC-WORD MAP

Sylvester and the Magic Pebble

STUDENTS' IDEAS

bumpy	smooth	rough	pointy	heavy	mine	pretty
collect	big	sand	candy	ugly	pebble	hard
granite	crystal	cold	diamond	ore	jewel	gold
throw	skip	shiny	luster	wet	valuable	polish
boulder	little	fall on you		rock-and-roll		salt

ATTRIBUTES

bumpy	rough
hard	smooth
shiny	heavy
cold	valuable
pointy	luster
wet	

THINGS YOU DO

throw
skip
collect
polish
mine

OTHER NAMES

pebble
boulder
sand
ore

ROCKS

UNIQUE ANSWERS

rock-and-roll
candy
fall on you

KIND

gold	granite
diamond	salt
jewel	crystal

LOOKS

pretty
little
ugly
big

DURING-STORY PRESENTATION

Directed Reading/Thinking Activity

Read to where Sylvester turns himself into a rock and confuses the lion. Have the students predict what the lion might be thinking. Write these predictions where all students can see them. Then read to where Sylvester's father and mother go on a picnic and find the pebble. Have the students predict what Sylvester's father will do with the pebble. Again, write these predictions where all students can see them.

Questioning

See the instructions on pages 23–24 for asking questions about the following figurative-language examples:

- The chance was *one in a billion* at best.

- Life *had no meaning* for them anymore.

- He was *stone dumb*.

Extension

After reading the sentence, "His thoughts began to race like mad," use the following extension to clarify *race like mad*: "Yes, he was thinking so many things at once that it was like a race." Provide an example from your own experience: "All of the students raced like mad to get to their free ice cream cones at the fair." Then ask students, "When have your thoughts raced like mad or when have you raced like mad?"

POSTSTORY PRESENTATION

Think Alouds

After reading the story, state, "Sylvester panicked and turned himself into a rock when he saw the lion. What are some other things he could have wished for if he had been thinking clearly?" Conduct a discussion about think-aloud questions. Compare students' responses before the story was read with the actual story events.

Question-Answer Relationships

See the instructions on page 35 for the question-answer relationships strategy. The following are examples of questions to test students' comprehension of *Sylvester and the Magic Pebble* (question type is indicated in parentheses after each example):

- What did the magic pebble look like? (Right There)

- How did Sylvester feel when he met the lion? (Right There)

- What else could Sylvester have wished for when he met the lion? (Author and You)

- What things did the parents do to find Sylvester? (Think and Search)

- How much time passed while Sylvester was a rock? (Think and Search)

- Why was Sylvester sleeping more and more? (Author and You)

- Why did Mr. Duncan put the pebble in the safe? (Author and You)

- What does a rock smell like? (On Your Own)

- What would you wish for if you found a magic pebble? Why? (On Your Own)

Word Substitution

See the instructions on pages 40–41 for the word-substitution strategy. The following are example sentences with their target words emphasized, followed by lists of synonyms:

- They concluded that something *dreadful* must have happened and that they would probably never see their son again.

  > *dreadful*
  > bad
  > awful
  > terrible
  > horrible

• On a rainy Saturday, during vacation, he found a quite *extraordinary* one.

extraordinary

interesting

fantastic

unique

unusual

remarkable

Story Map

See the instructions on page 38 for using a story map. The following is an example of a story map for *Sylvester and the Magic Pebble*.

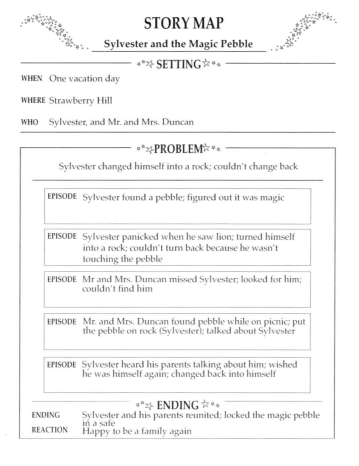

STORY MAP

Sylvester and the Magic Pebble

————————— ✳✳ **SETTING** ✩✳✳ —————————

WHEN   One vacation day

WHERE   Strawberry Hill

WHO   Sylvester, and Mr. and Mrs. Duncan

————————— ✳✳ **PROBLEM** ✩✳✳ —————————

Sylvester changed himself into a rock; couldn't change back

EPISODE	Sylvester found a pebble; figured out it was magic

EPISODE	Sylvester panicked when he saw lion; turned himself into a rock; couldn't turn back because he wasn't touching the pebble

EPISODE	Mr and Mrs. Duncan missed Sylvester; looked for him; couldn't find him

EPISODE	Mr. and Mrs. Duncan found pebble while on picnic; put the pebble on rock (Sylvester); talked about Sylvester

EPISODE	Sylvester heard his parents talking about him; wished he was himself again; changed back into himself

————————— ✳✳ **ENDING** ✩✳✳ —————————

ENDING   Sylvester and his parents reunited; locked the magic pebble in a safe

REACTION   Happy to be a family again

Internal-States Chart

See the instructions on pages 32–33 for developing an internal-states chart. Engage the students in dialogue like the following regarding the characters' feelings:

Educator: How did Sylvester feel when he found the magic pebble?

Students: He felt happy and excited.

Educator: Why did he feel happy?

Students: Because the rock was magic and he could make it do whatever he wished for.

The following is an example of an internal-states chart for *Sylvester and the Magic Pebble*.

INTERNAL-STATES CHART
Sylvester and the Magic Pebble

CHARACTER(S)	WHEN	FEELING	WHY
Sylvester	Found rock	Excited	Rock was magic
Sylvester	Saw lion	Frightened	Lion was going to eat him
Sylvester	As a rock	Lonely; hopeless; bored	Nobody to talk to or play with
Mr. and Mrs. Duncan	At home	Worried	Couldn't find Sylvester
Mr. and Mrs. Duncan	One year later	Sad; lonely	Missed Sylvester
Parents	Sylvester returned	Happy; excited	Son was back

Art Activity

Art materials needed:

- One rock for each student
- One or two sets of tempera paints (depending on the number of students in the group)
- One paintbrush per student

Give each student a clean rock about the size of an adult hand. Have students pretend that each rock was originally an animal that was changed into a rock by magic. Have students paint and decorate their rocks to resemble the animals they were before. Have them describe the attributes of their pet rocks.

Story Retelling

Have students retell the story in small groups by playing "Pass the Rock." As each student gets the rock, have them add another episode to the story. Allow students to use their story maps as guides.

Have the students retell the story to a partner and then to the group. Tape-record their retellings, if desired, and let them listen to the recordings. Have the students transcribe their stories from the recordings and help them edit their work.

Journals

To prepare for this journal activity, have each student choose a solitary place on the playground. Instruct students to curl into a tight ball as though they were a rock, eyes closed, with no movement or talking for three minutes. Encourage them to notice their surroundings using their senses of smell, hearing, and feeling.

Have students write about their experiences as "rocks" in their journals. The following are example questions for journal entries:

- How did you feel as a rock?

- What was going on around you?

- What did you notice about nature when you were a rock?

- Write about "a day in my life as a rock."

Unit 8M   THE BAKER'S DOZEN: A COLONIAL AMERICAN TALE

Retold by Heather Forest (1988). San Diego, CA: Harcourt Brace.
Unit developed by Kristin L. Walton.

A baker created a special cookie and became famous. He then became greedy and decreased the quality of his cookies so he could make more money. An old woman came to buy a dozen of his famous cookies. When she was given only 12 cookies, she became upset and told him that a dozen meant 13. The baker refused to give her 13, and from then on everything he made turned out poorly. His bad luck continued, and his greed eventually led to the loss of his fortune. When the old woman came back to his shop, he learned about how generosity could lead to good fortune, and the tradition of a "baker's dozen" spread. (The story is written in rhyme.)

MATERIALS NEEDED

- Obtain different kinds of bakery goods (e.g., bread, rolls, doughnuts, bagels, cookies, etc.) and pictures taken in a bakery.

- Make 12 photocopies of the vocabulary card illustration for Unit 8M (see Appendix D), or more or less depending on the number of target words selected (see preparatory set discussion in this unit).

- Photocopy a blank, five-category semantic-word map on an overhead transparency (or enlarge the map so all students can see it), or copy enough maps for all students in the group (see Appendix C).

- Photocopy a blank four-episode map on an overhead transparency (or enlarge the map so all students can see it), or copy enough maps for all students in the group (see Appendix C).

- Photocopy a blank internal-states chart on an overhead transparency (or enlarge the chart so all students can see it), or copy enough charts for all students in the group (see Appendix C).

- Obtain a tape recorder (see story retelling discussion in this unit).

- Photocopy a blank story-grammar cue chart on an overhead transparency (or enlarge the chart so all students can see it), or copy enough charts for all students in the group (see Appendix C).

PRESTORY PRESENTATION

Preparatory Set

Conduct a food-tasting activity and discussion in which students can compare and contrast different pastries, cookies, and breads. The following are examples of foods to include:

- breads that have yeast and those that do not

- cookies that are sweet and those that are salty

- cookies that are hard and those that are soft

See the instructions on page 18 for teaching selected story vocabulary words. Use the following vocabulary words selected for you, or select words appropriate for your specific students.

- inspired
- passerby
- custom

- prosperous
- merchants
- greed

Write each word on a vocabulary card illustration and write the corresponding definition on another card. After all cards have been created, have students match each word to its corresponding definition.

Think Alouds

Point to the cover and say, "I know that this book is about a happy baker who makes a Santa cookie for Christmas. How do I know this?"

Read the title and say, "The title of this story is *The Baker's Dozen*." Then, either model a prediction for the students (e.g., "I predict that this story will be about a baker who gives away a dozen cookies to his favorite customer") or ask a prediction question (e.g., "What do you think this story will be about?").

Scan the illustrations only. Stop at selected points of the story to model a prediction or to ask prediction questions based only on the illustrations:

- What do you think the man is thinking about as he is counting all of his money?

- What do you suppose the man and the woman are discussing? They look angry. Do you think they are yelling at each other? What are they saying to each other?

Write down the students' responses for discussion and compare with actual events after reading the story. Stop the prestory think-aloud strategy where the old woman comes back to purchase another dozen cookies so the end of the story will not be revealed.

Semantic-Word Map

Talk about bakers and bakeries:

- What is a baker?

- Where do bakers work?

- What kinds of food do you find in bakeries?

- What is a baker's dozen?

Use photographs taken in a bakery. Have the students list what is found in bakeries and everything they know about bakeries: location; types of employees; types of food, tools, and ingredients used by bakers. Using a semantic-word map, categorize all responses to show relationships. The following is an example of a semantic-word map for *The Baker's Dozen.*

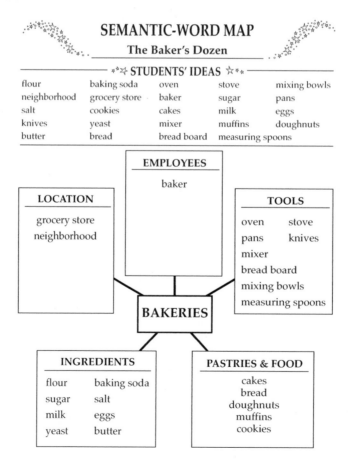

DURING-STORY PRESENTATION

Think Alouds

Confusing Information—Read to where the old woman counts her cookies and accuses the baker of being a greedy man. Say, "I don't understand why the woman wants 13 cookies. A dozen really does mean 12. This is different than what I would expect. I would expect that she would be happy with 12 cookies. What would you expect?"

Mental Picture—Read to where the woman leaves the shop and tells the baker that he will be sorry and state, "I wonder what she means when she says he will be sorry. The idea that I am getting is that she will tell all of the townspeople that the baker is greedy and then everyone will stop buying his goods. What do you think she will do?"

Analogy—Read to where the baker's cookies are really hard and state, "This reminds me of the time I made cookies and I used too much flour. The cookies were so hard that when I bit into one, my loose tooth fell out. Has something like this ever happened to you?"

Repair Strategy—Read to where the old woman returns and asks for a dozen St. Nicholas cookies and state, "I don't understand why the old woman wants to buy cookies from Van Amsterdam. Everyone knows that his cookies, cakes, pies, and muffins no longer taste good. I'd better read on to see what she is going to do with the cookies. What do you think she will do? Do you think Van Amsterdam will give her 12 or 13 cookies this time?"

Extension

After reading the sentence, "The next morning when Van Amsterdam took his loaves from the oven, he was shocked to discover that his bread tasted salty," use the following extension to clarify *shocked to discover*: "Yes, he was surprised that it tasted that way. He didn't expect it to be bad." Provide an example from your own experience:

"I was shocked to discover how much it had snowed during the night. When I went to bed, it was warm, but when I woke up, I saw three feet of snow." Then ask the students, "Is there anything you have ever been shocked to discover?"

POSTSTORY PRESENTATION

Think Alouds

After reading the story, state, "Van Amsterdam had to learn the hard way that being greedy only brings bad fortune. What could he have done to prevent losing his customers and his good reputation?" Conduct a discussion about think-aloud questions. Compare students' responses before the story was read with the actual story events.

Question-Answer Relationships

See the instructions on page 35 for the question-answer relationships strategy. The following are examples of questions to test students' comprehension of *The Baker's Dozen* (question type is indicated in parentheses after each example):

- What does the phrase *great renown* mean? (Author and You)

- What kind of cookie made Van Amsterdam famous? (Right There)

- What did Van Amsterdam decide to do so he could make more money? (Right There)

- What is the meaning of *swept out of his shop?* (Author and You)

- Why did Van Amsterdam begin having bad luck? (Think and Search)

- What did Van Amsterdam do that brought him good fortune? (Think and Search)

- What is wrong with being greedy? (On Your Own)

- What can you do to help a person who is greedy? (On Your Own)

Episode Map

See the instructions on pages 29–30 for using an episode map. The following is an example of an episode map for *The Baker's Dozen*.

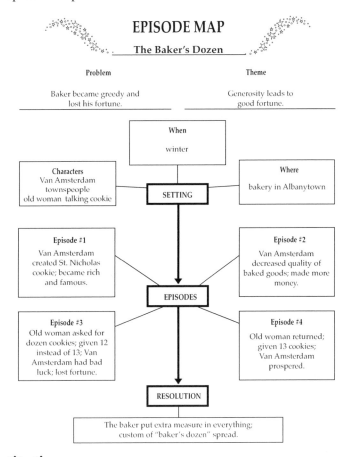

Word Substitution

See the instructions on pages 40–41 for the word-substitution strategy. The following are example sentences with their target words emphasized, followed by lists of synonyms:

• Before long, the St. Nicholas cookie had become *famous*.

> *famous*
>
> celebrated
>
> well-known
>
> important

- Van Amsterdam grew quite *prosperous*…

    prosperous
    successful
    rich
    well off
    wealthy

- A dozen means 13, and you're a *greedy* man!

    greedy
    selfish
    miserly

- The custom spread throughout the colonies, for merchants had discovered that when *generosity* replaces greed, good fortune follows.

    generosity
    kindness
    unselfishness

Journals

Show students an example of a reading/response journal as a model (see Chapter 2, pages 33–34). Offer suggestions for questions that students might respond to in their journals:

- What did you like/dislike about the old woman in the story?

- What did you like/dislike about the baker?

- What did you think about the baker changing his recipes to make more money?

- What do you think about the"baker's dozen" equaling 13?

- How do you think the people felt when they tasted the baker's food that was sour, salty, and hard?

- Why do you think the baker acted like he did?

- What was the moral of this story?

Internal-States Chart

See the instructions on pages 32–33 for using an internal-states chart. Engage students in dialogue like the following regarding the characters' feelings:

Educator: How did the baker feel when people came from far and wide to buy his bakery goods?

Students: Delighted; happy

Educator: Why did he feel so happy?

Students: Because he was earning lots of money.

The following is an example of an internal-states chart for *The Baker's Dozen*.

INTERNAL-STATES CHART
The Baker's Dozen

CHARACTER(S)	WHEN	FEELING	WHY
Passersby	Made St. Nicholas cookie	Pleased	Good cookies
Old woman	Given only 12 cookies, not 13	Upset; cheated	Baker was greedy
Baker	Old woman argued with him	Angry	Old woman called him greedy
People	Baker used less ingredients	Disappointed	Quality of baked goods was poor
Baker	People stopped buying	Despair	Lost fortune
People	Put extra measure in	Happy	Dozen meant 13 cookies

213

Story Retelling

Divide students into pairs. Give each pair a tape recorder and have the students retell the story together into the tape recorder, using the episode map for cues if needed. Let students listen to the different retellings.

Story-Grammar Cue Chart

See the instructions on page 37 for developing a story-grammar cue chart. The following is an example of a story-grammar cue chart for *The Baker's Dozen*.

STORY-GRAMMAR CUE CHART
The Baker's Dozen

STORY GRAMMAR	STORY	CHECK-OFF
Setting:		
When:	Winter, Christmas	
Where:	Albanytown, bakery	
Who:	Baker, townspeople, old woman, talking cookie	☐
Problem:	Baker became greedy	☐
Episode #1:	Baker made St. Nicholas cookie; townspeople bought baked goods; baker became famous; decreased quality	☐
Internal Response:	Excited, happy	
Episode #2:	Old woman wanted dozen cookies; baker gave her 12; old woman said a dozen meant 13; told him he was greedy	☐
Internal Response:	Angry	
Episode #3:	Baked goods turned out horribly; people stopped buying; lost fortune	☐
Internal Response:	Sad, unhappy, distraught	
Episode #4:	Old woman came back to buy a dozen cookies; baker gave her 13; word spread; baker baked again; customers came back	☐
Internal Response:	Happy, prosperous	
Ending:	Put extra measure in all baked goods; a dozen meant 13	☐
Reaction:	"Baker's dozen" custom spread throughout the colonies	

Unit 9M
THE RAINBABIES

By L.K. Melmed (1992). New York: Lothrop, Lee & Shepard.
Unit developed by Maggie S. Harris.

An honest, hardworking couple longed for a child to brighten their lonely days. After standing in a magic moonshower, they were given a dozen tiny rainbabies to care for. While caring for these babies, the old couple faced danger and challenges, which were really tests of their devotion and love for the rainbabies. Although the rainbabies had to return to Mother Moonshower, the old couple were rewarded with a baby girl to raise as their own.

MATERIALS NEEDED

- Make 18 photocopies of the vocabulary card illustration for Unit 9M (see Appendix D), or more or less depending on the number of target words selected (see preparatory set discussion in this unit).

- Photocopy a blank flow chart on an overhead transparency (or enlarge the chart so all students can see it), or copy enough charts for all students in the group (see Appendix C).

- Obtain art materials (magazines or coloring books that include pictures of children at different stages of development, scissors, large sheet of butcher paper or newsprint, tape, pencils, adhesive labels).

- Photocopy a blank story-grammar cue chart on an overhead transparency (or enlarge the chart so all students can see it), or copy enough charts for all students in the group (see Appendix C).

PRESTORY PRESENTATION

Preparatory Set

Discuss the nurturing and physical care required by babies. List student ideas where everyone can see them. Discuss the skills that parents need to care for and nurture babies. List these ideas where everyone can see them as well. Then draw lines from each baby need to the corresponding parent skill that will satisfy that need. Briefly review the relationship between the two lists.

- Discuss the consequences of not caring for and nurturing an infant.

- Ask how men and women learn good parenting skills. List students' ideas. Show a book about parenting skills. Point out that often men and women learn parenting skills from their own parents.

See the instructions on page 18 for teaching selected story vocabulary words. Use the following vocabulary words selected for you, or select words appropriate for your specific students.

- extinguish
- exhausted
- subdued
- whirlpool
- befall
- turnip
- gesturing
- moonstone
- weasel

Write each word on a vocabulary card illustration and write the corresponding definition on another card. After all cards have been created, have students match each word to its corresponding definition.

Music

Invite a mother with an infant or small child to visit the classroom and sing a lullaby to her baby. The mother can emphasize how singing a lullaby makes the baby feel loved and secure. Write the words of the lullaby where everyone can see them. Have the students identify words that convey love and nurturing.

Think Alouds

Point to the cover and say, "I know that this book is about a woman who is taking care of some very small babies. She loves the babies very much and feels very happy. How do I know this?"

Read the title and say, "The title of this story is *The Rainbabies*." Then, either model a prediction for the students (e.g., "I predict that this story will be about some babies and how much they like the rain") or ask a prediction question (e.g., "What do you think this story will be about?").

Scan the illustrations only. Stop at selected points of the story to model a prediction or to ask prediction questions based only on the illustrations:

- What do you think the couple are doing outside in the rainstorm? What could they be looking for?

• What do you suppose the man in the black cloak has come to tell the man? Do you think it is good or bad news? Why?

Write down the students' responses for discussion and comparison with actual events after reading the story. Stop the prestory think-aloud activity before the cloaked man turns into Mother Moonshower so the ending of the story is not revealed.

DURING-STORY PRESENTATION

Think Alouds

Confusing Information—Read to where the old couple find the babies in the grass. Say, "I don't know where those babies came from. There is not a person around except the old couple. This is different than what I would expect. I would expect that there would be someone hiding behind a tree or standing nearby. What would you expect?"

Mental Picture—Read to where the basket of babies gets swept overboard while the old couple are fishing and state, "I wonder what will happen to the babies. The idea that I have is that they will be swept down the river and the old couple will never see them again. What do you think will happen to them?"

Repair Strategy—Read to where Mother Moonshower comes to get the rainbabies from the old couple and state, "I don't understand why the couple have to give the rainbabies back. They have been good parents. I'd better read on to see whether Mother Moonshower will give them something to replace the rainbabies. What do you think will happen?"

Analogy—Read to where the old couple felt much joy with their new baby and state, "This reminds me of when my little sister was born. My mother and father were so happy and felt a lot of love for her. Have you ever felt like that toward someone?"

Questioning

See the instructions on pages 23–24 for asking questions about the following figurative-language examples:

- If children *grew in flowerpots* or blew down the chimney with the March wind, what a lucky woman I would be!

- Though she could hear the *steady tattoo of rainfall* on the rooftop, her gaze met the *white face of the full moon*...

- His heart *pounded like a hammer.*

- The next day dawned *blue as chicory.*

- She had *hair like the midnight sky,* and she smiled up at them with *shining gray eyes.*

- Her *laughter warmed* the small house.

Summarizing

See the instructions on page 24 for summarizing after story reading. Use a cloze procedure like the following to prompt a summary:

In the beginning, the old couple were very _____ (lonely). Then one night during a _____ (moonshower), they found some _____ (rainbabies) and took care of them. They protected the rainbabies from _____ (water), _____ (fire), and dangerous _____ (animals). Then a stranger came and offered them a precious _____ (moonstone) for their babies.

Extension

After reading the sentence, "Like all children, she brought her parents great joy and a bit of heartache too…," use the following extension to clarify *a bit of heartache*: "Yes, children sometimes do things to make their parents happy or cause them joy. Children also do things that make their parents sad or cause them heartache." Provide an example

from your own experience: "When I ran away from home, I caused my parents a bit of heartache." Then ask the students, "Have you ever caused a bit of heartache for your parents?"

POSTSTORY PRESENTATION

Think Alouds

After reading the story, state, "Mother Moonshower gave the old couple many tests to see if they could be worthy parents. Can you think of some other tests they could have faced as parents of the rainbabies?" Conduct a discussion about think-aloud questions. Compare students' responses before the story was read with the actual story events.

Question-Answer Relationships

See the instructions on page 35 for the question-answer relationships strategy. The following are examples of questions to test students' comprehension of *The Rainbabies* (question type is indicated in parentheses after each example):

- Why was the couple happy to find the rainbabies? (Think and Search)

- What was one good parenting skill used by the old couple? (Author and You)

- Who was the stranger underneath the disguise? (Right There)

- What was one dangerous event that happened to the rainbabies? (Think and Search)

- How was the old couple rewarded for their tender care of the rainbabies? (Right There)

- Why did the old couple call their daughter Rayna? (Author and You)

- What would you do if you found a baby that had been left alone? (On Your Own)

- What would you do if your baby brother or sister was in danger—for example, playing in the middle of the street? (On Your Own)

Flow Chart

See the instructions on pages 31–32 for developing a flow chart. The following is an example of a flow chart for *The Rainbabies*.

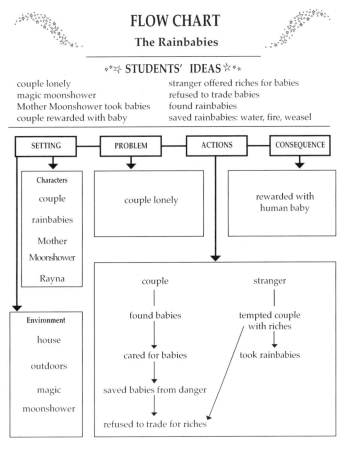

FLOW CHART

The Rainbabies

✶✷ STUDENTS' IDEAS ☆✷✷

couple lonely	stranger offered riches for babies
magic moonshower	refused to trade babies
Mother Moonshower took babies	found rainbabies
couple rewarded with baby	saved rainbabies: water, fire, weasel

SETTING	PROBLEM	ACTIONS	CONSEQUENCE

Characters

couple

rainbabies

Mother Moonshower

Rayna

couple lonely

rewarded with human baby

Environment

house

outdoors

magic moonshower

couple	stranger
found babies	tempted couple with riches
cared for babies	took rainbabies
saved babies from danger	
refused to trade for riches	

Art Activity

Art materials needed:

- Magazines or coloring books that include pictures of children at different stages of development
- Scissors
- Large sheet of white butcher paper or newsprint for a mural
- Tape, pencils
- Adhesive labels

To create a mural, pin a large sheet of butcher paper or newsprint to a bulletin board or tape it to a wall. Have students find and cut out pictures from magazines or coloring books depicting children at different stages of development: infant, crawler, toddler, preschooler, young school age, and older school age. Then have students tape these on a wall mural showing development horizontally.

Help students write the word for each stage of development on a label; have them stick the labels on the mural as well. Have students describe the attributes of children at each stage of development.

Story-Grammar Cue Chart

See the instructions on page 37 for using the story-grammar cue chart. An example of a story-grammar cue chart for *The Rainbabies* is provided on the following page.

Story Retelling

Have the students retell the story as a group. Use the flow chart as a prompt. Using the story-grammar cue chart, have students write the story on paper. Assist them in editing their stories and writing a final draft.

Story Generation

See the instructions on pages 35–37 for the story-generation strategy. Have the students write a story about a baby animal or bird that they might find and adopt. First, as a group, have them generate a list of possible baby animals/birds that they might find. Tell each student to select one baby for the story and to list some words that describe that baby. Discuss possible needs of the baby. Proceed with the suggestions for story generation found in Chapter 2.

STORY-GRAMMAR CUE CHART
The Rainbabies

STORY GRAMMAR	STORY	CHECK-OFF
Setting:		☐
When:	One rainy night, several days	
Where:	Small house, meadow	
Who:	Old couple, rainbabies, Mother Moonshower, Rayna	
Problem:	Couple lonely; wanted a child	☐
Episode #1:	Couple stood in magic moonshower; found rainbabies; cared for them	☐
Internal Response:	Excited, joyful, contented, satisfied	
Episode #2:	Rainbabies washed overboard and then lightening struck near rainbabies; man jumped in water and into fire; saved the rainbabies both times	☐
Internal Response:	Relieved, tired	
Episode #3:	Weasel stole rainbaby; woman ran after weasel; threw turnip; saved the rainbaby	☐
Internal Response:	Tired, relieved	
Episode #4:	Stranger offered riches for babies; couple refused to trade; stranger became Mother Moonshower; must take rainbabies	☐
Internal Response:	Surprised, sad, frightened	
Ending:	Couple given human baby as a reward	☐
Reaction:	Joyful, happy, sad, surprised	

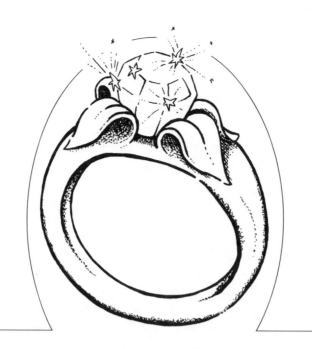

Unit 10M
TOO MANY TAMALES

By Gary Soto (1993). New York: Putnam.
Unit developed by Kelly Hoggan North.

Maria wanted to be grown-up. She especially wanted to wear her mother's sparkling diamond ring. While helping make tamales for a family Christmas party, Maria tried the ring on and lost it in the tamale dough (masa). Maria did not realize that she had lost the ring until all of the tamales were made. Instead of telling her mother what she had done, she and her cousins tried to find the ring by eating the tamales. They ate all 24 and still did not find it. Maria decided to tell her mother about her mistake and found that the ring was on her mother's finger. Maria's relatives pitched in to make a new batch of tamales for the Christmas celebration. Maria learned a hard lesson about borrowing without asking permission.

MATERIALS NEEDED

- Make 12 photocopies of the vocabulary card illustration for Unit 10M (see Appendix D), or more or less depending on the number of target words selected (see preparatory set discussion in this unit).

- Photocopy a blank internal-states chart on an overhead transparency (or enlarge the chart so all students can see it), or copy enough charts for all students in the group (see Appendix C).

- Photocopy a blank four-episode map on an overhead transparency (or enlarge the map so all students can see it), or copy enough maps for all students in the group (see Appendix C).

- Photocopy a blank story-grammar cue chart on an overhead transparency (or enlarge the chart so all students can see it), or copy enough charts for all students in the group (see Appendix C).

PRESTORY PRESENTATION

Preparatory Set

Talk about the responsibilities of being a grown-up. Have the students name some of their parents' responsibilities. Ask the students if they think they are grown-up enough to accept responsibilities.

Discuss the importance of caring for your belongings. Discuss the consequences of using others' belongings without asking for permission first. Ask the students to think of a time when they took something that didn't belong to them. Tell them to share any problems caused by taking things without asking for permission.

See the instructions on page 18 for teaching selected story vocabulary words. Use the following vocabulary words selected for you, or select words appropriate for your specific students.

- glittered
- platter
- knead
- masa
- chattered
- nudge

Write each word on a vocabulary card illustration and write the corresponding definition on another card. After all cards have been created, have students match each word to its corresponding definition.

Think Alouds

Point to the cover and say, "I know that this book is about a girl who likes tamales. How do you think I know this?"

Read the title and say, "The title of this story is *Too Many Tamales.*" Then, either model a prediction for the students (e.g., "I predict that this story will be about a girl who likes tamales so much that she eats too many and gets a stomachache") or ask a prediction question (e.g., "What do you think this story will be about?").

Scan the illustrations only. Stop at selected points of the story to model a prediction or to ask prediction questions based only on the illustrations:

- What time of year do you think it could be? How do you know?

- Why is the girl looking at that ring? What do you suppose she could be thinking? What is she going to do with the ring?

- Why does the girl look so shocked? What do you suppose she is thinking about?"

Write down the students' responses for discussion and comparison with actual events after reading the story. Stop the prestory think-aloud strategy where Danny is showing his tummy so the end of the story will not be revealed.

Music

Teach the song *Feliz Navidad* to the students. Explain that the song is a Spanish Christmas song. Ask the students whether they can figure out what *Feliz Navidad* means in Spanish.

DURING-STORY PRESENTATION

Think Alouds

Mental Picture—Read to where Maria realizes that she no longer has her mother's ring. Say, "Maria ran to the kitchen because she realized that her mother's ring was missing. I wonder where it could be. The idea that I have is that it fell on the floor. Where do you think the ring could be?"

Confusing Information—Read to where Danny states that he thinks he swallowed something hard and say, "I don't know how Danny could swallow something hard and not know that it was in his mouth before he swallowed it. This is different than I would expect. I would expect him to realize that the ring was in his mouth while he was chewing. What would you expect? Do you think he really ate it?"

Analogy—Read to where Maria and the children eat all of the tamales and say, "They have eaten all of the tamales and are feeling sick. This reminds me of a Thanksgiving dinner when I ate too much and had a bad stomachache the rest of the day. I was so full that I had a hard time moving. Has something like this ever happened to you?"

Repair Strategy—Read to where Maria realizes that the ring is on her mother's finger and say, "I don't understand how the ring got from the masa to her mother's finger. I'd better read on to see if Maria's mother will explain where she found the ring. What do you think she will say to Maria?"

Extension

After reading the sentence, "As Maria was snipping out a picture of a pearl necklace, a shock spread through her body," use the following extension to clarify *shock spread through her body:* "Yes, she realized that the ring was missing and she was shocked." Provide an example from your own experience: "Shock spread through my body one time when I realized I had gotten stung by a bee." Then ask the students, "Can you think of a time when shock spread through your body?"

Questioning

See the instructions on pages 23–24 for asking questions about the following figurative-language examples:

- They made 24 tamales as the windows *grew white with delicious-smelling curls of steam.*

- Maria cried, her eyes *big with worry.*

- She could feel tears *pressing to get out* as she walked into the living room where the grown-ups sat talking.

- Her mother moved the ring a little on her finger. *It winked a silvery light.*

POSTSTORY PRESENTATION

Think Alouds

After reading the story, state, "Maria and her cousins had to eat all of the tamales to find that her mother had the ring. What could she have done to find the ring before she made her cousins eat all of the tamales?" Conduct a discussion about think-aloud questions. Compare students' responses before the story was read with the actual story events.

Question-Answer Relationships

See the instructions on page 35 for the question-answer relationships strategy. The following are examples of questions to test students' comprehension of *Too Many Tamales* (question type is indicated in parentheses after each example):

- What was Maria helping her mother make? (Right There)

- How did it make Maria feel to help her mother? (Think and Search)

- Why did Maria want to wear her mother's ring? (Think and Search)

- How long did Maria plan to wear the ring when she first took it? (Right There)

- What should Maria have done when she realized that she no longer had the ring? (Author and You)

- Why did Maria's cousins help her by eating the tamales? (Author and You)

- What can you do to prevent losing something that is not yours? (On Your Own)

- What should you do if you lose something that is not yours? (On Your Own)

Internal-States Chart

See the instructions on pages 32–33 for developing an internal-states chart. Engage the students in dialogue like the following regarding the characters' feelings:

Educator: How did Maria feel when she was helping with the masa?

Students: Maria felt grown-up.

Educator: Why did she feel grown-up?

Students: Because she was helping her mother with a grown-up job.

The following is an example of an internal-states chart for *Too Many Tamales*.

INTERNAL-STATES CHART
Too Many Tamales

CHARACTER(S)	WHEN	FEELING	WHY
Maria	Helping with masa	Proud; grown up	Able to help her mother
Maria	Looking at ring	Wishful	Thought ring was beautiful
Maria	Discovered ring gone	Shocked	She knew it was her fault
Cousins	Eating the tamales	Sick	Ate too many tamales
Maria	Told her mother	Scared	Thought she would get into trouble
Mother	Maria told her	Patient	Knew the ring wasn't gone

Episode Map

See the instructions on pages 29–30 for using an episode map. The following is an example of an episode map for *Too Many Tamales*.

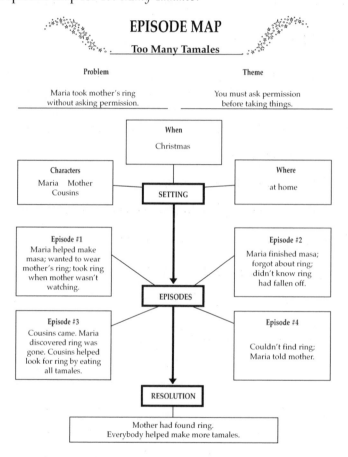

EPISODE MAP

Too Many Tamales

Problem
Maria took mother's ring without asking permission.

Theme
You must ask permission before taking things.

When
Christmas

Characters
Maria   Mother
Cousins

SETTING

Where
at home

Episode #1
Maria helped make masa; wanted to wear mother's ring; took ring when mother wasn't watching.

Episode #2
Maria finished masa; forgot about ring; didn't know ring had fallen off.

EPISODES

Episode #3
Cousins came. Maria discovered ring was gone. Cousins helped look for ring by eating all tamales.

Episode #4
Couldn't find ring; Maria told mother.

RESOLUTION

Mother had found ring.
Everybody helped make more tamales.

Story Retelling

Follow the instructions provided on pages 39–40 for story retelling. Model a retelling for the students using the episode map. Then provide a scaffold for a group retelling using the following cloze prompts:

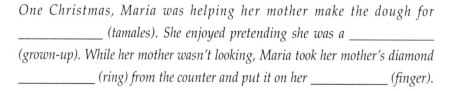

One Christmas, Maria was helping her mother make the dough for _____ (tamales). She enjoyed pretending she was a _____ (grown-up). While her mother wasn't looking, Maria took her mother's diamond _____ (ring) from the counter and put it on her _____ (finger).

Maria finished making the _____ (tamales) and forgot about the _____ (ring). When Maria was playing with her cousins, she suddenly realized that the ring was not on her _____ (finger). She raced to the kitchen and saw the big stack of _____ (tamales). She and her cousins ate all of the _____ (tamales) because they were trying to find the _____ (ring). The ring wasn't there, so Maria had to tell her _____ (mother). To her surprise, the ring was on her mother's _____ (finger). Everybody helped make more _____ (tamales). Maria learned that she shouldn't take other people's belongings without _____ (asking).

Story-Grammar Cue Chart

See the instructions on page 37 for using the story-grammar cue chart. The following is an example of a story-grammar cue chart for *Too Many Tamales*.

STORY-GRAMMAR CUE CHART
Too Many Tamales

STORY GRAMMAR	STORY	CHECK-OFF
Setting:		☐
When:	One evening, Christmas time	
Where:	Maria's house	
Who:	Maria, mother, cousins	
Problem:	Maria wore mother's ring without asking permission	☐
Episode #1:	Mother and Maria made tamales together; took ring when mother not watching; ring fell off when making masa	☐
Internal Response:	Happy to help mother, didn't know ring gone	
Episode #2:	Cousins arrived; played with Maria; Maria cut out pictures of jewelry; realized ring was gone	☐
Internal Response:	Shocked	
Episode #3:	Cousins helped Maria look for ring; ate all tamales; tamales gone; ring not found	☐
Internal Response:	Full, sick from tamales, upset	
Episode #4:	Maria decided to tell mother; saw ring on hand; her mother explained she had found ring in dough	☐
Internal Response:	Happy, relieved	
Ending:	Everyone helped make a new batch of tamales	☐
Reaction:	Happy	

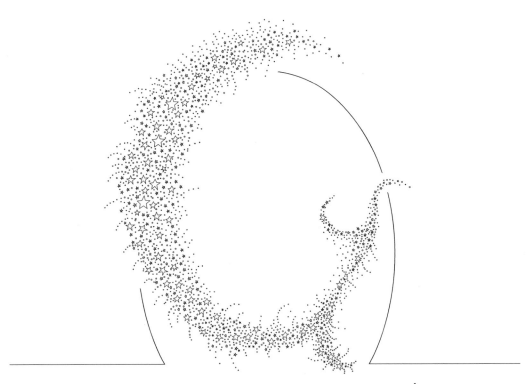

STORIES FOR UPPER-ELEMENTARY/MIDDLE-SCHOOL GRADES (Grades 5 through 7)

Unit 1U
A DAY'S WORK

By Eve Bunting (1994). Boston: Houghton Mifflin.
Unit developed by Kelly Hoggan North.

Francisco took his grandfather, who was new to America, to find a day's work. To get work, Francisco lied by telling an employer that his grandfather was a fine gardener. They worked all day at weeding a large bank of land only to find out at the end that they had pulled out the flowers instead of the weeds. Francisco did not want to return the next day to do the job right, but his grandfather insisted and also refused to be paid until the job was complete. The employer was impressed with grandfather's integrity and told them that he had more than a day's work for them.

MATERIALS NEEDED

- Make 12 photocopies of the vocabulary card illustration for Unit 1U (see Appendix D), or more or less depending on the number of target words selected (see preparatory set discussion in this unit).

- Construct a compare/contrast chart where all students can see it (see compare/contrast chart discussion in this unit).

- Photocopy a blank, four-category episode map on an overhead transparency (or enlarge the map so all students can see it), or copy enough maps for all students in the group (see Appendix C).

- Photocopy a blank story-grammar cue chart on an overhead transparency (or enlarge the chart so all students can see it), or copy enough charts for all students in the group (see Appendix C).

PRESTORY PRESENTATION

Preparatory Set

Talk about the migration of immigrants to America and the problems that they face here. Discuss the language barriers, housing accommodations, work environments, and employment challenges. Explain to the students that America is known as a safe haven for immigrants and that they are welcomed if they can provide appropriate identification and can support themselves.

Also discuss the importance of honesty in work and in our dealings with others. List the consequences of dishonesty and ask the students to think of a time they have been dishonest. Discuss the way they felt and what they did to resolve the problems caused by their dishonesty.

See the instructions on page 18 for teaching selected story vocabulary words. Use the following vocabulary words selected for you, or select words appropriate for your specific students.

- appreciate
- fortune
- chorizos
- honesty
- integrity
- omen

Write each word on a vocabulary card illustration and write the corresponding definition on another card. After all cards have been created, have students match each word to its corresponding definition.

Think Alouds

Show the cover and say, "From the cover, I know that this book is about an old man and a little boy. I wonder who that old man is and if he is related to the boy. Who do you think the old man could be?"

Point to the title and state, "The title of this story is *A Day's Work*." Either model a prediction for the students (e.g., "I predict that this story will be about the old man providing a day of work for the little boy so he can earn some money to buy a toy") or ask a prediction question (e.g., "What do you think this story will be about?").

Scan the illustrations only. Stop at selected points of the story to model a prediction or to ask prediction questions based only on the illustrations:

- Why do you think those men are running to get into that truck? Where could the truck be going?

- The man is pointing to a bank of weeds and flowers. What do you suppose he is telling the old man and boy to do?

Write down students' responses for discussion and comparison with actual events after reading the story. Stop the prestory think-aloud activity before Ben discovers that they have pulled out flowers instead of weeds so the ending is not revealed.

DURING-STORY PRESENTATION

Directed Reading/Thinking Activity

Read to where Francisco tells his grandfather that he lied to get a day's work. Have the students predict what the grandfather will do. Also, ask the students what Ben will do. Write these predictions where all students can see them.

At the story's end, encourage reflection about actual versus predicted events. Ask the students which predictions were correct.

Compare/Contrast Chart

While reading, have the students take notes of all the Spanish words they hear. Stop after each word and help the students determine the English interpretations. The following is an example of a compare/contrast chart for Spanish words and their English translations.

Spanish Words	English Meaning
1. Hace frio	1. It's cold
2. Abuelo	2. Grandfather
3. Señora	3. Lady
4. Gracias	4. Thank you
5. Bueno	5. Good
6. Muy bonito	6. Very beautiful

Extension

After reading the sentence, "The important things your grandfather knows already. And I can teach him gardening," use the following extension to clarify *important things*: "Yes, the important things grandfather already knew were honesty and integrity in

his work and dealings with other people." Provide an example from your own experience: "I learned the important things about working when I got my first job. I learned to start on time, work hard the whole time I was there, and to be honest with my employer and coworkers." Then ask the students, "Can you think of some important things you know about how to treat other people?"

Questioning

See the instructions on pages 23–24 for asking questions about the following figurative-language examples:

- His *breath was coming fast.*

- It is the *price of a lie.*

- Francisco sat by the window *in huddled silence.*

- His throat *burned with tears.*

POSTSTORY PRESENTATION

Think Alouds

After reading the story, state, "Ben decided to give Francisco and his grandfather more work because of grandfather's integrity and honesty. What other things could Ben have done to show Francisco that honesty and integrity were important values?" Conduct a discussion about think-aloud questions. Compare students' responses before the story was read with the actual story events.

Question-Answer Relationships

See the instructions on page 35 for the question-answer relationships strategy. The following are examples of questions to test students' comprehension of *A Day's Work* (question type is indicated in parentheses after each example):

- Why were several men standing in the large parking lot? (Think and Search)

- What type of job did Francisco and his grandfather get? (Right There)

- Why did Francisco lie about his grandfather knowing how to garden? (Author and You)

- Where did the van take Francisco and his grandfather? (Think and Search)

- What did Ben tell Francisco and his grandfather to do? (Right There)

- What should Francisco have told Ben before they were hired to garden? (Author and You)

- If you didn't speak English, what would you do to communicate? (On Your Own)

- Why is it important to be honest with the people with whom you associate and work? (On Your Own)

Word Substitution

See the instructions on pages 40–41 for the word-substitution strategy. The following is an example sentence with its target word emphasized, followed by a list of synonyms:

- Francisco wanted to laugh, Ben seemed so *shocked*.

shocked
astounded
astonished
stunned
surprised

Episode Map

See the instructions on pages 29–30 for using an episode map. Use the episode map to teach the students each element of the story (i.e., setting, problem/goal, major episodes, theme, and resolution). Have the students help map out the story's episodes where all students can see. An example of an episode map for *A Day's Work* is provided on the following page.

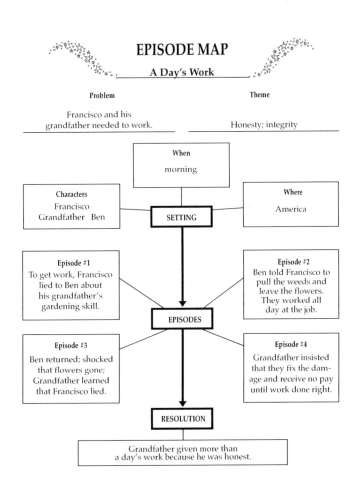

EPISODE MAP

A Day's Work

Problem	Theme
Francisco and his grandfather needed to work.	Honesty; integrity

When
morning

Characters
Francisco
Grandfather Ben

SETTING

Where
America

Episode #1
To get work, Francisco lied to Ben about his grandfather's gardening skill.

Episode #2
Ben told Francisco to pull the weeds and leave the flowers. They worked all day at the job.

EPISODES

Episode #3
Ben returned; shocked that flowers gone; Grandfather learned that Francisco lied.

Episode #4
Grandfather insisted that they fix the damage and receive no pay until work done right.

RESOLUTION

Grandfather given more than a day's work because he was honest.

Story Retelling

Model a story retelling of *A Day's Work* for the students. Use the episode map as a retelling guide. Place the students in pairs and have them practice retelling the story to each other. Next, have each student retell the story to the group. As an option, tape-record and transcribe their retellings. Have them read their own stories during the next session and allow them to change their initial retellings.

Story-Grammar Cue Chart

See the instructions on page 37 for using the story-grammar cue chart. An example of a story-grammar cue chart for *A Day's Work* is provided on the next page.

STORY-GRAMMAR CUE CHART
A Day's Work

STORY GRAMMAR	STORY	CHECK-OFF
Setting:		☐
When:	One morning	
Where:	America	
Who:	Francisco, Grandfather, Ben	
Problem:	Francisco and Grandfather needed a day's work	☐
Episode #1:	Francisco and Grandfather tried to find job; Francisco lied about Grandfather; got the job	☐
Internal Response:	Happy, excited	
Episode #2:	Ben instructed to pull weeds and leave flowers; pulled the flowers; left the weeds; hillside clean	☐
Internal Response:	Proud	
Episode #3:	Ben returned and yelled at them because flowers were gone; Grandfather found out Francisco lied	☐
Internal Response:	Angry, disappointed	
Episode #4:	Ben tried to pay half day's work; Grandfather insisted on fixing damage and refused pay until work done right	☐
Internal Response:	Surprised	
Ending:	Ben offered them more than a day's work	☐
Reaction:	Satisfied, happy, Francisco learned about honesty	

Story Generation

Work with the students as a group to create a new story about an American who goes to a new country as an exchange student. Have them include challenges such as language barriers, a new family, new friends, and using a second language while learning academics.

Unit 2U
ANNIE AND THE OLD ONE

By Miska Miles (1971). New York: Little, Brown and Company.
Unit developed by Jennifer Abbott and Gina A. Hollinger.

A Navajo girl named Annie lived with her mother, father, and grandmother in a small hogan in the desert. Annie loved her grandmother and spent her free time talking with the older woman. Annie's family earned money by raising livestock, making jewelry, and weaving rugs on a loom. One day, Annie's grandmother announced to the family that she would return to Mother Earth when the rug on the loom was finished. Knowing that her grandmother would die when the rug was finished, Annie tried to sabotage the weaving of the rug. After her attempts failed, Grandmother spoke with Annie and explained that she should not try to hold back time. Annie finally accepted that there are some things that cannot be changed, and she began to weave the rug.

MATERIALS NEEDED

- Make 12 photocopies of the vocabulary card illustration for Unit 2U (see Appendix D), or more or less depending on the number of target words selected (see preparatory set discussion in this unit).

- Obtain art materials (balloon[s]; one-inch strips of newsprint; liquid starch, wallpaper paste, or flour-and-water mixture; piece[s] of cardboard; glue; land-scaping materials [e.g., sand, yarn, sticks]).

- Obtain an audiotape of tribal music from your library, preferably one that includes the Navajo culture.

- Obtain books, magazines, and pictures about Native American life, preferably ones that include the Navajo culture.

- Photocopy a blank, four-category semantic-word map on an overhead transparency (or enlarge the map so all students can see it), or copy enough maps for all students in the group (see Appendix C).

- Photocopy a blank discussion web on an overhead transparency (or enlarge the web so all students can see it), or copy enough webs for all students in the group (see Appendix C).

- Photocopy a blank flow chart on an overhead transparency (or enlarge the chart so all students can see it), or copy enough charts for all students in the group (see Appendix C).

- Photocopy a blank internal-states chart on an overhead transparency (or enlarge the chart so all students can see it), or copy enough charts for all students in the group (see Appendix C).

- Photocopy a blank story-grammar cue chart on an overhead transparency (or enlarge the chart so all students can see it), or copy enough charts for all students in the group (see Appendix C).

PRESTORY PRESENTATION

Preparatory Set

Conduct a discussion about grandparents. Provide a model for the students by telling them about your own grandparents and why they are special to you. Then prompt students to tell about their grandparents and how they feel about them. Have students tell of experiences they have shared with their grandparents.

See the instructions on page 18 for teaching selected story vocabulary words. Use the following vocabulary words selected for you, or select words appropriate for your specific students.

- hogan
- mellow
- mesa
- harmony
- bluffs
- loom

Write each word on a vocabulary card illustration and write the corresponding definition on another card. After all cards have been created, have students match each word to its corresponding definition.

Think Alouds

Show the cover and say, "From the cover, I know that this book is about a girl who lives in the desert in a hogan. How do I know this?"

Point to the title and state, "The title of this story is *Annie and the Old One*." Either model a prediction for the students (e.g., "I predict that this story will be about a girl named Annie who takes care of her grandmother when she is old") or ask a prediction question (e.g., "What do you think this story will be about?").

Scan the illustrations only. Stop at selected points of the story to model a prediction or to ask questions based only on the illustrations:

- The girl is laying her head on her grandmother's lap. What do you think she is feeling for her grandmother? Why?

- Annie is running to catch the school bus. Why do you think she is running? What do you suppose made her late?

Write down students' responses for discussion and comparison with actual events after reading the story. Stop the prestory think-aloud strategy where Annie is unraveling the rug on the loom so the end of the story will not be revealed.

Art Activity

Art materials needed:

- Balloon(s)
- One-inch strips of newsprint
- Liquid starch, wallpaper paste, or flour-and-water mixture
- Piece(s) of cardboard
- Glue
- Landscaping materials (e.g., sand, yarn, sticks)

To make a papier-mâché hogan, blow up a round balloon and tie it off. Provide students with torn strips of newspaper.

Work as a class or in small groups and have students create a three-dimensional hogan out of papier-mâché. First, have students dip the strips in liquid starch, wallpaper paste, or flour water. Have them cover the entire balloon with these strips. Allow drying time between layers. When all layers are completely dry, cut off the bottom one-third of the balloon to make the hogan's shape.

Attach the hogan to a piece of cardboard with glue and let the students landscape the area surrounding the hogan with sand, yarn, sticks, etc. Discuss the differences between the hogan and their own homes.

Music

Play an audiotape of tribal music. Ask students to tap their desks or stomp their feet to the beat of the music. Ask students when or how they think the music would by used by Native Americans.

Semantic-Word Map

Obtain some books, magazines, and pictures on Native American life. Have students scan the materials. Instruct them to call out any words that are related to Native Americans or Native American life. Assist the students in organizing the words into categories. The following is an example of a semantic-word map for *Annie and the Old One*.

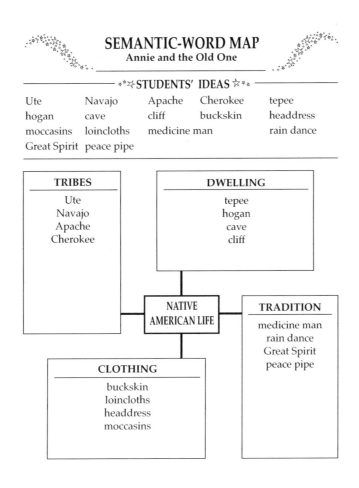

DURING-STORY PRESENTATION

Think Alouds

Confusing Information—Read to where the grandmother announces that she will die when the new rug is taken from the loom and say, "I don't understand how the grandmother knows when she will die. This is different than what I would expect. I would expect that she would say something like, 'I am old and will die soon.' What did you expect her to say?"

Analogy—Read to where Annie causes mischief at school by taking her teacher's shoe and say, "This reminds me of the time I hid my teacher's keys because I was angry at her for telling me to be quiet. When she finally found them, I felt guilty for taking them and I confessed. I had to stay in from recess for three days as my punishment. Have you ever caused mischief at school? Why did you do it and what were the consequences of your behavior?"

Repair Strategy—Read to where Annie wakes in the middle of the night to unwind the loom and state, "I don't understand why Annie thinks that unwinding the loom will prolong her grandmother's life. I'd better read on to see if she is successful in her efforts. Do you think she will be? Why?"

Mental Picture—Read to where Annie and her grandmother are sitting on the small mesa and state, "Annie and her grandmother are going to discuss something very important. The idea that I have is that they will talk about Annie's behavior and that there are some things in life that can't be changed. What do you think the grandmother will say to Annie?"

Questioning

See the instructions on pages 23–24 for asking questions about the following figurative-language examples:

- A girl *who had seen no more than 9 or 10 harvestings*.

- The sky was *dark and secret*.

- "My children, when the new rug is taken from the loom, I will *go to Mother Earth*."

Journals

Ask a question related to the day's reading such as, "Would you like to live in a hogan and do chores?" Have students write their responses in their journals and provide reasons to support their answers.

POSTSTORY PRESENTATION

Question-Answer Relationships

See the instructions on page 35 for the question-answer relationships strategy. The following are examples of questions to test students' comprehension of *Annie and the Old One* (question type is indicated in parentheses after each example):

- What did Annie let out of the pen at night? (Right There)

- How did Annie feel about her grandmother? (Think and Search)

- Why did Annie take the teacher's shoe? (Think and Search)

- What are some other things Annie could have done to keep the rug from being finished? (Author and You)

- If you were Annie and thought your grandmother was going to die, how would you feel? Why? (Author and You)

- Who gave Annie advice? What was it? (Right There)

- How would you feel if someone you love died? (On Your Own)

- What are some things or people that you would not want to lose? Why? (On Your Own)

Discussion Web

See the instructions on pages 26–27 for the discussion-web strategy. The following is an example of a discussion web for *Annie and the Old One*.

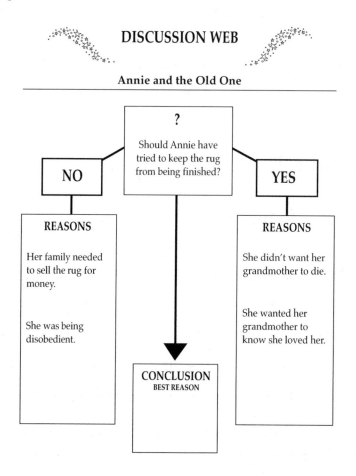

DISCUSSION WEB

Annie and the Old One

?

Should Annie have tried to keep the rug from being finished?

NO

YES

REASONS

Her family needed to sell the rug for money.

She was being disobedient.

REASONS

She didn't want her grandmother to die.

She wanted her grandmother to know she loved her.

CONCLUSION
BEST REASON

Flow Chart

See the instructions on pages 31–32 for using a flow chart. An example of a flow chart for *Annie and the Old One* is provided on the following page.

FLOW CHART

Annie and the Old One

⋆ STUDENTS' IDEAS ⋆

Grandmother told family she is going to die
Annie stole the teacher's shoe
Annie let the sheep out of the pen
Annie undid the rug

Grandmother caught Annie
Annie and Grandmother talked
Annie started to weave

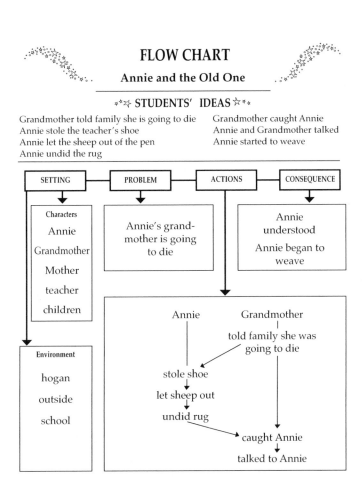

Internal-States Chart

See the instructions on pages 32–33 for using an internal-states chart. Engage students in dialogue like the following regarding the characters' feelings:

Educator:	How did Annie feel when she found out that her grandmother was going to die?
Students:	She couldn't believe it. She denied it.
Educator:	Why did she deny it?
Students:	Because she did not want her grandmother to die.

The following is an example of an internal-states chart for *Annie and the Old One*.

INTERNAL-STATES CHART

Annie and the Old One

CHARACTER(S)	WHEN	FEELING	WHY
Annie	Found out her grandmother was going to die	Denial	Did not want her to die
Mother	Found out her mother was going to die	Acceptance	Understood; some things can't be changed
Annie	Mother wanted her to weave	Scared	Did not want to grow up
Annie	Talked to teacher	Timid	Did something wrong
Annie	Let sheep out of pen	Hopeful	Wanted to stop rug
Mother	Discovered sheep missing	Upset	Thought sheep were lost
Grandmother	Caught Annie undoing rug	Patient	Knew Annie was only little girl
Annie	Realized can't hold back time	Peaceful	Understood some things can't be changed

Story-Grammar Cue Chart

See the instructions on page 37 for using the story-grammar cue chart. An example of a story-grammar cue chart for *Annie and the Old One* is provided on the following page.

STORY-GRAMMAR CUE CHART
Annie and the Old One

STORY GRAMMAR	STORY	CHECK-OFF
Setting:		☐
When:	Over several days	
Where:	Mesa	
Who:	Annie, Grandmother, Mother, Father, teacher	
Problem:	Grandmother said she would die when rug done	☐
Episode #1:	Grandmother getting old; told family she was going to die; family chose gifts from Grandmother	☐
Internal Response:	Sad, quiet, respectful	
Episode #2:	Annie didn't want rug to be finished; stole teacher's shoe; plan didn't work; rug became higher than Annie's waist	☐
Internal Response:	Defiant, determined, hopeful, desperate	
Episode #3:	Annie didn't want rug to be finished; let sheep out of pen; plan didn't work; unraveled rug; rug only as high as Annie's waist again	☐
Internal Response:	Hopeful, excited, scared, devious	
Episode #4:	Annie didn't want rug to be finished; went to unravel rug; Grandmother stopped her; they talked; Annie accepted that Grandmother would die	☐
Internal Response:	Understanding	
Ending:	Annie started to weave	☐
Reaction:	Understanding, love, acceptance, maturation	

Unit 3U   HUMPHREY THE LOST WHALE: A TRUE STORY

By Wendy Tokuda and Richard Hall (1992). Torrance, CA: Heian.
Unit developed by Rod Bullock.

Humphrey, a whale, entered San Francisco Bay and made a mistake by swimming up the Sacramento River instead of back out to sea. Humphrey continued up the river until he became stuck in a tiny stream. Because the water was fresh rather than salt water, he was also sick. With the help of scientists, the Coast Guard, and many citizens, Humphrey turned around and swam back out to the ocean.

MATERIALS NEEDED

- Obtain books, magazines, and pictures about oceans from the library.

- Make 22 photocopies of the vocabulary card illustration for Unit 3U (see Appendix D), or more or less depending on the number of target words selected (see preparatory set discussion in this unit).

- Photocopy a blank, four-category semantic-word map on an overhead transparency (or enlarge the map so all students can see it), or copy enough maps for all students in the group (see Appendix C).

- Obtain a map of North and South America (or use a globe).

- Obtain a videotape or an audiotape of whale songs from your library.

- Photocopy a blank, four-category episode map on an overhead transparency (or enlarge the map so all students can see it), or copy enough maps for all students in the group (see Appendix C).

- Photocopy a blank internal-states chart on an overhead transparency (or enlarge the chart so all students can see it), or copy enough charts for all students in the group (see Appendix C).

- Photocopy a blank story-grammar cue chart on an overhead transparency (or enlarge the chart so all students can see it), or copy enough charts for all students in the group (see Appendix C).

PRESTORY PRESENTATION

Preparatory Set

Talk about the ocean and what it would be like to swim in it. Have students share experiences they have had at the ocean or at lakes.

Look at magazines and books about the ocean. A particularly good award-winning book is *Whales* (Jeunesse, Delafosse, Fuhr, and Sautai, 1991). Discuss the following topics:

- Different oceans and their locations

- Different types of whales and their characteristics

- Endangered species

See the instructions on page 18 for teaching selected story vocabulary words. Use the following vocabulary words selected for you, or select words appropriate for your specific students.

- pod
- magnificent
- intelligent
- logged

- spectacular
- scientist
- broadcast
- flotilla

- thrashed
- rescue
- ordeal

Write each word on a vocabulary card illustration and write the corresponding definition on another card. After all cards have been created, have students match each word to its corresponding definition.

Think Alouds

Point to the cover and say, "I know that this book is about a whale that likes to jump out of the water and flip over. How do I know this?"

Read the title and say, "The title of this story is *Humphrey the Lost Whale.*" Either model a prediction (e.g., "I predict that the story will be about a whale named Humphrey that becomes separated from his whale family and gets lost") or ask a prediction question (e.g., "What do you think this story will be about?").

Scan the illustrations only. Stop at selected points of the story to model a prediction or ask prediction questions based only on the illustrations:

- Humphrey is swimming near the Golden Gate Bridge. Where do you think Humphrey is headed? Why?

- Humphrey is in a small river. How do you think he got there? Why are there people stopping to look at him?

Write down students' responses for discussion and comparison with actual events after reading the story. Stop the prestory think-aloud strategy before the men use the crane to help Humphrey so the end of the story will not be revealed.

Semantic-Word Map

Have students suggest words that describe the ocean, that name animals that live in the ocean, and that name ocean plant life. List the responses where all students can see them. Help students categorize their suggestions. The following is an example of a semantic-word map for *Humphrey the Lost Whale*.

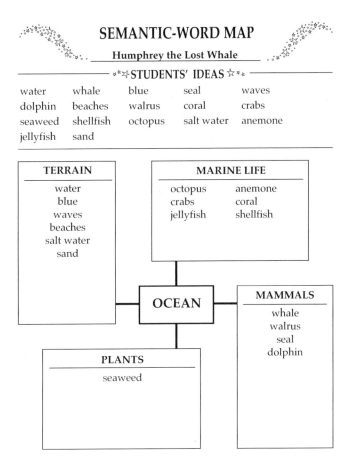

Place a map of North and South America where all students can see it, or provide a globe. First, point out where your students live. Point out California and San Francisco Bay. Show students the whales' migratory route from Alaska to Mexico (i.e., Alaska; Canada; the United States; Baja, California; Mexico). Use the maps located at the end of *Humphrey the Lost Whale* as well. Refer to the maps (or globe) throughout the unit to point out the location of the Golden Gate Bridge and the Sacramento River.

Music

Locate a videotape or audiotape of whale songs and play a segment. Suggested videotapes include:

NOVA: Signs of the Apes, Songs of the Whales (WGBH Television, 1984)

Gift of the Whales (Nickman and Phelan, 1989)

DURING-STORY PRESENTATION

Think Alouds

Analogy—Read to where hundreds of people came to see Humphrey in the river and say, "This reminds me of the time we were on vacation in Florida and dozens of cars were stopped along the road to look at an alligator. Have you ever seen an animal in an unusual place?"

Mental Picture—Read to where Humphrey swam to the river beyond the bridge where the water is shallow and say, "Humphrey looks very sick. The idea that I have is that he will die in the stream because it is too shallow and it is fresh water rather than salt water. What do you think will happen to Humphrey?"

Confusing Information—Read to where Humphrey cannot get back under the small bridge and state, "I don't understand why Humphrey can't find his way back under the small bridge. This is different than what I would expect. I would expect that he would be able to get through easily because it was so easy for him to get through the first time. How do you think he will actually get through?"

Repair Strategy—Read to where Humphrey spends one whole day in the San Francisco Bay happily swimming and say, "I don't understand why Humphrey spent an entire day in the bay. I would expect him to be in a hurry to get back to his whale family. I'd better read on to see if he will be able to find his family once he gets out into the ocean. Do you think he will find them? Why?"

Extension

After reading the sentence, "Humphrey seemed flustered," use the following extension to clarify the word *flustered*: "Yes Humphrey was flustered. He couldn't get under the bridge and the noise from the banging pipes was annoying. I'm sure he was very frustrated." Provide an example from your own experience: "I was flustered the other day when I couldn't thread a needle to sew a button on my shirt. I tried and tried, but I just kept poking myself." Then ask the students, "Have you ever been flustered? When? Why?"

Questioning

See the instructions on pages 23–24 for asking questions about the following figurative-language examples:

- He *broke free* from the pilings.
- He would come up to breathe, appearing *as if by magic…*
- Time was *running out.*

POSTSTORY PRESENTATION

Think Alouds

After reading the story, state, "Humphrey swam clear up into the Sacramento River before the scientists tried to help him back to the ocean. Why do you think they waited so long to try to turn him around? Do you think another whale would be able to swim upstream that far again without anyone doing something about it?" Conduct a discussion about think-aloud questions. Compare students' responses before the story was read with the actual story events.

Question-Answer Relationships

See the instructions on page 35 for the question-answer relationships strategy. The following are examples of questions to test students' comprehension of *Humphrey the Lost Whale* (question type is indicated in parentheses after each example):

- Where was the pod of whales traveling for the winter? (Right There)

- Why would people stop what they were doing to watch Humphrey? (Right There)

- Why would Humphrey die if he didn't get back to the ocean? (Think and Search)

- What did people try to do to get Humphrey to head back toward the ocean? (Think and Search)

- Why did Humphrey spend one whole day swimming around San Francisco Bay before heading out to sea? (Author and You)

- Why is salt water better than fresh water for Humphrey? (Author and You)

- Why do whales migrate north for the summer? (On Your Own)

- Why do whales migrate south for the winter? (On Your Own)

Word Substitution

See the instructions on pages 40–41 for the word-substitution strategy. The following are example sentences with their target words emphasized, followed by lists of synonyms:

- Humpback whales are *magnificent* creatures.

    magnificent
    extraordinary
    splendid
    impressive
    grand

- Many times during his *ordeal*, Humphrey could have simply flicked his tail and overturned boats carrying the people who were trying to help him.

    ordeal
    difficulty
    trial
    tribulation

Episode Map

See the instructions on pages 29–30 for developing an episode map. The following is an example of an episode map for *Humphrey the Lost Whale*.

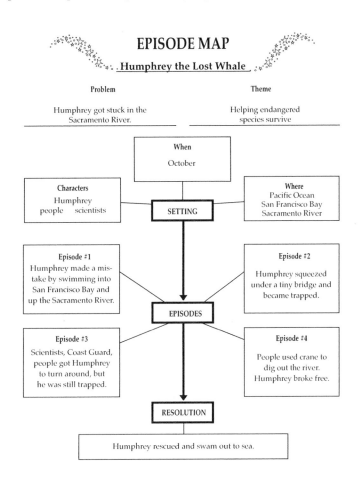

Internal-States Chart

See the instructions on pages 32–33 for using an internal-states chart. Engage students in dialogue like the following regarding the characters' feelings:

Educator: How did the people feel when Humphrey entered the San Francisco Bay?

Students: They felt surprised.

Educator: Why were they surprised?

Students: Because whales usually stay out in the ocean and do not come into the bay.

The following is an example of an internal-states chart for *Humphrey the Lost Whale*.

INTERNAL-STATES CHART
Humphrey the Lost Whale

CHARACTER(S)	WHEN	FEELING	WHY
People	Humphrey entered the bay	Surprised	Whales usually stay in ocean
People	Humphrey went up the river	Worried	Humphrey could die
Humphrey	At bridge	Afraid; flustered	No space to get through
Humphrey	At bridge	Nervous	Humphrey's last chance
People	Humphrey started down the river	Relieved	Humphrey might be saved
Humphrey	In the bay	Happy	Was free

Story-Grammar Cue Chart

See the instructions on page 37 for using the story-grammar cue chart. The following is an example of a story-grammar cue chart for *Humphrey the Lost Whale*.

STORY-GRAMMAR CUE CHART
Humphrey the Lost Whale

STORY GRAMMAR	STORY	CHECK-OFF
Setting: When: Where: Who:	October, sunny day Pacific Ocean, San Francisco Bay, Sacramento River Humphrey, people, scientists, Coast Guard	☐
Problem:	Humphrey stuck in river	☐
Episode #1:	Humphrey made mistake; swam up river; Humphrey lost	☐
Internal Response:	People excited, then worried	
Episode #2:	Humphrey stuck behind bridge	☐
Internal Response:	Humphrey felt sick	
Episode #3:	Scientists and others got Humphrey to turn around; still trapped	☐
Internal Response:	People worried, Humphrey flustered	
Episode #4:	Used crane to dig out river; Humphrey tired; made it through	☐
Internal Response:	People relieved, Humphrey happy	
Ending: **Reaction:**	Humphrey made it back to the bay and out to sea; people learned about whales People happy	☐

Unit 4U   MUFARO'S BEAUTIFUL DAUGHTERS: AN AFRICAN TALE

By John Steptoe (1987). New York: Lothrop, Lee & Shepard.
Unit developed by Judy Armstrong, Anne Elsweiler, and Ann McKeehan.

Mufaro and his two daughters lived in an African village. A king, who decided to take a wife, invited "the most worthy and beautiful daughters in the land" to appear before him in the city. Mufaro's daughters, Manyara and Nyasha, were very different from each other. Their differences became apparent as they individually traveled to the city to meet the king. The kind and selfless spirit of Nyasha was rewarded in the end when the king chose her for his wife.

MATERIALS NEEDED

- Make 24 photocopies of the vocabulary card illustration for Unit 4U (see Appendix D), or more or less depending on the number of target words selected (see preparatory set discussion in this unit).

- Obtain the *Reading Rainbow* videotape of *Mufaro's Beautiful Daughters* from a library.

- Obtain maps of Africa (or a globe) and magazines and books about Africa.

- Photocopy a blank, six-category semantic-word map on an overhead transparency (or enlarge the map so all students can see it), or copy enough maps for all students in the group (see Appendix C).

- Construct a compare/contrast chart where all students can see it (see compare/contrast chart discussion in this unit).

- Photocopy a blank, four-episode map on an overhead transparency (or enlarge the map so all students can see it), or copy enough maps for all students in the group (see Appendix C).

- Obtain necessary art materials (one necktie; wadded tissue paper or cotton batting; glue gun, ticky-tacky glue, or needle and thread; two buttons [for eyes] and small piece of red felt [cut in shape of snake's tongue]; beads and feathers).

PRESTORY PRESENTATION

Preparatory Set

Read the background for the story found on the book's front page. Discuss the meanings of the African names. Ask the students whether they know what their own names mean.

See the instructions on page 18 for teaching selected story vocabulary words. Use the following vocabulary words selected for you, or select words appropriate for your specific students.

- village
- journey
- clever
- weakness
- worthy
- greed
- descended
- commotion
- relief
- destination
- anxious
- hysterical

Write each word on a vocabulary card illustration and write the corresponding definition on another card. After all cards have been created, have students match each word to its corresponding definition.

Music

View the celebration of African music portion from the *Reading Rainbow* videotape of *Mufaro's Beautiful Daughters* (Krauss, 1989). Discuss the different dances performed.

Think Alouds

Point to the cover and say, "I know that this book is about an African woman who is very beautiful. How do I know this?"

Read the title and subtitle and say, "The title of this story is *Mufaro's Beautiful Daughters*, and the subtitle is *An African Tale*." Ask the students what they know about specific words in the title (e.g., Mufaro must be the father; he has more than one daughter; his daughters are not ugly, they are beautiful). Ask students the following questions and write responses where all students can see them:

- Where do you think this story takes place?

- Whom do you think this story is about?

- What do you know from the pictures about the characters' personalities?

- When do you think the story took place?

Scan the illustrations only. Stop at selected points of the story to model a prediction or ask prediction questions based only on the illustrations:

- The woman has her hands on her hips. She looks angry. What do you suppose has caused her to feel that way? What is she saying to the other woman?

- There is a woman hiding in the bush. What do you suppose she is going to do? Why is she there?

Write down students' responses for discussion and comparison with actual events after reading the story. Stop the prestory think-aloud strategy where Nyasha is talking to the snake in the palace so the end of the story will not be revealed.

Semantic-Word Map

Provide maps of Africa (or a globe) as well as magazines and books about Africa. Divide the students into small groups and have each group suggest words that describe Africa from such categories as animals, terrain, people, occupations, culture, and products. List the responses where all students can see them. With the students, form natural groupings for their ideas. An example of a semantic-word map for *Mufaro's Beautiful Daughters* is provided on the following page.

DURING-STORY PRESENTATION

Think Alouds

Confusing Information—Read to where Nyasha tells her sister that she would be pleased to serve her if Manyara were to be made queen and say, "I don't understand why Nyasha would be pleased to serve her sister. Her sister is mean and inconsiderate to her. This is different than what I would expect. I would expect that Nyasha would not want to be a servant to her sister. Why do you suppose she would be pleased to serve her sister?"

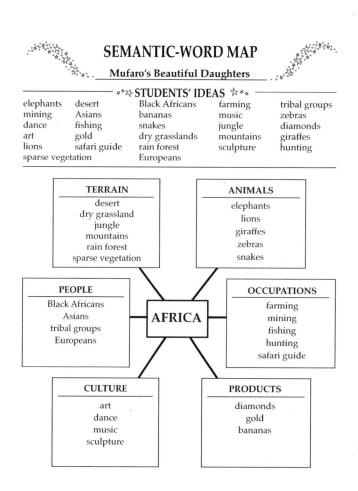

SEMANTIC-WORD MAP

Mufaro's Beautiful Daughters

★✦STUDENTS' IDEAS ☆✦★

elephants	desert	Black Africans	farming	tribal groups
mining	Asians	bananas	music	zebras
dance	fishing	snakes	jungle	diamonds
art	gold	dry grasslands	mountains	giraffes
lions	safari guide	rain forest	sculpture	hunting
sparse vegetation		Europeans		

TERRAIN
desert
dry grassland
jungle
mountains
rain forest
sparse vegetation

ANIMALS
elephants
lions
giraffes
zebras
snakes

PEOPLE
Black Africans
Asians
tribal groups
Europeans

AFRICA

OCCUPATIONS
farming
mining
fishing
hunting
safari guide

CULTURE
art
dance
music
sculpture

PRODUCTS
diamonds
gold
bananas

Mental Picture—Read to where Mufaro receives the message that the king wanted a wife and state, "The king is looking for a wife, and Nyasha and Manyara will go to his home to try to become the queen. The idea that I have is that Manyara will become his wife because she has dreamed all her life of becoming the queen. Whom do you think the king will choose for his wife? Why?"

Repair Strategy—Read to where Manyara warns her sister not to go into the king's home and state, "I don't understand why Manyara is warning Nyasha not to go into the king's home. She has been very selfish throughout the whole story. I'd better read on to see if Manyara's warning is genuine. Do you think she is really concerned about her sister's welfare? Why?"

Analogy—Read to where the king has chosen Nyasha to be his wife and the wedding preparations are taking place. State, "This reminds me of when I got married. Everyone was hustling around trying to take care of the details and formalities of the wedding. I felt really happy. How do you think Nyasha is feeling right now? Could she be nervous? Why?"

Extension

After reading the sentence, "Manyara was almost always in a bad temper," use the following extension to clarify *in a bad temper:* "Yes, it seemed as if she was always in a bad mood. She was easily irritated by small things." Provide an example from your own experience: "I was in a bad temper last week when I found out that I owed money on my income taxes." Then ask the students, "Have you ever felt in a bad temper?"

After reading the sentence, "She stood transfixed at her first sight of the city," use the following extension to clarify *stood transfixed:* "Yes, all she could do was stare because the city was so beautiful. It was as if she were in a trance." Provide an example from your experience: "I stood transfixed at the sight of my wrecked car." Have students name a sight that would cause them to be transfixed.

POSTSTORY PRESENTATION

Think Alouds

After reading the story, state, "Manyara didn't know that the king had magical powers and that he was testing her worth as a queen throughout the entire story. Do you think it was fair to deceive Manyara in this manner? Why?" Conduct a discussion about think-aloud questions. Compare students' responses before the story was read with the actual story events.

Journals

Have the students write a letter to Manyara telling her how she should behave in the village if she wants to be liked as Nyasha is.

Episode Map

See the instructions on pages 29–30 for using an episode map. The following is an example of an episode map for *Mufaro's Beautiful Daughters*.

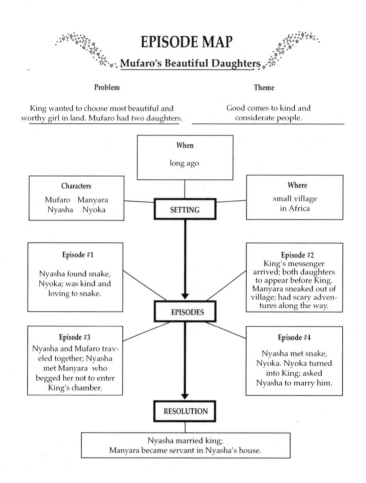

Compare/Contrast Chart

Summarize what happened to the sisters in the city by developing a compare/contrast chart. An example of a compare/contrast chart for *Mufaro's Beautiful Daughters* is provided on the following page.

Manyara	Nyasha
Saw monster snake with five heads	Saw a beautiful place
Afraid of being swallowed alive	Found her friend, the snake
Ran	Saw snake change into king
Begged Nyasha not to go inside gate	Found out small boy and old woman were really handsome king
Became servant for queen	King asked her to marry him; wedding; became queen

Art Activity/Story Retelling

Art materials needed:

- One necktie
- Wadded tissue paper or cotton batting
- Glue gun, ticky-tacky glue, or needle and thread
- Two buttons (for eyes) and small piece of red felt (cut in shape of snake's tongue)
- Beads and feathers

Make a snake out of a man's necktie:

- Open the tie at the widest part, stuff the area under the triangular flap of cloth with paper or cotton batting. Tuck it in and either sew or glue the area closed. Glue eyes and a tongue on the head.

- Discuss why the snake was a key character in the story. Compare and contrast how Nyasha treated the snake when she first met it and how Manyara might have treated the snake if she had met it in the garden at the beginning of the story.

- Because the snake is really a king, have the students decorate the snake with beads and feathers, discussing texture, size, and color as they glue the ornaments in place. Discuss which of these decorations might be available to an

African king and how a king might wear different clothing and decorations than others in his kingdom.

Retell the story for the students without the book. Then, using the episode map as a guide, have students take turns retelling what happens in the different episodes. Pass the snake from student to student as they retell the story. When everyone has had a chance to describe an episode, have each student retell the story and tape-record the retellings. Let the students listen to their tape-recorded retellings.

Story Generation

Assign small groups of students to make up a different story, with at least two episodes, about Mufaro and his family. Using the episode map that was generated, maintain the same theme and problem, but change the map to create a new story that will be different in setting and episodes from the original story. Provide verbal scaffolding to assist students with generating ideas.

Begin with the setting. Provide students with examples such as the following:

- A long time age in an isolated spot in Alaska, a man named Mufaro lived with his two daughters. They lived two days' journey, by sled, away from a larger village, where a kind and famous chief lived.

- Recently, in Hollywood, there was a small house. This house was across the freeway and an hour's journey, through the traffic, to where a movie star lived. A man named Mufaro lived in this house with his two daughters.

Have students cooperatively select one setting for their group story. Encourage students to elaborate on the setting by writing down ideas that fit with the proposed beginning. Then, assist students in generating two episodes for the story. Finally, assist students in generating a resolution for the story.

After students generate ideas, help them put their ideas together into paragraphs to develop the new story. Have one student write the paragraphs for the whole group where all can see. Have the group then tell the new story about Mufaro's family to another group of students.

Unit 5U   PROFESSOR PUFFENDORF'S SECRET POTIONS

By Robin Tzannes and Korky Paul (1992). New York: Checkerboard Press.
Unit developed by Susie Yoakum.

Professor Puffendorf's inventions made her rich and famous. While she attended a conference, her lazy and jealous assistant found the key and combination to her top secret cabinet, where several mysterious potions were hidden. Because the formulas had not been tested, the assistant tried the potions on the professor's guinea pig. He gave the first potion, for instant hair, to the guinea pig, and the guinea pig grew hair. He gave the second potion, for a beautiful voice, to the guinea pig, and the guinea pig sang beautifully. The assistant then stole the potions from the professor and greedily gave the third potion, for a best wish, to the guinea pig. The guinea pig made his best wish, which was to trade places with the assistant. The potion for a best wish worked, and the assistant got what he deserved.

MATERIALS NEEDED

- Obtain tangible objects from home that can be discussed as inventions.

- Obtain books about inventions from the library.

- Make 12 photocopies of the vocabulary card illustration for Unit 5U (see Appendix D), or more or less depending on the number of target words selected (see preparatory set discussion in this unit).

- Photocopy a blank, six-category semantic-word map on an overhead transparency (or enlarge the map so all students can see it), or copy enough maps for all students in the group (see Appendix C).

- Obtain necessary utensils and ingredients for a potion that students will invent (see dramatic play discussion in this unit).

- Photocopy a blank internal-states chart on an overhead transparency (or enlarge the chart so all students can see it), or copy enough charts for all students in the group (see Appendix C).

- Obtain necessary art materials (one piece of construction paper per student, colored pencils or markers).

- Photocopy a blank four-episode map on an overhead transparency (or enlarge the map so all students can see it), or copy enough maps for all students in the group (see Appendix C).

PRESTORY PRESENTATION

Preparatory Set

Provide students with tangible objects (e.g., light bulb, telephone, Polaroid camera). Discuss what an invention is (i.e., something new and useful). Ask the following questions:

- What is a scientist?

Professor Puffendorf's Secret Potions

- What are some famous inventions?

- Who invented them?

- What inventions do you have in your home?

The book *Mistakes That Worked* (Jones and O'Brien, 1991) provides illustrations and descriptions of inventions that are of interest to school-age students. This information can be used in the preparatory set or as support material for the semantic-word map.

See the instructions on page 18 for teaching selected story vocabulary words. Use the following vocabulary words selected for you, or select words appropriate for your specific students.

- potion
- laboratory
- assistant
- linoleum
- hesitated
- prance

Write each word on a vocabulary card illustration and write the corresponding definition on another card. After all cards have been created, have students match each word to its corresponding definition.

Think Alouds

Point to the cover and say, "I know that this book is about a scientist who is making some kind of potion. What type of potion could she be making?"

Read the title and say, "The title of this story is *Professor Puffendorf's Secret Potions*." Either model a prediction (e.g., "I predict that this story will be about a secret potion that Professor Puffendorf makes. I think the other person on the cover of the book will steal the secret potion and sell it") or ask a prediction question (e.g., "What do you think the story will be about?").

Scan the illustrations only. Stop at selected points of the story to model a prediction or to ask prediction questions based only on the illustrations:

- Professor Puffendorf is holding her guinea pig near her face. How do you think she feels about him?

275

• That man has broken into the secret potion safe. What types of potions do you think he will find there?

Write down students' responses for discussion and comparison with actual events after reading the story. Stop the prestory think-aloud activity before Slag and Chip trade places so the ending of the story will not be revealed.

Semantic-Word Map

Write the word *inventions* where all students can see it. Provide categories for types of inventions. Ask students to think of inventions for each category, and write their suggestions down. Use the book *Mistakes That Worked* by Jones and O'Brien (1991) for assistance if needed. The following is an example of a semantic-word map for *Professor Puffendorf's Secret Potions.*

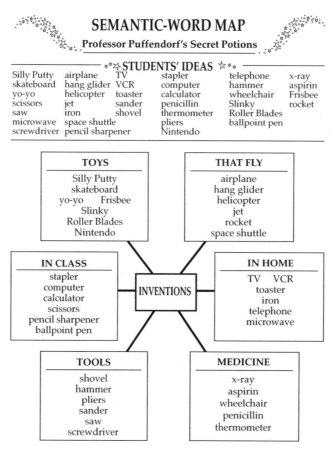

SEMANTIC-WORD MAP
Professor Puffendorf's Secret Potions

STUDENTS' IDEAS

Silly Putty	airplane	TV	stapler	telephone	x-ray
skateboard	hang glider	VCR	computer	hammer	aspirin
yo-yo	helicopter	toaster	calculator	wheelchair	Frisbee
scissors	jet	sander	penicillin	Slinky	rocket
saw	iron	shovel	thermometer	Roller Blades	
microwave	space shuttle		pliers	ballpoint pen	
screwdriver	pencil sharpener		Nintendo		

TOYS
Silly Putty
skateboard
yo-yo   Frisbee
Slinky
Roller Blades
Nintendo

THAT FLY
airplane
hang glider
helicopter
jet
rocket
space shuttle

IN CLASS
stapler
computer
calculator
scissors
pencil sharpener
ballpoint pen

INVENTIONS

IN HOME
TV   VCR
toaster
iron
telephone
microwave

TOOLS
shovel
hammer
pliers
sander
saw
screwdriver

MEDICINE
x-ray
aspirin
wheelchair
penicillin
thermometer

DURING-STORY PRESENTATION

Directed Reading/Thinking Activity

Read to where the guinea pig drinks the potion for a best wish. Have the students predict what they think will happen when the guinea pig drinks the potion. Write these predictions where all students can see them.

Questioning

See the instructions on pages 23–24 for asking questions about the following figurative-language examples:

- Suddenly his *eye fell* on a cabinet marked *top secret!*

- Chip began to sing *with a voice so rich and melodious* that tears came into Slag's eyes.

- Slag's greedy eyes *nearly popped out of his head.*

- Slag looked at Chip *with an evil glint in his eye.*

POSTSTORY PRESENTATION

Think Alouds

After reading the story, state, "Slag was able to break into Professor Puffendorf's secret potion safe and use the potions. List on your own paper some precautions Professor Puffendorf could have taken to prevent this from happening." After students have written down some precautions, have them share these with the group. Conduct a discussion about think-aloud questions. Compare students' responses before the story was read with the actual story events.

Dramatic Play

Have students work in small groups to invent a potion that they will make. Have them decide on the type and quantity of ingredients they would like to put into a magic potion. Tell students that you will bring the ingredients and necessary utensils to the next session and they will make the potion using their recipe as a guide. Remind students that they will be trying out their potion, so they should include ingredients that are drinkable. Write their recipe where all students can see it. Have them also plan the utensils that will be needed to make their potion.

At the next session, have the ingredients available along with necessary utensils. Have students work together in small groups, following their recipe to make the potion. Have students test-drink their concoction and evaluate it. What changes would they make if they were to create it again?

Word Substitution

See the instructions on pages 40–41 for the word-substitution strategy. The following is an example sentence with its target word emphasized, followed by a list of synonyms:

Then Slag had a *wicked* idea…try it on the guinea pig.

wicked

evil

rotten

terrible

sinful

lousy

Question-Answer Relationships

See the instructions on page 35 for the question-answer relationships strategy. The following are examples of questions to test students' comprehension of *Professor Puffendorf's Secret Potions* (question type is indicated in parentheses after each example):

- Where were the potions hidden? (Right There)

- What was one thing that happened to Chip after drinking one of the potions? (Think and Search)

- How did Slag manage to get the top secret cabinet open? (Think and Search)

- Why didn't Slag want to drink the potion? (Right There)

- Do you think Slag did the right thing by giving Chip the potion first? Why? (Author and You)

- Do you think the professor was angry with Slag when she found out what he had done? Why? (Author and You)

- What should you do when your friend steals something that does not belong to him? (On Your Own)

- Is it okay to conduct experiments on animals even if it is harmful to them? Why? (On Your Own)

Internal-States Chart

See the instructions on pages 32–33 for using an internal-states chart. Engage students in dialogue like the following regarding the characters' feelings:

Educator: How did Slag feel when he started to drink the potion?

Students: He felt scared.

Educator: Why did he feel scared?

Students: Because he didn't know if the potion was poisoned.

An example of an internal-states chart for *Professor Puffendorf's Secret Potions* is provided on the following page.

INTERNAL-STATES CHART
Professor Puffendorf's Secret Potions

CHARACTER(S)	WHEN	FEELING	WHY
Slag	Started to drink potion	Scared	Didn't want to be poisoned
Chip	Slag gave him potion	Upset; mad	Didn't think Slag should make him drink potion
Slag	Chip's hair turned red and curly	Excited	Thought he would be rich and famous

Art Activity/Journals

Art materials needed:

- One piece of white construction paper per student
- Colored pencils or markers

Have the students think about a wacky or serious idea for something they would like to invent. Have them draw pictures of their inventions. After the drawings are completed, have the students make up names for their inventions and label them on their papers (e.g., Unburnable Toast, Bananamatic, Smell-O-Telephone).

Have students write about their inventions in their journals using the following writing prompts:

- What is the name of your invention?

- What does your invention look like?

- What does your invention do?

- How much will it cost for someone to buy it?

- Include the name of the inventor, where it was invented, and the date it was invented.

Episode Map

See the instructions on pages 29–30 for using an episode map. The following is an example of an episode map for *Professor Puffendorf's Secret Potions*.

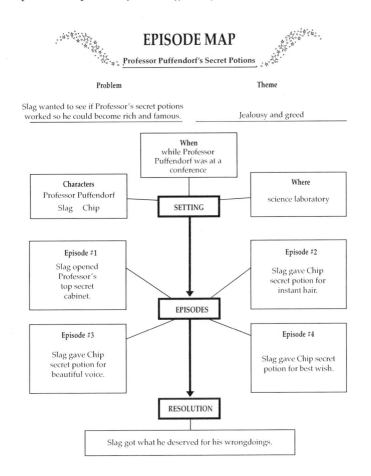

Unit 6U
THE ELEVENTH HOUR: A CURIOUS MYSTERY

By Graeme Base (1988). New York: Harry N. Abrams.
Unit developed by Kelly Majeroni and Heather Moran.

Horace the elephant decided to throw a huge party for all of his animal friends on his 11th birthday. He prepared a feast of fine desserts for his 11 friends. When all of the guests arrived, Horace presented the food and they were all very impressed. However, he insisted that they would not eat until the 11th hour. To pass the time, the animals engaged in 11 party games and were thoroughly exhausted and famished by the 11th hour. When the animals filed into the banquet room, they were shocked to find that someone had already eaten all of the food. Horace saved the day by making a large stack of sandwiches, but they never solved the mystery of who stole the feast. (The story is written in rhyme.)

MATERIALS NEEDED

- Make 24 photocopies of the vocabulary card illustration for Unit 6U (see Appendix D), or more or less depending on the number of target words selected (see preparatory set discussion in this unit).

- Construct a compare/contrast chart where all students can see it (see compare/contrast chart discussion in this unit).

- Obtain art materials (sheets of colored construction paper, glue, colored markers or pencils, glitter, sequins, crepe paper, scissors).

- Obtain food and beverages and items needed for games for an end-of-unit party (see dramatic play/art activity discussion in this unit).

- Photocopy a blank, four-episode map on an overhead transparency (or enlarge the map so all students can see it), or copy enough maps for all students in the group (see Appendix C).

- Photocopy a blank story-grammar cue chart on an overhead transparency (or enlarge the chart so all students can see it), or copy enough charts for all students in the group (see Appendix C).

- Prepare index cards with one episode from the story written on each one.

PRESTORY PRESENTATION

Preparatory Set

Share an experience with students in which you planned something and a problem occurred (e.g., rain at a picnic, burning food when you had guests for dinner, running out of game prizes at a birthday party). Discuss what happened and the solutions used to overcome the problem. Discuss how you felt when the problem was solved. Ask the students to share a similar problem.

See the instructions on page 18 for teaching selected story vocabulary words. Use the following vocabulary words selected for you, or select words appropriate for your specific students.

- initiative
- clever
- contrived
- masquerading
- banquet
- disbelief
- celebration
- swagger
- immense
- devour
- satisfied
- curious

Write each word on a vocabulary card illustration and write the corresponding definition on another card. After all cards have been created, have students match each word to its corresponding definition.

Think Alouds

Show the cover and say, "From the cover, I know that this book is about a group of animals that are dressed up in costumes. Where do you think the animals are going all dressed up?"

Point to the title and state, "The title of this story is *The Eleventh Hour.*" Either model a prediction (e.g., "I predict that this story is about a costume party that starts at 11 o'clock") or ask a prediction question (e.g., "What do you think this story will be about?").

Scan the illustrations only. Stop at selected points to model a prediction or to ask prediction questions based only on the illustrations:

- What do you think the elephant is cooking?

- The animals are having a sack race. Who do you think will win?

Write down the students' responses for discussion and comparison with actual events after reading the story. Stop the prestory think-aloud activity before the animals discover that all of the food is missing so the ending of the story will not be revealed.

DURING-STORY PRESENTATION

Compare/Contrast Chart

Construct a compare/contrast chart where all students can see it. Provide a column for the characters' names, their party costumes, and their animal types. During story reading, complete the columns of information with the students' assistance. For three of the characters, the author provides no character names; instruct the students to invent names for these characters. The following is an example of a compare/contrast chart for *The Eleventh Hour*.

Characters' names	Party costumes	Animal types
Oliver	Admiral	Pig
Kilroy	Musketeer	Mouse
Horace	Centurion	Elephant
Eric	Punk	Zebra
—	Cleopatra	Cat
Thomas	Astronaut	Rhinoceros
Maxwell	Indian	Tiger
—	Princess	Swan
—	Angels	Giraffes (twins)
Sam	Judge	Crocodile

Directed Reading/Thinking Activity

Read to where the animals discover that all of the food has already been eaten. Have the students predict what the animals will do to solve the problem of the missing

food. Write these predictions where all students can see them. After the story reading, use the predictions for discussion and comparison with actual events.

Extension

After reading the sentence, "They set off at a cracking pace," use the following extension to clarify *cracking pace:* "Yes, all the animals started the race extremely fast." Provide an example from your own experience: "I started off the day at a cracking pace. I cleaned the house, raked the yard, and washed the car. By 10 a.m., I was tired." Then ask the students, "When is a time you did something at a cracking pace?"

Questioning

See the instructions on pages 23–24 for asking questions about the following figurative-language examples:

- No sooner had they entered than *a rumor filled the air.*

- And one by one the guests were *drawn within to feast their eyes.*

- The elephant was shaky: it appeared he'd *lost his nerve.*

- But every *mind was on the feast.*

POSTSTORY PRESENTATION

Question-Answer Relationships

See the instructions on page 35 for the question-answer relationships strategy. The following are examples of questions to test students' comprehension of *The Eleventh Hour* (question type is indicated in parentheses after each example):

- Why did Horace pick the eleventh hour for the time of the feast? (Right There)

- Why wasn't there a winner of the musical chair game? (Think and Search)

- How did the pig cheat while playing cards? (Author and You)

- Why did Horace miss his chance to make a speech? (Author and You)

- How did Horace save the day? (Think and Search)

- Why was the birthday cake safe? (Right There)

- What types of treats have you eaten at a party? (On Your Own)

- If it was your birthday, what kinds of activities would you plan for your friends? (On Your Own)

Dramatic Play/Art Activity

Instruct the students to plan an end-of-unit (or birthday) party. Tell them to make a menu and a list of the games that will be played. Ask students to volunteer for responsibilities at the party and to make a list of assigned tasks. Then, direct them to think of problems that might occur (e.g., not enough food or drinks, rainy day so outdoor party games can't be played, forgetting to buy birthday candles, a guest gets hurt during a party game). Discuss realistic solutions to the potential problems.

Art materials needed:

- Sheets of colored construction paper
- Glue
- Colored markers or pencils
- Glitter, sequins, crepe paper
- Scissors

Instruct the students to make party hats or costumes to wear at the party and to create their own invitations to the party. These can also be used to invite family members or friends to the party.

When the party day arrives, sabotage one of the games or one of the food items so the students have to solve the problem. After the party, discuss how it felt to have their plans disrupted and the adjustments that had to be made to have a successful party.

Episode Map

See the instructions on pages 29–30 for using an episode map. The following is an example of an episode map for *The Eleventh Hour*.

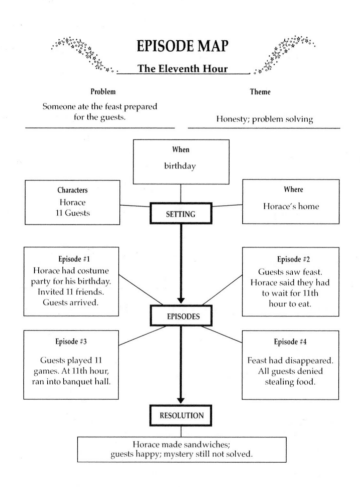

EPISODE MAP

The Eleventh Hour

Problem
Someone ate the feast prepared for the guests.

Theme
Honesty; problem solving

When
birthday

Characters
Horace
11 Guests

SETTING

Where
Horace's home

Episode #1
Horace had costume party for his birthday. Invited 11 friends. Guests arrived.

Episode #2
Guests saw feast. Horace said they had to wait for 11th hour to eat.

EPISODES

Episode #3
Guests played 11 games. At 11th hour, ran into banquet hall.

Episode #4
Feast had disappeared. All guests denied stealing food.

RESOLUTION

Horace made sandwiches; guests happy; mystery still not solved.

Think Alouds

After reading the story, state, "While all of the animals were playing the party games, someone ate the feast Horace had prepared for his friends. What could Horace have done to ensure that the food would not be eaten until the eleventh hour?" Conduct a discussion about think-aloud questions. Compare students' responses before the story was read with the actual story events.

Story-Grammar Cue Chart

See the instructions on page 37 for using the story-grammar cue chart. The following is an example of a story-grammar cue chart for *The Eleventh Hour*.

STORY-GRAMMAR CUE CHART
The Eleventh Hour

STORY GRAMMAR	STORY	CHECK-OFF
Setting: When: Horace's 11th birthday Where: Horace's house Who: Horace and his 11 friends		☐
Problem: Someone ate Horace's birthday feast		☐
Episode #1: Horace planned party; Horace sent invitations and made a feast; 11 friends arrived wearing costumes		☐
Internal Response: Happy, excited		
Episode #2: Guests entered the banquet hall; feast presented; everyone wanted to eat; had to wait until the 11th hour		☐
Internal Response: Disappointed		
Episode #3: Guests told to play games; everyone played 11 party games; time passed quickly		☐
Internal Response: Happy, had a good time		
Episode #4: 11th hour arrived; stopped games to eat feast; someone had already eaten the feast		☐
Internal Response: Shocked		
Ending: Horace made sandwiches and saved the day		☐
Reaction: Guests happy and satisfied, but the mystery remained		

Story Retelling

Give each student a card with an episode of the story written on it. As a group, the students can put the story together. Have each student tell his or her episode as it fits into the story.

Retell the story as a group. The episode map may be used as a guide to prompt retellings.

Unit 7U
THE GIRL WHO LOVED WILD HORSES

By Paul Goble (1978). New York: Macmillan.
Unit developed by Mary P. Scotese.

In a village lived a girl who loved horses. She and the village horses became lost one day after a terrible thunderstorm. They met a beautiful spotted stallion, the leader of some wild horses. The girl and the village horses stayed with the wild horses and were happy and free. A year later, she was caught by hunters from her village, and they returned her to her parents. But the girl was unhappy back in the village, so her parents let her return to the wild horses. The girl didn't forget her people and would come back each year to give her parents a colt. One year the girl did not return. Hunters later saw a beautiful mare galloping beside the stallion. It was believed that the girl had become one of the wild horses.

MATERIALS NEEDED

- Obtain books about wild horses from the library.

- Obtain a map of the western United States from the library.

- Make 16 photocopies of the vocabulary card illustration for Unit 7U (see Appendix D), or more or less depending on the number of target words selected (see preparatory set discussion in this unit).

- Photocopy a blank story map on an overhead transparency (or enlarge the map so all students can see it), or copy enough maps for all students in the group (see Appendix C).

- Photocopy two blank Venn diagrams on overhead transparencies (or enlarge the diagrams so all students can see them), or copy enough diagrams for all students in the group (see Appendix C).

- Obtain musical instruments from a music teacher or another source (see dramatic play / music / story retelling discussion in this unit); and a tape recorder.

PRESTORY PRESENTATION

Preparatory Set

Discuss the vocabulary words *wild* and *tame*. Ask the students if they have ever seen a wild horse. Have them imagine what it would be like to ride one. Write down their suggested descriptions where all students can see them. Use the list for discussion before having students write in their journals (see the journals discussion in this unit).

Look at books about wild horses. A children's book with photographs is *Last of the Wild Horses* (Harbury, 1986). An excellent teacher reference is *Wild Horses* (Moorhead, 1994). Discuss the following topics:

- origins of wild horses in the Western United States

- wild horse habitat, including the states where they are found (show on a map of the United States)

See the instructions on page 18 for teaching selected story vocabulary words. Use the following vocabulary words selected for you, or select words appropriate for your specific students.

- village
- terror
- colt
- neigh

- stallion
- gallop
- pursue
- defend

Write each word on a vocabulary card illustration and write the corresponding definition on another card. After all cards have been created, have students match each word to its corresponding definition.

Think Alouds

Show the students the book and indicate that the author and illustrator are the same person. Point out the Caldecott Medal and see if students know its significance. (Since 1938, this medal has been conferred annually by the American Library Association. It honors the illustrator of the most distinguished American picture book published in the United States [Jensen and Roser, 1993]). Show a few of the book's pictures, and ask the students why they think this book earned a medal.

Talk about the author's interest in Native Americans and their stories. Paul Goble wanted Native American children to be proud of their culture; therefore, he started writing Native American tales for children. Paul Goble provides pictures and words in his books that reflect Native American cultural heritage. He has been adopted by some Native American tribes.

Show the cover and say, "From the cover, I know that this book is about a Native American girl and her horse. I think she has a special friendship with the horse. How do I know this?"

Point to the title and say, "The title of this story is *The Girl Who Loved Wild Horses.*" Either model a prediction (e.g., "I predict that this story will be about a girl and

her efforts to protect wild horses") or ask a prediction question (e.g., "What do you think this story will be about?").

Scan the illustrations only. Stop at selected points to model a prediction or to ask prediction questions based only on the illustrations:

- The girl is riding one of the wild horses. Where is she going?

- Two men are waving to the girl, but it looks like she's running away from them! Where do you think she is going? Why?

Write down the students' responses for discussion and comparison with actual events after reading the story. Stop the prestory think-aloud strategy where the two hunters see the girl riding a horse and leading a colt so the end of the story will not be revealed.

DURING-STORY PRESENTATION

Directed Reading/Thinking Activity

Read to where the wild stallion asks the girl to live with him and the other wild horses. Have the students predict what the girl will do.

Read to where the stallion defends the horses from the hunters. Have the students predict what the hunters will do if they catch the girl.

Read to where the girl is back at the village and is very sad and lonely. Have the students predict what she will do.

Write students' predictions where all students can see them. After story reading, use these predictions for discussion and comparison with actual events.

Questioning

See the instructions on pages 23–24 for asking questions about the following figurative-language examples:

- …her voice was *lost in the thunder.*

- …*prancing to and fro.*

- His eyes *shone like cold stars.*

- …a mane and tail *floating like wispy clouds* about her.

- Our thoughts *fly with them.*

Extension

After reading the sentence, "If a horse was hurt she looked after it," use the following extension to clarify *looked after:* "Yes, she would take care of it until its wounds were healed." Provide an example from your own experience: "I looked after my grandfather after he had a stroke." Then ask the students, "What or whom have you looked after?"

POSTSTORY PRESENTATION

Think Alouds

After reading the story, state, "The hunters had to get their fastest horses to catch the girl. What could they have done to get her to return to the tribe without capturing her?" Conduct a discussion about think-aloud questions. Compare students' responses before the story was read with the actual story events.

Summarizing

See the instructions on page 24 for summarizing after story reading. Use an oral cloze procedure like the following with students:

In the _____ (village) lived a girl who loved _____ (wild horses). One hot day after she fell asleep, a terrible _____ (thunderstorm) filled the horses with _____ (terror). The girl jumped on a horse's back, and the herd _____ (galloped) away. The next morning, the girl saw a beautiful _____ (stallion). He asked the girl to live with _____ (him). A year

later, _____ (hunters) saw the girl with the wild horses. Men from the village _____ (captured) her, but the stallion _____ (defended) her and the colt. The girl was _____ (sad) and lonely back in the village. Each evening the _____ (stallion) would _____ (neigh) sadly from the hilltop above the village. In return for letting her live with the wild horses again, the girl gave her parents a _____ (colt).

Question-Answer Relationships

See the instructions on page 35 for the question-answer relationships strategy. The following are examples of questions to test students' comprehension of *The Girl Who Loved Wild Horses* (question type is indicated in parentheses after each example):

- Why did the village's horses run away? (Think and Search)

- How did the girl and horses become lost? (Think and Search)

- When the beautiful stallion first saw the girl, what did he say to her? (Right There)

- Why was the stallion protective of the girl and the colt? (Author and You)

- How did the girl feel when the hunters brought her back to live with her parents? (Right There)

- Why did the stallion neigh sadly from the hilltop above the village each evening? (Author and You)

- Why do thunder and lightning frighten horses? (On Your Own)

- What is your favorite animal? What makes that animal special to you? (On Your Own)

Journals

Review the list generated during the preparatory set from students' descriptions of what it would be like to ride a wild horse. Again have students imagine what it would be like to ride a wild horse; add new ideas to the previous list. Have the students choose

one of the following topics, or have them suggest their own topics to write about in their journals.

- If I were a wild horse, I would…

- If I were a hunter in the village, I'd like to catch and ride the wild stallion because…

- If I were the girl and the stallion died, I would (not) return to the village because…

Story Map

See the instructions on page 38 for creating a story map. The following is an example of a story map for *The Girl Who Loved Wild Horses*.

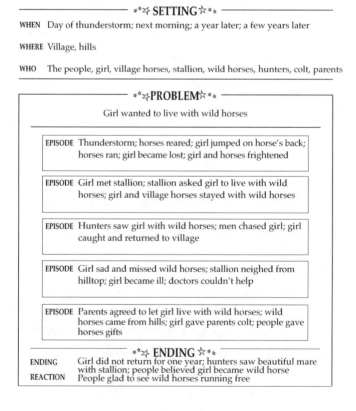

STORY MAP

The Girl Who Loved Wild Horses

SETTING

WHEN Day of thunderstorm; next morning; a year later; a few years later

WHERE Village, hills

WHO The people, girl, village horses, stallion, wild horses, hunters, colt, parents

PROBLEM

Girl wanted to live with wild horses

EPISODE Thunderstorm; horses reared; girl jumped on horse's back; horses ran; girl became lost; girl and horses frightened

EPISODE Girl met stallion; stallion asked girl to live with wild horses; girl and village horses stayed with wild horses

EPISODE Hunters saw girl with wild horses; men chased girl; girl caught and returned to village

EPISODE Girl sad and missed wild horses; stallion neighed from hilltop; girl became ill; doctors couldn't help

EPISODE Parents agreed to let girl live with wild horses; wild horses came from hills; girl gave parents colt; people gave horses gifts

ENDING

ENDING Girl did not return for one year; hunters saw beautiful mare with stallion; people believed girl became wild horse

REACTION People glad to see wild horses running free

Compare/Contrast Venn Diagram

See the instructions on page 16 for using a compare/contrast Venn diagram. The following diagram and the one on the next page are examples of compare/contrast Venn diagrams for *The Girl Who Loved Wild Horses*.

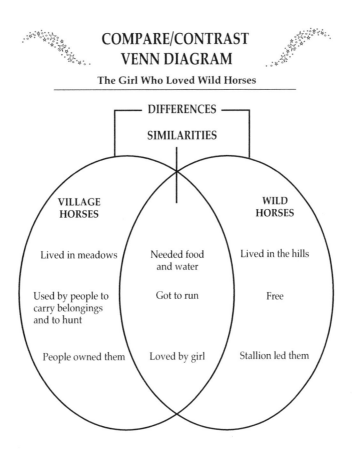

COMPARE/CONTRAST VENN DIAGRAM

The Girl Who Loved Wild Horses

DIFFERENCES

SIMILARITIES

VILLAGE HORSES

Lived in meadows

Used by people to carry belongings and to hunt

People owned them

Needed food and water

Got to run

Loved by girl

WILD HORSES

Lived in the hills

Free

Stallion led them

Dramatic Play/Music/Story Retelling

Have the students retell the story in an oral dramatic play that will be tape-recorded.

- Using the story map developed previously, work with the students in a group. For each of the episodes, ask students to decide if any characters should have speaking parts and what the characters will say. Write down their suggestions for dialogue for each of the episodes where all can see them.

COMPARE/CONTRAST
VENN DIAGRAM

The Girl Who Loved Wild Horses

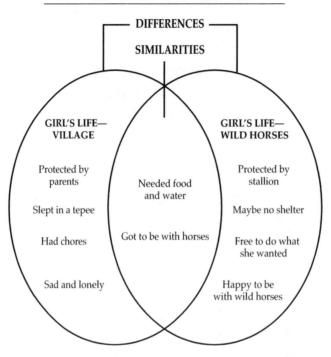

DIFFERENCES

SIMILARITIES

**GIRL'S LIFE—
VILLAGE**

**GIRL'S LIFE—
WILD HORSES**

Protected by
parents

Needed food
and water

Protected by
stallion

Slept in a tepee

Maybe no shelter

Had chores

Got to be with horses

Free to do what
she wanted

Sad and lonely

Happy to be
with wild horses

- Demonstrate the sounds produced by different musical instruments (e.g., drums, cymbals, harmonica, recorder, xylophone, triangle). Ask students to think of sound effects for each of the episodes in the story. Suggest that they use different instruments to represent the characters (e.g., drums for horses running during the storm and the chase; harmonica or recorder for neighing of the stallion; xylophone or triangle for the colt). If musical instruments are not available from a music teacher, suggest that students make sounds with their voices, bodies, or classroom objects.

- Instruct students to practice separate parts of the story before performing the play in its entirety. Tape-record these sessions; listen to them together with the students and provide them with feedback. Request suggestions from students for needed changes in the script or sound effects.

Unit 8U   THE GREAT KAPOK TREE:
A TALE OF THE AMAZON RAIN FOREST

By Lynne Cherry (1990). San Diego, CA: Harcourt Brace.
Unit developed by Kelly Hoggan North and Tobey Fields.

A man walked into the rain forest to chop down a Kapok tree. Soon, he grew tired from chopping and fell asleep. While sleeping, the forest animals told the man why he shouldn't cut down the tree. The great Kapok tree sustained many lives in the rain forest. When the man awoke, he looked at the animals surrounding him and decided not to chop down the tree. He dropped his ax and left the rain forest.

MATERIALS NEEDED

- Obtain picture books about rain forests from the library.

- Draw a large tree where all students can see it (see preparatory set discussion in this unit).

- Make 12 photocopies of the vocabulary card illustration for Unit 8U (see Appendix D), or more or less depending on the number of target words selected (see preparatory set discussion in this unit).

- Photocopy a blank, five-category semantic-word map on an overhead transparency (or enlarge the map so all students can see it), or copy enough maps for all students in the group (see Appendix C).

- Photocopy one blank discussion web on an overhead transparency (or enlarge the web so all students can see it), or copy enough webs for all students in the group (see Appendix C).

- Photocopy one blank story-grammar cue chart on an overhead transparency (or enlarge the chart so all students can see it), or copy enough charts for all students in the group (see Appendix C).

PRESTORY PRESENTATION

Preparatory Set

Talk about rain forests and the threats rain forests face today. Look at magazines and books about rain forests. A particularly good book is *The Rain Forest* (Jeunesse and Mettler, 1992). Talk about the following topics:

- rain forest locations (show map at front and back of book)

- resources received in America from rain forests

- layers of the rain forest and vegetation growing in each

- animal life in the rain forest

- deforestation, erosion, pollution—how these are affecting rain forests

- what we can do to preserve rain forests

Draw a large tree where all students can see it. Discuss with students the vegetation in each layer of the rain forest and label these layers on the drawing (i.e., emergent, canopy, middle, shrub, and herb layers).

See the instructions on page 18 for teaching selected story vocabulary words. Use the following vocabulary words selected for you, or select words appropriate for your specific students.

- underbrush
- troupe
- canopy

- hesitate
- lulled
- senhor

Write each word on a vocabulary card illustration and write the corresponding definition on another card. After all cards have been created, have students match each word to its corresponding definition.

Think Alouds

Show the cover and say, "From the cover, I know that this book is about a man who is going to cut down a large tree. Why do you think he wants to cut it down?"

Point to the title and say, "The title of this story is *The Great Kapok Tree*." Either model a prediction for the students (e.g., "I predict that this story will be about how the man works to cut down the tree") or ask a question (e.g., "What do you think this story will be about?").

Scan the illustrations only. Stop at selected points to model a prediction or to ask prediction questions based only on the illustrations:

- The man is wiping the sweat off of his forehead. How do you think he is feeling?

- The monkeys are surrounding the man. What do you think they are going to do?

Write down the students' responses for discussion and comparison with actual events after reading the story. Stop the prestory think-aloud activity before the man drops his ax and leaves the rain forest so the ending of the story will not be revealed.

Semantic-Word Map

Show students the pictures on the inside cover of *The Great Kapok Tree*. Have students identify some of the rain forest animals and list their suggestions where all can see them. Using the drawing of the tree constructed previously, help students organize the animals into categories representing the layers of the rain forest. Discuss why each animal lives in a particular layer. The following is an example of a semantic-word map for *The Great Kapok Tree*.

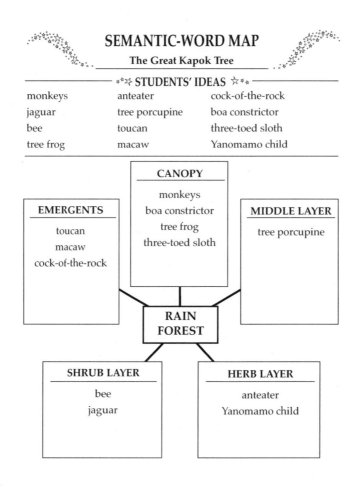

DURING-STORY PRESENTATION

Think Alouds

Analogy—Read to where the man gets tired and sits down at the base of the Kapok tree and say, "The man is already tired of chopping. This reminds me of the time I went to gather wood with my family. It was such hard work that I grew tired and fell asleep. What makes you so tired that you fall asleep?"

Confusing Information—Read to where the jaguar growls in the man's ear and state, "I don't understand how the man can sleep with a jaguar growling in his ear. This is different than what I would expect. How would you expect the man to respond to the growling?"

Repair Strategy—Read to where the man awakens from his sleep and say, "When the man awoke, all of the animals were staring at him. I don't understand why the animals didn't try to tell the man not to chop down the tree while he was awake. I'd better read on to see if the man will remember what the animals said to him while he was asleep. Do you think he will remember? Why?"

Mental Picture—Read to where the man is looking at all of the animals and state, "The man is looking at all the rain forest animals and thinking about them. The idea that I have is that he is remembering what they said and he will decide not to cut down the tree. What is your idea? What do you think the man will do?"

Extension

After reading the sentence, "You will leave many of us homeless if you chop down this great Kapok tree," use the following extension to clarify *many of us:* "Yes, the tree frogs would be homeless as well as the birds, monkeys, and anteater. Many of the animals would not have a home." Provide an example from your own experience: "Many of us would like a vacation." Then ask the student to use the phrase *many of us* in a sentence.

Questioning

See the instructions on pages 23–24 for asking questions about the following figurative-language examples:

- Soon the man *grew tired.*

- If you destroy the beauty of the rain forest, on what would you *feast your eyes?*

- Senhor, when you awake, please look upon us all *with new eyes.*

- Spots of bright light *glowed like jewels* amidst the dark green forest.

- The man smelled the *fragrant perfume of their flowers.*

Summarizing

Have the students take notes on what each animal said to the man. Students can use their written notes to summarize the story. Using their written notes, direct them to create sentences like the following for a partner to complete using a cloze procedure:

- The tree frog said to the man: "Senhor, a ruined rain forest means ruined _____ (lives)."

- The jaguar said, "Senhor, the Kapok tree is home to many birds and animals. If you cut it down, where will I find my _____ (dinner)?"

Direct partners to take turns retelling the story to each other.

POSTSTORY PRESENTATION

Think Alouds

After reading the story, state, "The man's boss told him to chop down the Kapok tree and he didn't. What reasons will he give to his boss for not cutting down the tree? Do you think he will be able to convince his boss that the rain forest is important? Why?"

Conduct a discussion about think-aloud questions. Compare students' responses before the story was read with the actual story events.

Word Substitution

See the instructions on pages 40–41 for the word-substitution strategy. The following is an example sentence with its target word emphasized, followed by lists of synonyms and antonyms:

They set fires to clear the underbrush, and soon the forest *disappears*.

disappears (synonym)	*disappears* (antonym)
fades	materializes
vanishes	appears
dissipates	evolves

Question-Answer Relationships

See the instructions on page 35 for the question-answer relationships strategy. The following are examples of questions to test students' comprehension of *The Great Kapok Tree* (question type is indicated in parentheses after each example):

- Why did the man go into the rain forest? (Right There)

- What made the man fall asleep? (Think and Search)

- What is the name of one animal that came down from the tree to talk to the man? (Right There)

- What were the rain forest creatures doing when the man awoke? (Think and Search)

- What was the man thinking when he looked at the rain forest animals as he was about to swing his ax? (Author and You)

- Where do you think the man was going when he left the rain forest? (Author and You)

- What is one thing the rain forests provide for us? (On Your Own)

- What can you do to preserve the rain forests? (On Your Own)

Discussion Web

See the instructions on pages 26–27 for the discussion-web strategy. The following is an example of a discussion web for *The Great Kapok Tree*.

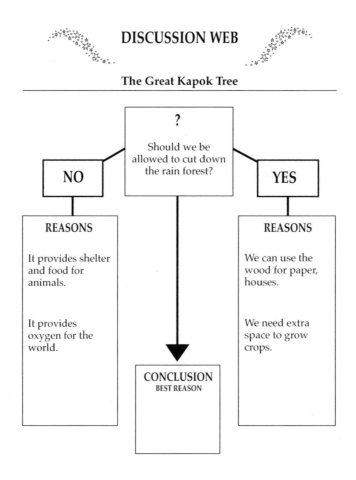

DISCUSSION WEB

The Great Kapok Tree

?
Should we be allowed to cut down the rain forest?

NO

YES

REASONS

It provides shelter and food for animals.

It provides oxygen for the world.

REASONS

We can use the wood for paper, houses.

We need extra space to grow crops.

CONCLUSION
BEST REASON

Story-Grammar Cue Chart

See the instructions on page 37 for using a story-grammar cue chart. The following is an example of a story-grammar cue chart for *The Great Kapok Tree.*

STORY-GRAMMAR CUE CHART
The Great Kapok Tree

STORY GRAMMAR	STORY	CHECK-OFF
Setting:		☐
When:	One afternoon	
Where:	Rain forest	
Who:	Man, forest animals, child	
Problem:	Rain forest disappearing; animals worried about shelter and food	☐
Episode #1:	Man chopping down Kapok tree; fell asleep; animals whispered to man not to chop tree	☐
	Boa constrictor said…	
	Bee said…	
	Monkeys said…	
	Birds said…	
	Tree frog said…	
	Jaguar said…	
	Tree porcupines said…	
	Anteaters said…	
	Three-toed sloth said…	
	Child said…	
Internal Response:	Animals worried; man tired	
Episode #2:	Man woke; saw beauty of forest and animals; picked up ax to chop; looked at animals and child	☐
Internal Response:	Man thought about what he was doing	
Ending:	Dropped ax; walked out of rain forest	☐
Reaction:	*	

* None provided in story. Ask students to write about how the animals and the child felt when the man walked out of the rain forest.

Unit 9U
THE STORY OF WALI DAD

By Kristina Rodanas (1988). New York: Lothrop, Lee & Shepard.
Unit developed by Shannan Smith and Lisa Stott.

Wali Dad, an elderly grasscutter in India, saved his money until it exceeded his needs. He chose to spend it on a lovely bracelet and to give the bracelet to the kindest and most beautiful woman in the land. His merchant friend delivered the gift to the Princess of Khaistan, who fit the desired description. To show her gratitude, the princess repaid the anonymous giver with an even greater gift. Having no need for luxuries, Wali Dad sent the gift on to the most honorable young prince in the land. The prince responded by returning an even more extravagant gift. The princess and the prince continued to exchange gifts unknowingly through Wali Dad until the princess decided she must meet Wali Dad. Upon her arrival, Wali Dad sent for the prince, and the two youths fell in love and were married. Happiest of all were not the receivers, but the giver.

MATERIALS NEEDED

- Obtain a map or globe of the world from the library.

- Make 18 photocopies of the vocabulary card illustration for Unit 9U (see Appendix D), or more or less depending on the number of target words selected (see preparatory set discussion in this unit).

- Obtain an audiotape of Indian music from the library.

- Obtain picture books or magazines that feature India from the library.

- Enlarge the vocabulary card illustration (see Appendix D) and photocopy enough enlargements for all students in the group.

- Photocopy one blank story map on an overhead transparency (or enlarge the map so all students can see it), or copy enough maps for all students in the group (see Appendix C).

- Photocopy one blank internal-states chart on an overhead transparency (or enlarge the chart so all students can see it), or copy enough charts for all students in the group (see Appendix C).

PRESTORY PRESENTATION

Preparatory Set

Talk about giving without expecting to receive. First, describe a time when you gave something secretly and how good it made you feel. Then, ask students to tell of an experience when they did something nice for somebody else and didn't tell anyone. Ask them to describe how they felt. Discuss why it is hard to do something for another without telling anyone or expecting to receive a reward for the good deed.

Discuss the geographic location of India. Have students locate India in relation to their geographical location on a globe.

See the instructions on page 18 for teaching selected story vocabulary words. Use the following vocabulary words selected for you, or select words appropriate for your specific students.

- gratitude
- profitable
- loyal
- dismayed
- beckoned
- caravan
- taxing
- persuade
- perplexed

Write each word on a vocabulary card illustration and write the corresponding definition on another card. After all cards have been created, have students match each word to its corresponding definition.

Think Alouds

Point to the cover and say, "From the cover, I know that this story is about a man from India who owns a herd of elephants, camels, and horses. How do I know this? Do you think this man is wealthy?"

Read the title and state, "The title of this story is *The Story of Wali Dad.*" Either model a prediction for the students (e.g., "I predict that this story will be about a man named Wali Dad and his life style") or ask a question (e.g., "What do you think this story will be about?").

Scan the illustrations only. Stop at selected points to model a prediction or to ask prediction questions based only on the illustrations:

- Wali Dad is counting his money. What is he planning to buy with his savings?

- Two men are in Wali Dad's tent. What do you think they are discussing?

Write down the students' responses for discussion and comparison with actual events after reading the story. Stop the prestory think-aloud strategy where the two men are in Wali Dad's tent so the end of the story will not be revealed.

Music/Semantic-Word Map

Locate an audiotape of Indian music at your public library (e.g., India's national anthem). Use the audiotape for background music as students prepare a map of India.

Give each student an enlarged photocopy of the vocabulary card illustration for this unit (i.e., an outline of India). Using a globe (or a map of India), a picture book, or a *National Geographic* issue focused on India, have the students identify:

- where India is located (Asian continent)

- the surrounding bodies of water (Indian Ocean, Arabian Sea, Bay of Bengal)

- animals found in India (horses, tigers, camels, elephants)

- types of climate (hot, dry, desert, and mountain)

- important natural features (Himalayas)

Help students fill in their maps with major landmarks.

DURING-STORY PRESENTATION

Directed Reading/Thinking Activity

Read to where the merchant agrees to deliver the bracelet to the princess. Have students predict whether the princess will give something to Wali Dad in return and what it might be.

Read to where the king asks Wali Dad if is true that he wants to marry his daughter. Have the students predict Wali Dad's response.

Write these predictions where all students can see them. After the story reading, use the predictions for discussion and comparison with actual events.

Extension

After reading the sentence, "The young prince was most grateful," use the following extension to clarify *most grateful*: "Yes, the prince was thankful to get such a wonderful gift from a stranger." Provide an example from your own experience: "I was most grateful for the extra money I received in my paycheck." Then ask the students, "Can you think of a time when you were most grateful for a gift that you received? Can you think of

a time when you really appreciated what someone did for you? Can you think of a time when you wished someone else had been more grateful for something you did?"

Questioning

See the instructions on pages 23–24 for asking questions about the following figurative-language examples:

- These presents must be *taxing the resources* of the generous stranger.

- He *blinked his eyes in disbelief.*

- The lawn was *ablaze with beautiful gardens…*

POSTSTORY PRESENTATION

Think Alouds

After reading the story, state, "Wali Dad started all of the gift giving by giving a simple bracelet to the princess. What could he have done to ensure that the gift giving stopped after one gift?" Conduct a discussion about think-aloud questions. Compare students' responses before the story was read with the actual story events.

Question-Answer Relationships

See the instructions on page 35 for the question-answer relationships strategy. The following are examples of questions to test students' comprehension of *The Story of Wali Dad* (question type is indicated in parentheses after each example):

- Why did Wali Dad give away the bracelet? (Right There)

- Who delivered all the presents to the prince and princess for Wali Dad? (Right There)

- What is one gift that the princess gave to Wali Dad? (Think and Search)

- What is one gift that the prince gave to Wali Dad? (Think and Search)

- Why did the princess ask her father for advice? (Author and You)

- Why was Wali Dad happiest of all when he saw the princess wearing the bracelet? (Author and You)

- What would you do if someone you didn't know gave you an expensive gift? (On Your Own)

- How does it make you feel when someone gives you a gift or does something nice for you? Why? (On Your Own)

Story Map

See the instructions on page 38 for developing a story map. The following is an example of a story map for *The Story of Wali Dad*.

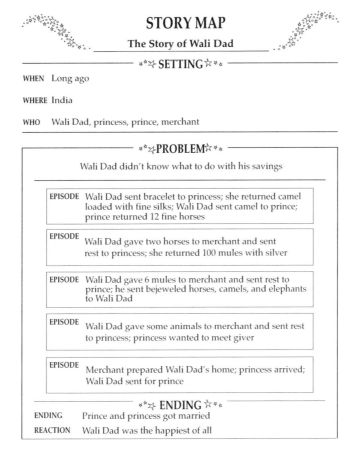

STORY MAP

The Story of Wali Dad

━━ SETTING ☆ ━━

WHEN Long ago

WHERE India

WHO Wali Dad, princess, prince, merchant

━━ PROBLEM ☆ ━━

Wali Dad didn't know what to do with his savings

EPISODE	Wali Dad sent bracelet to princess; she returned camel loaded with fine silks; Wali Dad sent camel to prince; prince returned 12 fine horses
EPISODE	Wali Dad gave two horses to merchant and sent rest to princess; she returned 100 mules with silver
EPISODE	Wali Dad gave 6 mules to merchant and sent rest to prince; he sent bejeweled horses, camels, and elephants to Wali Dad
EPISODE	Wali Dad gave some animals to merchant and sent rest to princess; princess wanted to meet giver
EPISODE	Merchant prepared Wali Dad's home; princess arrived; Wali Dad sent for prince

━━ ENDING ☆ ━━

ENDING Prince and princess got married

REACTION Wali Dad was the happiest of all

Internal-States Chart

See the instructions on pages 32–33 for developing an internal-states chart. Engage students in dialogue like the following regarding the characters' feelings:

Educator: How did Wali Dad feel when he gave the bracelet to the princess?

Students: He felt generous.

Educator: Why did he feel generous?

Students: Because he wanted to share his good fortune with someone else.

The following is an example of an internal-states chart for *The Story of Wali Dad*.

INTERNAL-STATES CHART
The Story of Wali Dad

CHARACTER(S)	WHEN	FEELING	WHY
Wali Dad	Gave bracelet to princess	Generous	Wanted to share
Prince	After receiving silver-laden mules	Embarrassed	Thought presents too generous
Merchant	Led princess to Wali Dad's home	Reluctant	Knew Wali Dad was poor; princess did not know this
Princess	Met the prince	Love	Prince was honorable and kind

Word Substitution

See the instructions on pages 40–41 for the word-substitution strategy. The following are example sentences with their target words emphasized, followed by lists of synonyms:

The old grasscutter was *astonished* when the *spirited* horses pranced into his yard.

astonished	*spirited*
surprised	lively
shocked	energetic
amazed	active

Journals

Have students draw pictures of the main character of the story in their journals. Ask them to write a response below their pictures for one of the following prompts:

- Describe Wali Dad for someone who hasn't heard or read *The Story of Wali Dad.*

- How do you feel about Wali Dad?

- Does Wali Dad remind you of someone? If so, who and why?

- What have you learned from this story?

- What did you dislike about this story?

Story Retelling

Model story retelling for the students using the story map as a prompt. Then have each student retell the story using the story map. Tape-record their retellings, if desired. Have students listen to their retellings and make revisions.

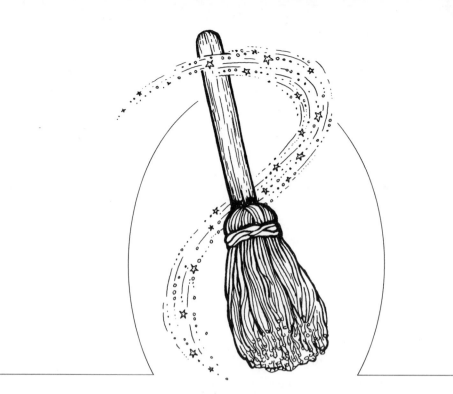

Unit 10U
THE WIDOW'S BROOM

By Chris Van Allsburg (1992). Boston: Houghton Mifflin.
Unit developed by Kimberly Buckner and Janette Robinson.

A lonely widow, named Minna Shaw, found an injured witch while out gardening. To her surprise, the witch disappeared and left her broom behind. She thought the broom was ordinary, but Minna Shaw discovered the broom's magical powers. The broom provided her with companionship and assistance, which she desperately needed. Soon, her neighbors found out about the broom's powers. They believed the broom was evil and sought to destroy it. The neighbors took a broom and burned it. However, Minna Shaw was not willing to give up the magic broom's companionship, so she had devised a plan to keep it. Her plot scared the neighbors; they moved away and she kept the broom.

MATERIALS NEEDED

- Make 18 photocopies of the vocabulary card illustration for Unit 10U (see Appendix D), or more or less depending on the number of target words selected (see preparatory set discussion in this unit).

- Photocopy the game-board pattern (see page 319) for all students in the group. Also make an additional 40 photocopies of the vocabulary card illustration (i.e., the broom) to use with the game board. Obtain tokens from another board game to use as markers. Obtain a spinner from another board game (or have a coin available for flipping).

- Photocopy one blank internal-states chart on an overhead transparency (or enlarge the chart so all students can see it), or copy enough charts for all students in the group (see Appendix C).

- Photocopy one blank discussion web on an overhead transparency (or enlarge the web so all students can see it), or copy enough webs for all students in the group (see Appendix C).

- Photocopy one blank flow chart on an overhead transparency (or enlarge the chart so all students can see it), or copy enough charts for all students in the group (see Appendix C).

- Photocopy one blank story-grammar cue chart on an overhead transparency (or enlarge the chart so all students can see it), or copy enough charts for all students in the group (see Appendix C).

PRESTORY PRESENTATION

Preparatory Set

Discuss what a widow (and widower) is and how someone becomes a widow (or widower). Ask the students if they know any widows or widowers. Talk about the feelings

(e.g., loneliness, sadness) or needs (e.g., help with yard work, automobile repair, or child care) that a widow (or widower) might have.

Have the students recall stories and movies in which objects came to life (e.g., *Beauty and the Beast, Fantasia*). Discuss magic and who can perform magic tricks. Perform a magic trick to illustrate how people can be tricked. A good source is *Now You See It, Now You Don't* (Esterreicher, 1992).

See the instructions on page 18 for teaching selected story vocabulary words. Use the following vocabulary words selected for you, or select words appropriate for your specific students.

- rare
- wicked
- gesturing
- innocent
- ordinary
- amuse
- convince
- stake
- possessions

Write each word on a vocabulary card illustration and write the corresponding definition on another card. After all cards have been created, have students match each word to its corresponding definition.

Duplicate and use the game board on the following page to reinforce and enhance understanding of the targeted vocabulary words. Make enough photocopies of the vocabulary card illustration (i.e., broom) to use as rewards for correct responses. Provide students with tokens (pawns) from another board game.

To move their tokens, direct students to flip a coin (heads = move one space forward; tails = move two spaces forward) or use a spinner from another game. To play the game, instruct students to formulate responses to the directions on the game board. The object of the game is to earn the most brooms.

Think Alouds

Point to the cover and say, "From the cover, I know that this story is about a broom. How do I know this?"

Read the title and state, "The title of this story is *The Widow's Broom*." Either model a prediction for the students (e.g., "I predict that this story will be about a widow

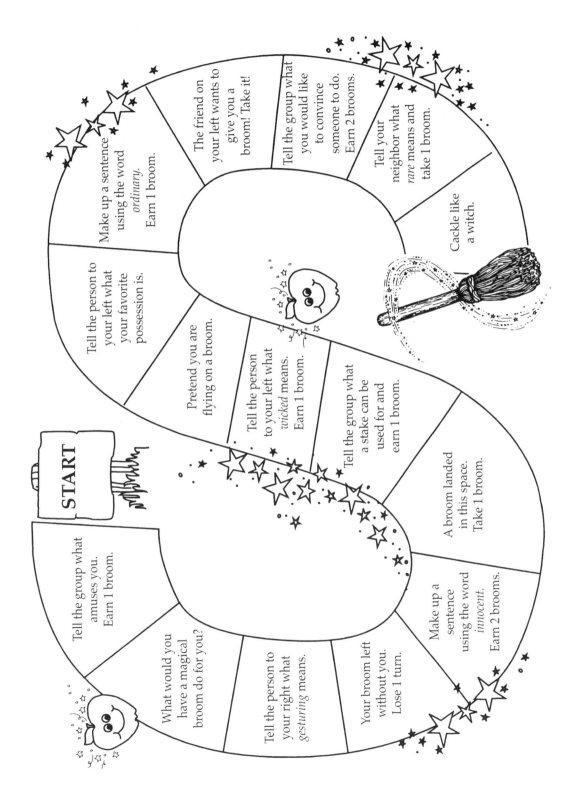

The friend on your left wants to give you a broom! Take it!

Tell the group what you would like to convince someone to do. Earn 2 brooms.

Tell your neighbor what *rare* means and take 1 broom.

Make up a sentence using the word *ordinary*. Earn 1 broom.

Cackle like a witch.

Tell the person to your left what your favorite possession is.

Pretend you are flying on a broom.

Tell the person to your left what *wicked* means. Earn 1 broom.

Tell the group what a stake can be used for and earn 1 broom.

A broom landed in this space. Take 1 broom.

START

Tell the group what amuses you. Earn 1 broom.

What would you have a magical broom do for you?

Tell the person to your right what *gesturing* means.

Your broom left without you. Lose 1 turn.

Make up a sentence using the word *innocent*. Earn 2 brooms.

who finds a broom that has magical powers") or ask a question (e.g., "What do you think this story will be about?").

Scan the illustrations only. Stop at selected points to model a prediction or to ask prediction questions based only on the illustrations:

- The witch is falling from the sky. What do you think has happened to make her fall?

- The broom is standing on its own. What do you think it is going to do?

Write down the students' responses for discussion and comparison with actual events after reading the story. Stop the prestory think-aloud strategy before showing the picture of the man reaching for the broom so the ending of the story will not be revealed.

DURING-STORY PRESENTATION

Directed Reading/Thinking Activity

Read to where the witch is falling from the sky. Have the students predict where the witch will land.

Read to where the men come to take the broom. Have the students predict whether Minna will let them have it.

Read to where the broom is in the woods holding the ax. Have the students predict what the broom will do.

Write these predictions where all students can see them. After the story reading, use the predictions for discussion and comparison with actual events.

Questioning

See the instructions on pages 23–24 for asking questions about the following figurative-language examples:

- She peeked in and saw something that *made her heart jump.*

- Minna Shaw was asleep in a chair by the fireplace, where *embers of a dying fire glowed on the hearth.*

- It could even *pick out simple tunes* on the piano.

POSTSTORY PRESENTATION

Think Alouds

After reading the story, state, "All of Minna Shaw's neighbors thought that her broom was evil. List some things Minna could have done to show them that her broom was friendly." Conduct a discussion about think-aloud questions. Compare students' responses before the story was read with the actual story events.

Question-Answer Relationships

See the instructions on page 35 for the question-answer relationships strategy. The following are examples of questions to test students' comprehension of *The Widow's Broom* (question type is indicated in parentheses after each example):

- How do you feel when someone teases you? (On Your Own)

- Why was Minna Shaw so happy with the broom? (Think and Search)

- What is something mean that the Spiveys did to the broom? (Right There)

- How do you feel when someone helps you? (On Your Own)

- How was the broom disguised? (Right There)

- How would you feel if you were the broom and everyone thought you were wicked? (Author and You)

- What would have happened if the magic broom had been burned? (Think and Search)

- Why would you keep the broom if you were Minna Shaw? (Author and You)

Internal-States Chart

See the instructions on pages 32–33 for using the internal-states chart. Engage students in dialogue like the following regarding the characters' feelings:

Educator: How did Minna feel when she found the witch?

Students: She felt scared.

Educator: Why did she feel scared?

Students: Because witches are scary.

The following is an example of an internal-states chart for *The Widow's Broom.*

INTERNAL-STATES CHART
The Widow's Broom

CHARACTER(S)	WHEN	FEELING	WHY
Minna Shaw	Found witch in garden	Afraid	Witches are scary
Minna Shaw	Saw broom sweeping	Surprised; frightened	Broom can't sweep by itself
Mr. Spivey	Discovered broom	Horrified; afraid	Broom was evil
Neighbors	Discovered broom	Shocked	Broom was magic
Minna Shaw	Reported broom was ghost	Mischievous	Wanted to trick men
Minna Shaw	Spiveys moved away	Happy	Broom could stay

Discussion Web

See the instructions on pages 26–27 for using the discussion-web strategy. The following is an example of a discussion web for *The Widow's Broom*.

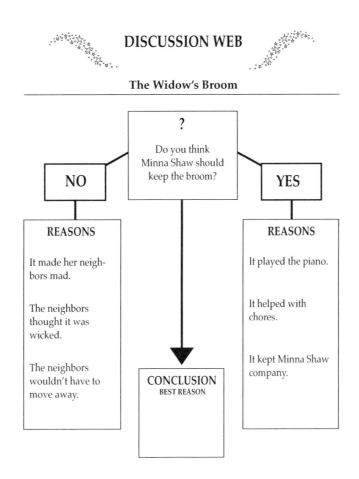

Journals

Provide a model of a journal entry for the students. Have students write a response to one of the following prompts:

- The Spivey boys teased the broom. Describe a time when you were teased and how you felt.

323

• The widow could tell by the men's faces that there was nothing she could do to stop them from taking the broom. Describe a time when you could tell it would do no good to argue with somebody, and that you had to give in.

Flow Chart

See the instructions on pages 31–32 for using the flow chart. The following is an example of a flow chart for *The Widow's Broom*.

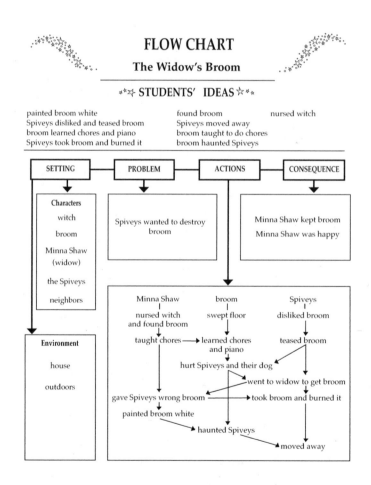

FLOW CHART

The Widow's Broom

STUDENTS' IDEAS

painted broom white	found broom nursed witch
Spiveys disliked and teased broom	Spiveys moved away
broom learned chores and piano	broom taught to do chores
Spiveys took broom and burned it	broom haunted Spiveys

SETTING	PROBLEM	ACTIONS	CONSEQUENCE

Characters

witch

broom

Minna Shaw (widow)

the Spiveys

neighbors

Spiveys wanted to destroy broom

Minna Shaw kept broom

Minna Shaw was happy

Environment

house

outdoors

Minna Shaw — nursed witch and found broom → taught chores → learned chores and piano

broom — swept floor

Spiveys — disliked broom → teased broom

hurt Spiveys and their dog

went to widow to get broom

gave Spiveys wrong broom → took broom and burned it

painted broom white

haunted Spiveys

moved away

Story-Grammar Cue Chart

See the instructions on page 37 for using the story-grammar cue chart. The following is an example of a story-grammar cue chart for *The Widow's Broom*.

STORY-GRAMMAR CUE CHART
The Widow's Broom

STORY GRAMMAR	STORY	CHECK-OFF
Setting:		
When:	Cold autumn night many years ago	
Where:	Farmhouse and outdoors	
Who:	Witch, Minna Shaw, broom, Spiveys	☐
Problem:	Spiveys afraid of widow's broom	☐
Episode #1:	Magic broom lost its power; broom and witch fell; Minna Shaw found them; witch was wounded; Minna Shaw helped witch; witch left broom	☐
Internal Response:	Afraid, surprised	
Episode #2:	Minna Shaw found broom sweeping floor; taught broom to do chores and play piano	☐
Internal Response:	Happy	
Episode #3:	Neighbors found out about broom; Spivey boys and dog teased broom; broom hit them and tossed the dog; Mr. Spivey angry; Mr. Spivey and men tied broom to stake; lit fire; burned broom	☐
Internal Response:	Mad, hurt, satisfied	
Episode #4:	Minna Shaw painted broom white; ghost broom circled Spivey's house; they moved	☐
Internal Response:	Happy, satisfied	
Ending:	Minna kept broom friend	☐
Reaction:	Happy and content	

Story Generation

Have students create a story about an object that they would like to come to life. Follow these steps:

- Draw a story line where all students can see it. Together with the students, recount what happened in *The Widow's Broom*, going from left to right: First, a witch's broom lost its power and the witch fell into the widow's garden. Next…

- Model a brief story (two to three episodes) of your own about an object that comes to life.

- List the students' names where all students can see them. Have students think of their favorite things. List their ideas underneath their names. Have them select/identify the one object that they like best and say why.

- Help students list words that relate to their selected object. Help students categorize their ideas (e.g., color, shape, why the object is a favorite).

- Have students draw their own story line on sheets of paper and use their lines to plan their own brief stories (i.e., only two or three episodes) about their selected object.

- Using their story lines, direct students to work in pairs and tell their stories to their partners.

- Allow time for students to write their brief stories.

- Have students read their stories aloud to their partners. Direct students to edit and revise their stories. Ask them to read their stories for the group.

APPENDICES

CLASSROOM LANGUAGE QUESTIONNAIRE

Use the classroom language questionnaire provided on pages 330–331 to record observations about a particular student. The most reliable and complete information is obtained from the student's teacher or someone who can observe the student at different times during the day and in different instructional activities (individual, small group, and entire class).

Use the guidelines below to complete the questionnaire:

- Observe the student several times over the course of an instructional unit, not just once.

- Record observations as soon as possible to avoid problems with remembering the student's behaviors in a given learning situation.

- Evaluate each item within a skill area (e.g., speaking skills) separately. That is, do not evaluate speaking skills globally for a given student (e.g., "This student has poor speaking skills, so I will check No for all items").

Use the obtained information, along with assessment information gleaned from oral and/or written narrative samples, to write both long-term goals and short-term objectives for your individualized education programs.

CLASSROOM LANGUAGE QUESTIONNAIRE

Student _____   Teacher _____

Age _____   Birth Date_____   Date _____

Teacher: Use this form to record information about the student's speaking, reading, writing, listening, and learning skills. Place a check mark under Yes, No, or Sometimes for each item observed. Record additional comments at the bottom of the form.

Speaking Skills	Yes	No	Sometimes
1. Volunteers information and contributes to class discussions.			
2. Conveys information in an organized, related manner.			
3. Answers questions appropriately.			
4. Asks questions appropriately.			
5. Uses humor, sarcasm, and figurative language appropriately.			
6. Uses complex sentences that contain subordinate clauses.			
7. Uses specific vocabulary rather than general words (*thing, stuff*).			
8. Takes conversational turns appropriately.			
9. Maintains a topic appropriately.			
10. Provides relevant information when retelling a story.			
11. Sequences events appropriately.			
Reading Skills	Yes	No	Sometimes
1. Recalls ideas or facts from print.			
2. Uses titles, pictures, and graphic information to make predictions.			
3. Uses prior knowledge to understand new information.			
4. Summarizes main ideas.			

Writing Skills	Yes	No	Sometimes
1. Responds to questions and provides opinions in writing.			
2. Writes a book report and sequences the events appropriately.			
3. Plans, generates, edits, and revises a story.			
4. Uses appropriate grammar and vocabulary in written assignments.			
5. Self-monitors written communication.			
Listening Skills	Yes	No	Sometimes
1. Follows oral directions.			
2. Pays attention.			
3. Understands the meaning of what is said.			
4. Grasps main ideas.			
5. Understands jokes, sarcasm, and figurative language.			
6. Listens for specific information.			
7. Self-monitors listening comprehension.			
Learning Skills	Yes	No	Sometimes
1. Compares and contrasts information.			
2. Plans and organizes information.			
3. Plans and organizes assignments.			

Comments

Some items adapted from Bouffler (1993), Morrow and Smith (1990), and Rhodes (1993).

EXAMPLES OF IEP GOALS AND OBJECTIVES

Long-Term Goals

The student will:

1. Retell a story with three episodes (including setting, problem, events, and ending) orally and/or in writing.

2. Plan, generate, edit, and revise a written story with at least two episodes when provided with a story-generation prompt.

3. Participate in classroom discussion by listening, volunteering information, and responding to and asking questions appropriately.

4. Demonstrate comprehension and use of vocabulary and figurative language related to the story units.

5. Organize and retrieve information using charts, maps, and diagrams.

Short-Term Objectives

The student will:

1. Retell a story orally in the correct sequence with the assistance of an episode map, story map, or flow chart.

2. Generate predictions about story outcomes using available information.

3. Answer the four types of question-answer relationship questions.

4. Organize information into categories using a semantic map.

5. Respond to a journal writing prompt by generating three sentences.

6. Use vocabulary or figurative language correctly in a sentence.

SEMANTIC-WORD MAP

_____

──── STUDENTS' IDEAS ────

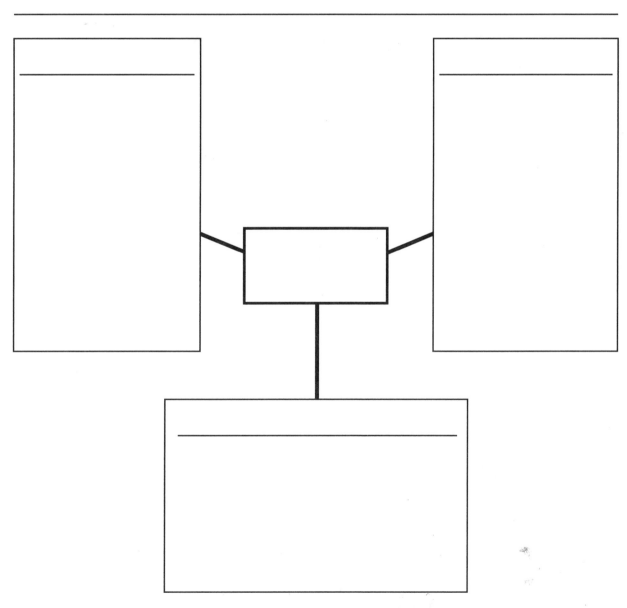

SEMANTIC-WORD MAP

_____

★*☆ STUDENTS' IDEAS ☆*★

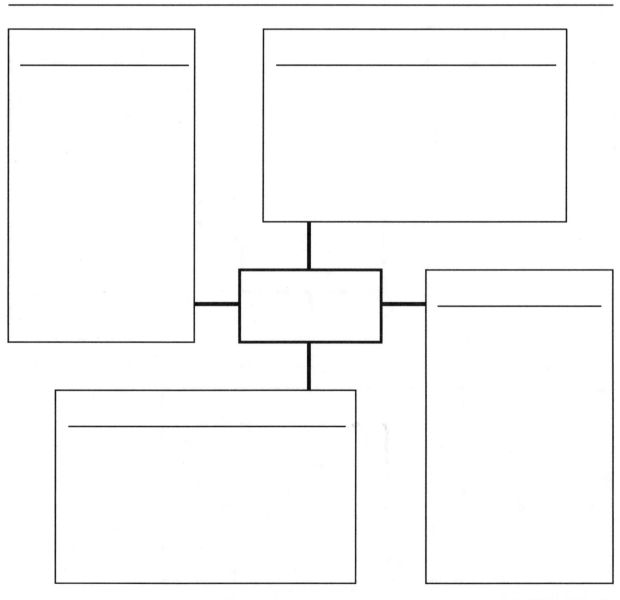

SEMANTIC-WORD MAP

_____

⋆⋆☆ STUDENTS' IDEAS ☆⋆⋆

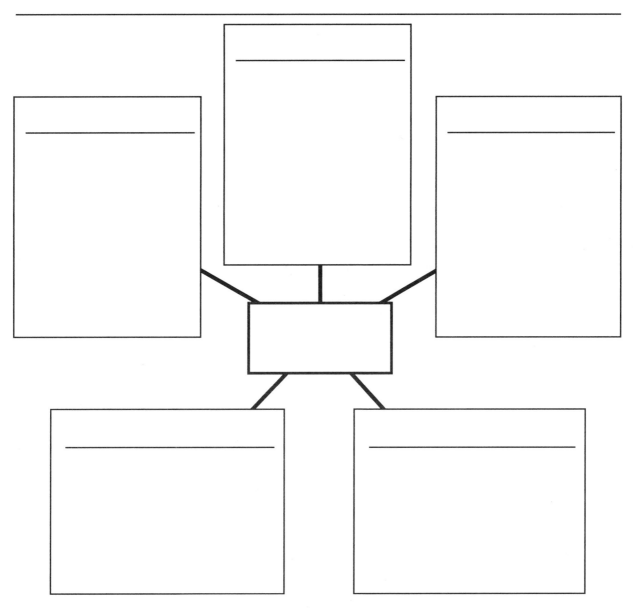

SEMANTIC-WORD MAP

_____

—————— ☆*☆ STUDENTS' IDEAS ☆☆* ——————

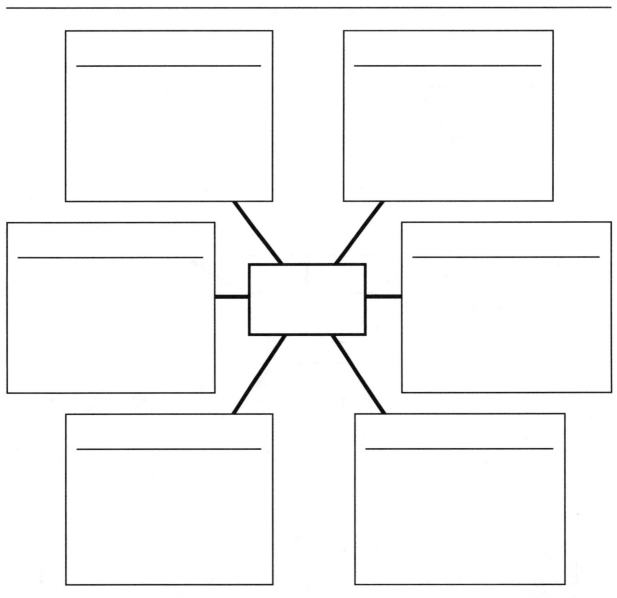

DISCUSSION WEB

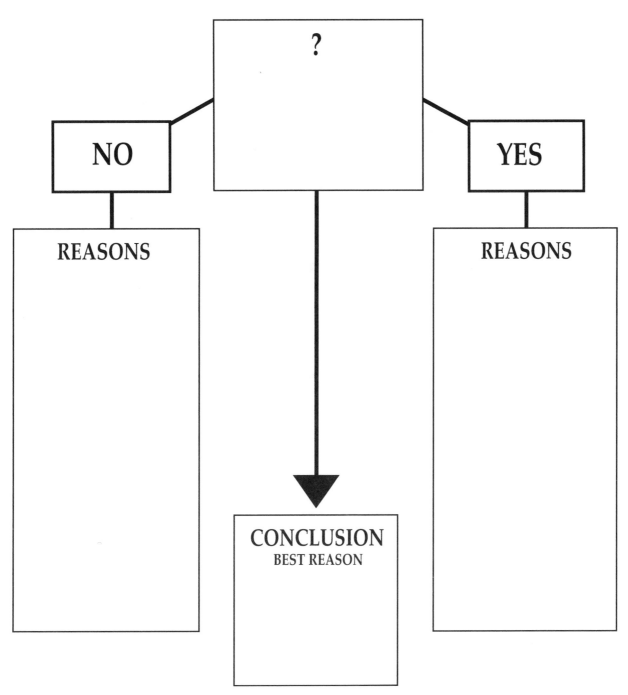

?

NO

YES

REASONS

REASONS

CONCLUSION
BEST REASON

EPISODE MAP

_____

Problem   Theme

_____   _____

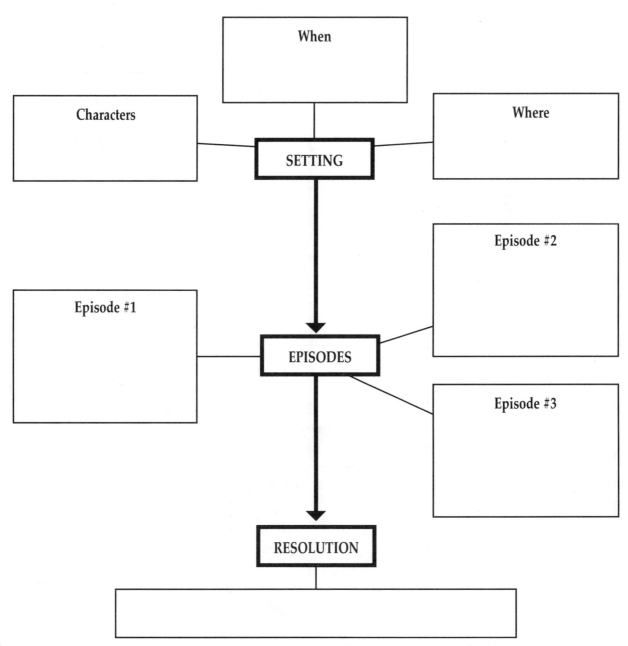

When

Characters   Where

SETTING

Episode #2

Episode #1

EPISODES

Episode #3

RESOLUTION

EPISODE MAP

Problem   Theme

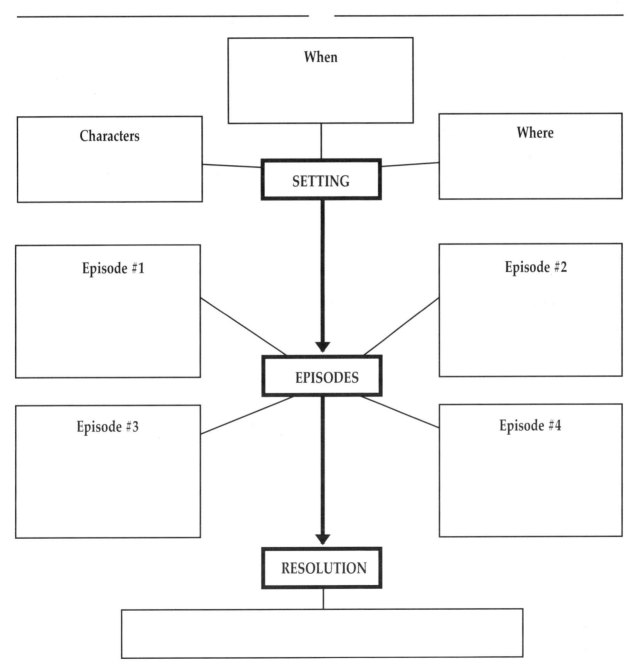

STORY MAP

_____

⁕⁕✺ SETTING ☆⁕⁕

WHEN

WHERE

WHO

⁕⁕✺ PROBLEM ☆⁕⁕

_____

EPISODE

EPISODE

EPISODE

EPISODE

EPISODE

⁕⁕✺ ENDING ☆⁕⁕

ENDING

REACTION

FLOW CHART

_____

⋆⋆✧ STUDENTS' IDEAS ✧⋆⋆

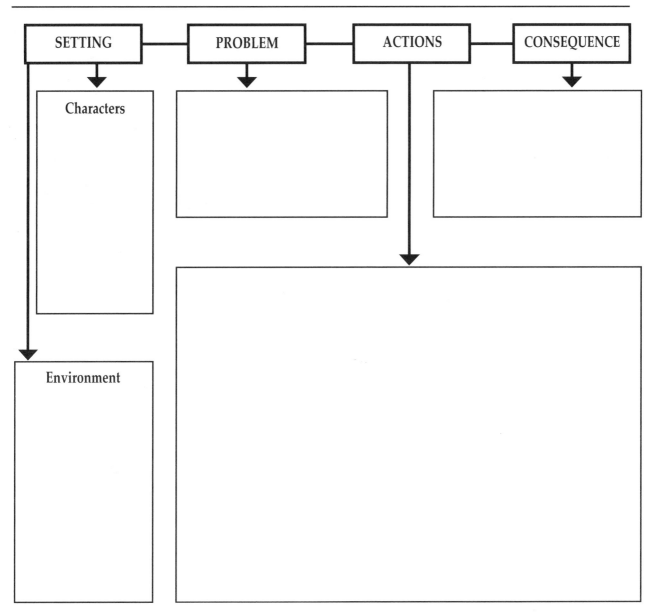

| SETTING | → | PROBLEM | | ACTIONS | | CONSEQUENCE |

Characters

Environment

INTERNAL-STATES CHART

_____

CHARACTER(S)	WHEN	FEELING	WHY

STORY-GRAMMAR CUE CHART

STORY GRAMMAR	STORY	CHECK-OFF

Setting:
  When:
  Where:
  Who:
		☐

Problem:		☐
Episode #1:		☐
Internal Response:		
Episode #2:		☐
Internal Response:		
Episode #3:		☐
Internal Response:		
Episode #4:		☐
Internal Response:		
Ending: Reaction:		☐

COMPARE/CONTRAST
VENN DIAGRAM

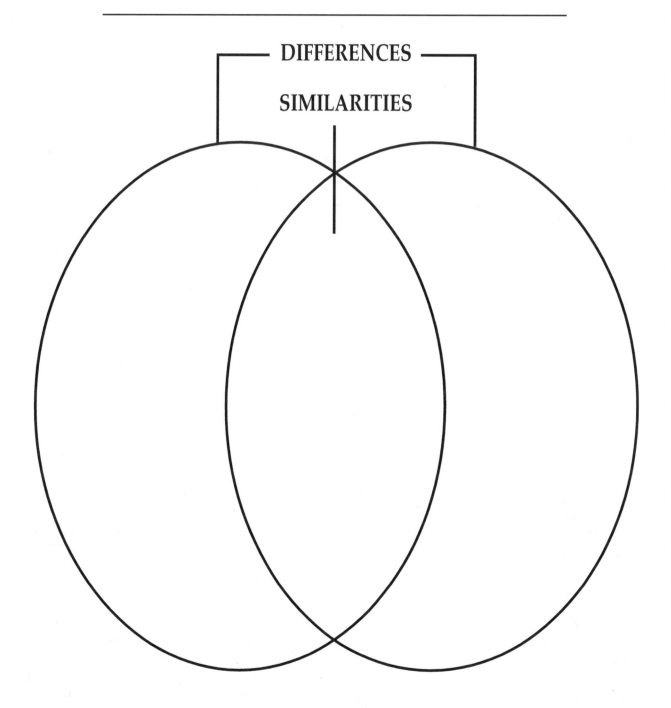

DIFFERENCES

SIMILARITIES

Unit 7M

Unit 8M

Unit 9M

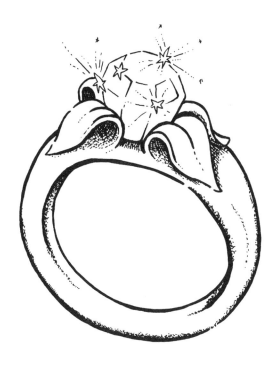

Unit 10M

Unit 5U

Unit 6U

Unit 7U

Unit 8U

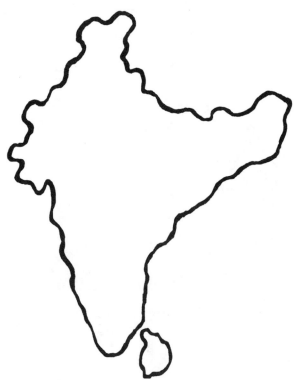

LIST OF PUBLISHERS FOR STORIES IN NARRATIVE UNITS

Amazing Grace	Dial Books for Young Readers 375 Hudson Street New York, NY 10014-3657
Annie and the Old One	Little, Brown and Company Time & Life Bldg. 1271 Avenue of the Americas New York, NY 10020
The Baker's Dozen: A Colonial American Tale	Harcourt Brace 1250 Sixth Avenue San Diego, CA 92101
The Biggest Bear	Houghton Mifflin 222 Berkeley St. Boston, MA 02116
A Day's Work	Houghton Mifflin 222 Berkeley St. Boston, MA 02116
The Eleventh Hour: A Curious Mystery	Harry N. Abrams 100 Fifth Ave. New York, NY 10011
Eyes of the Dragon	Lothrop, Lee & Shepard 1340 Avenue of the Americas New York, NY 10019
The Girl Who Loved Wild Horses	Macmillan 866 Third Avenue New York, NY 10022
The Great Kapok Tree: A Tale of the Amazon Rain Forest	Harcourt Brace 1250 Sixth Avenue San Diego, CA 92101
Great White Bear	Armstrong Publishing 55 Old Post Road No. 2 P. O. Box 1678 Greenwich, CT 06836-1678

Gregory, the Terrible Eater	Scholastic 555 Broadway New York, NY 10012-3999
Heckedy Peg	Harcourt Brace 1250 Sixth Avenue San Diego, CA 92101
Humphrey the Lost Whale: *A True Story*	Heian 1815 W. 205 Street, Suite 301 Torrance, CA 90501
Mufaro's Beautiful Daughters: *An African Tale*	Lothrop, Lee & Shepard 1350 Avenue of the Americas New York, NY 10019
Professor Puffendorf's Secret Potions	Checkerboard Press 30 Vesey Street New York, NY 10007
The Proud and Fearless Lion	Barron's Educational Series 113 Crossways Park Drive Woodbury, NY 11797
The Puppy Who Wanted a Boy	William Morrow 1350 Avenue of the Americas New York, NY 10019
The Rainbabies	Lothrop, Lee & Shepard 1350 Avenue of the Americas New York, NY 10019
The Rainbow Fish	North-South Books 1133 Broadway, Suite 1016 New York, NY 10010
Rude Giants	Harcourt Brace 1250 Sixth Avenue San Diego, CA 92101
Sam, Bangs & Moonshine	Holt, Rinehart & Winston 1120 S. Capital of Texas Hwy. No II-100 Austin, TX 78746-6487
Sam Is My Half Brother	Viking Penguin 375 Hudson St. New York, NY 10014

The Show-and-Tell Frog	Bantam Books 666 Fifth Avenue New York, NY 10103
"Stand Back," Said the Elephant, *"I'm Going to Sneeze!"*	Lothrop, Lee & Shepard 1350 Avenue of the Americas New York, NY 10019
Stellaluna	Harcourt Brace 1250 Sixth Avenue San Diego, CA 92101
The Story of Wali Dad	Lothrop, Lee & Shepard 1350 Avenue of the Americas New York, NY 10019
Strega Nona	Scholastic 555 Broadway New York, NY 10012-3999
Sylvester and the Magic Pebble	Simon and Schuster 1230 Avenue of the Americas New York, NY 10020
The Widow's Broom	Houghton Mifflin 222 Berkeley St. Boston, MA 02116
Too Many Tamales	Putnam 200 Madison Avenue New York, NY 10016

REFERENCES

Alvermann, D. (1991). The discussion web: A graphic aid for learning across the curriculum. *The Reading Teacher, 45*(2), 92–99.

Alvermann, D.E., Smith, L.C., and Readence, J.E. (1985). Prior knowledge activation and the comprehension of compatible and incompatible text. *Reading Research Quarterly, 20,* 420–436.

Atwell, N. (1987). Building a dining room table: Dialogue journals about reading. In T. Fulwiler (Ed.), *The journal book* (pp. 157–170). Portsmouth, NH: Heinemann.

Ausubel, D.P. (1960). The use of advance organizers in the learning and retention of meaningful verbal material. *Journal of Educational Psychology, 51,* 267–272.

Barclay, K.D., and Walwer, L. (1992). Linking lyrics and literacy through song picture books. *Young Children, 14*(4), 76–85.

Barnes, S., Gutfreund, M., Satterly, D., and Wells, G. (1983). Characteristics of adult speech which predict children's language development. *Journal of Child Language, 10*(1), 65–84.

Bartelo, D.M. (1984). *Getting the picture of reading and writing: A look at the drawings, composing, and oral language of limited English proficiency children.* Durham, University of New Hampshire: Research in the Teaching of Writing. (ERIC Document Reproduction Service No. ED 245 533)

Beaumont, C. (1992). Language intervention strategies for Hispanic LLD students. In H. W. Langdon and L. L. Cheng (Eds.), *Hispanic children and adults with communication disorders* (pp. 272–325). San Diego, CA: Aspen.

Beck, J., and McKeown, M. (1981). Developing questions that promote comprehension: The story map. *Language Arts, 58,* 913–918.

Berney, T.D., and Barrera, M. (1990). *Language development through holistic learning.* New York: Office of Research, Evaluation, and Assessment. (ERIC Document Reproduction Service No. ED 319 235)

Blank, M., and White, S. (1986). Questions: A powerful but misused form of classroom exchange. *Topics in Language Disorders, 6*(2), 1–12.

Blaska, J.K., and Lynch, E.C. (1993). Inclusion and depiction of persons with disabilities in children's literature. *Communicator, 19*(4), 9.

Bouffler, C. (Ed.). (1993). *Literacy evaluation.* Portsmouth, NH: Heinemann.

Brown, J.E., Phillips, L.B., and Stephens, E.C. (1993). *Toward literacy: Theory and applications for teaching writing in the content areas.* Belmont, CA: Wadsworth.

Brown, M.H., Althouse, R., and Anfin, C. (1993). Guided dramatization: Fostering social development in children with disabilities. *Young Children, 48*(2), 68–71.

Camp, B.W., and Bash, M.A. (1981). *Think aloud: Increasing social and cognitive skills — A problem solving approach for children.* Champaign, IL: Research Press.

Cerf, C. (1993). Healthy food. On *Sesame Road* [Cassette]. Racine, WI: Western Publishing.

Christie, J.F. (1987). Play and story comprehension: A critique of recent training research. *Journal of Research and Development in Education, 21*(1), 36–43.

Culatta, B. (1994). Representational play and story enactments. In J. F. Duchan, L. E. Hewitt, and R. M. Sonnenmeier (Eds.), *Pragmatics: From theory to practice* (pp. 105–119). Englewood Cliffs, NJ: Prentice Hall.

Davey, B. (1983). Think aloud: Modeling the cognitive process of reading comprehension. *Journal of Reading, 27*(1), 44–47.

Davis, Z.T., and McPherson, M. D. (1989). Story map instruction: A road map for reading comprehension. *The Reading Teacher, 43*, 232–240.

Dollaghan, C., and Kaston, N. (1986). A comprehension monitoring program for language-impaired children. *Journal of Speech and Hearing Disorders, 51*, 264–271.

Dunning, D.B. (1992). *Instructional questions that clarify story characters' feelings and motivations: Their effect on students' narrative comprehension.* Urbana, IL: Center for the Study of Reading. (ERIC Document Reproduction Service No. ED 350 579)

Duthie, J. (1986). The web: A powerful tool for the teaching and evaluation of expository essay. *The History and Social Science Teacher, 21*, 232–236.

Esterreicher, C. (1992). *Now you see it, now you don't.* Austin, TX: Pro-Ed.

Evans, D.D., and Strong, C.J. (in press). Narrative intervention for students with disabilities. *Teaching Exceptional Children.*

Gebers, J.L. (1990). *Books are for talking too! A sourcebook for using children's literature in speech and language remediation.* Tucson, AZ: Communication Skill Builders.

Geva, E. (1983). Facilitating reading comprehension through flow charting. *Reading Research Quarterly, 18*, 384–405.

Graves, A., and Montague, M. (1991). Using story-grammar cueing to improve the writing of students with learning disabilities. *Learning Disabilities Research and Practice, 6*, 246–250.

Hamayan, E.V. (1989). *Teaching writing to potentially English proficient students using whole language approaches.* (Program Information Guide Series, Number 11) Washington, DC: Office of Bilingual Education and Minority Language Affairs. (ERIC Document Reproduction Service No. ED 337 038)

Hansen, J. (1981). The effects of inference training and practice on young children's comprehension. *Reading Research Quarterly, 16,* 391–417.

Harbury, M. (1986). *Last of the wild horses.* New York: Arrowood Press.

Harp, B. (1988). Why are your kids singing during reading time? *The Reading Teacher, 41,* 454–456.

Heath, S.B. (1982). What no bedtime story means: Narrative skills at home and school. *Language in Society, 11*(1), 49–76.

Hedberg, N.L., and Westby, C.E. (1993). *Analyzing storytelling skills.* San Antonio, TX: Communication Skill Builders.

Heimlich, J.E., and Pittelman, S.D. (1986). *Semantic mapping: Classroom applications.* Newark, DE: International Reading Association.

Herrmann, B.A. (Ed.). (1994). *The volunteer tutor's toolbox.* Newark, DE: International Reading Association.

Hewitt, L.E. (1994). Narrative comprehension: The importance of subjectivity. In J. F. Duchan, L. E. Hewitt, and R. M. Sonnenmeier (Eds.), *Pragmatics: From theory to practice* (pp. 88–104). Englewood Cliffs, NJ: Prentice Hall.

Hoggan, K.C., and Strong, C.J. (1994). The magic of "once upon a time": Narrative teaching strategies. *Language, Speech, and Hearing Services in Schools, 25,* 76–89.

Holdaway, D. (1979). *The foundations of literacy.* Sydney, Australia: Ashton Scholastic.

Hughes, D., McGillivray, L., and Schmidek, M. (in press). *Sourcebook for narrative language: Procedures for assessment.* Eau Claire, WI: Thinking Publications.

Hutson-Nechkash, P. (1990). *Storybuilding: A guide to structuring oral narratives.* Eau Claire, WI: Thinking Publications.

Idol, L. (1987). Group story mapping: A comprehension strategy for both skilled and unskilled readers. *Journal of Learning Disabilities, 20,* 196–205.

Idol, L., and Croll, V. (1985). Story-mapping training as a means of improving reading comprehension. *Learning Disability Quarterly, 10,* 214–229.

Jensen, J. M., and Roser, N. L. (Eds.) (1993). *Adventuring with books: A booklist for pre-k—grade 6* (10th ed.), Urbana, IL: National Council of Teachers of English.

Jeunesse, G., and Bour, L. (1989). *Bears.* New York: Scholastic.

Jeunesse, G., Delafosse, C., Fuhr, U., and Sautai, R. (1991). *Whales.* New York: Scholastic.

Jeunesse, G., Delafosse, C., and Mettler, R. (1993). *Birds.* New York: Scholastic.

Jeunesse, G., and Mettler, R. (1992). *The rain forest*. New York: Scholastic.

Jones, C.F., and O'Brien, J. (1991). *Mistakes that worked*. New York: Delacorte Press.

Koppenhaver, D.A., Coleman, P. P., Kalman, S. L., and Yoder, D. E. (1991). The implications of emergent literacy research for children with developmental disabilities. *American Journal of Speech-Language Pathology, 1*(1), 38–44.

Krauss, R. (Producer). (1989). *Mufaro's beautiful daughters* [Videotape]. Lincoln, NE: Great Plains National WNED TV of Buffalo.

Lahey, M. (1988). *Language disorders and language development*. New York: Macmillan.

Langdon, H.W., and Cheng, L.L. (1992). *Hispanic children and adults with communication disorders: Assessment and intervention*. Gaithersburg, MD: Aspen.

Langer, J.A. (1984). Examining background knowledge and text comprehension. *Reading Research Quarterly, 19*, 468–481.

McCabe, A., and Rollins, P.R. (1994). Assessment of preschool narrative skills. *American Journal of Speech-Language Pathology, 3*(1), 45–56.

McCracken, R.A., and McCracken, M.J. (1986). *Stories, songs and poetry to teach reading and writing: Literacy through language*. New York: Teachers College Press.

McEachern, W.R. (1990). *Supporting emergent literacy among young American Indian students*. Charleston, WV: Appalachia Educational Lab.

Michaels, S. (1981). "Sharing time": Children's narrative styles and differential access to literacy. *Language in Society, 10*, 423–442.

Milosky, L. M. (1987). Narratives in the classroom. *Seminars in Speech and Language, 8*, 329–343.

Moorhead, C. A. (1994). *Wild horses*. Niwot, CO: Roberts Rinehart.

Morrow, C. M. (1985). Retelling stories: The strategy for improving children's comprehension, concept of story structure, and oral language complexity. *Elementary School Journal, 85*, 647–661.

Morrow, L. M. (1989). *Literacy development in the early years: Helping children read and write*. Englewood Cliffs, NJ: Prentice Hall.

Morrow, L. M., and Smith, J. K. (Eds.). (1990). *Assessment for instruction in early literacy*. Englewood Cliffs, NJ: Prentice Hall.

Muma, J. R. (1971). Language intervention: Ten techniques. *Language, Speech, and Hearing Services in Schools, 2*(1), 7–17.

Nagy, W. (1988). *Teaching vocabulary to improve reading comprehension.* Urbana, IL: National Council of Teachers of English.

Nelson, N.W. (1988). *Planning individualized speech and language intervention programs: Objectives for infants, children, and adolescents.* Tucson, AZ: Communication Skill Builders.

Nessel, D. (1989). Do your students think when they read? *Learning, 17*(8), 55–58.

Nessel, D., Jones, M., and Dixon, D. (1989). *Thinking through the language arts.* New York: Macmillan.

Nickman, J.C. (Producer), and Phelan, K. (Director). (1989). *Gift of the whales* [Videotape]. Seattle, WA: Miramar Legend Series.

Nippold, M.A. (1985). Comprehension of figurative language in youth. *Topics in Language Disorders, 5*(3), 1–20.

Norris, J.A. (1991). From frog to prince: Using written language as a context for language learning. *Topics in Language Disorders, 12*(1), 66–81.

Ollmann, H.E. (1989). Cause and effect in the real world. *Journal of Reading, 33,* 224–225.

Page, J.L., and Stewart, S.R. (1985). Story grammar skills in school-age children. *Topics in Language Disorders, 5*(2), 16–30.

Panofsky, C. (1986, December). *The functions of language in parent-child bookreading events.* Paper presented at the National Reading Conference, Austin, TX.

Pearson, P.D., Hansen, J., and Gordon, C. (1979). The effect of background knowledge on young children's comprehension of explicit and implicit information. *Journal of Reading Behavior, 11,* 201–209.

Peck, J. (1989). Using story telling to promote language and literacy development. *The Reading Teacher, 42,* 138–141.

Putnam, L. (1991). Dramatizing nonfiction with emerging readers. *Language Arts, 68,* 463–469.

Raphael, T.E. (1984). Teaching learners about sources of information for answering comprehension questions. *Journal of Reading, 27,* 303–311.

Raphael, T.E. (1986). Teaching question-answer relationships, revisited. *The Reading Teacher, 40,* 516–522.

Raphael, T.E., and Pearson, P.D. (1982). *The effect of metacognitive training on children's question-answering behavior.* Urbana, IL: Center for the Study of Reading. (ERIC Document Reproduction Service No. ED 215 315)

Readence, J.E., Bean, T.W., and Baldwin, R.S. (1992). *Content area reading* (4th ed.). Dubuque, IA: Kendall/Hunt.

Reutzel, D. (1984). Story mapping: An alternative approach to communication. *Reading World, 24*(2), 16–25.

Reutzel, D. (1986). Clozing in on comprehension: The cloze story map. *The Reading Teacher, 39*, 524–528.

Rhodes, L.K. (Ed.). (1993). *Literacy assessment: A handbook of instruments.* Portsmouth, NH: Heinemann.

Richardson, J.S., and Morgan, R.F. (1990). *Reading to learn in the content areas.* Belmont, CA: Wadsworth.

Ripich, D.N., and Griffith, P. L. (1985, November). *Story structure, cohesion, and propositions in learning disabled children.* Paper presented at the annual convention of the American Speech-Language-Hearing Association, Washington, DC.

Roth, F.P. (1986). Oral narrative abilities of learning-disabled students. *Topics in Language Disorders, 7*(1), 21–30.

Rudman, M.K. (1994). *Children's literature: An issues approach.* New York: Longman.

Savage, S. (1995). *Frog.* New York: Thomson Learning.

Schieffelin, B.B., and Cochran-Smith, M. (1984). Learning to read culturally: Literacy before schooling. In H. Goelman, A. Oberg, and F. Smith (Eds.), *Awakening to literacy* (pp. 3–23). Portsmouth, NH: Heinemann.

Schmelzer, R., and Dickey, J.P. (1990). *Using story grammar to teach literature: Episodic mapping.* Richmond, KY: Eastern Kentucky University. (ERIC Document Reproduction Service No. ED 322 482)

Sharmat, M. (1980). *Gregory, the terrible eater.* New York: Scholastic.

Shebar, S. (1990). *Bats.* New York: Franklin Watts.

Slapin, B., and Seale, D. (Eds.). (1992). *Through Indian eyes: The native experience in books for children.* Philadelphia: New Society.

Staton, J. (1985). Using dialogue journals for developing thinking, reading, and writing with hearing-impaired students. *The Volta Review, 87*, 127–154.

Stauffer, R. (1981). *Directing the reading-thinking process.* New York: Harper and Row.

Stein, N.L., and Glenn, C.G. (1979). An analysis of story comprehension in elementary school children. In R. O. Freedle (Ed.), *New directions in discourse processing* (Vol. 2, pp. 53–120). Norwood, NJ: Ablex.

Stein, N.L., and Glenn, C.G. (1982). Children's concept of time: The development of a story schema. In W. J. Friedman (Ed.), *The developmental psychology of time* (pp. 255–282). New York: Academic Press.

Strickland, D.S., and Morrow, L.M. (1989). Interactive experiences with storybook reading. *The Reading Teacher, 42*, 322–323.

Strong, C.J. (1994). *Elicitation instructions and tape-recorded stimuli for retold narrative samples. Unpublished manuscript,* Utah State University at Logan, Department of Communicative Disorders and Deaf Education.

Strong, C.J., and Strong, W. (1995). *Rhythm, rhyme, and rap: Developmental sentence-combining exercises*. Tucson, AZ: Communication Skill Builders.

Teale, W.H. (1984). Reading to young children: Its significance for literacy development. In H. Goelman, A. Oberg, and F. Smith (Eds.), *Awakening to literacy* (pp. 110–121). Portsmouth, NH: Heinemann.

Teale, W.H., and Sulzby, E. (Eds.). (1986). *Emergent literacy: Writing and reading*. Norwood, NJ: Ablex.

Trelease, J. (1989a). *The new read-aloud handbook*. New York: Penguin.

Trelease, J. (1989b). Jim Trelease speaks on reading aloud to children. *The Reading Teacher, 43*, 200–206.

Trousdale, A.M. (1990). Interactive storytelling: Scaffolding children's early narratives. *Language Arts, 67*, 164–173.

Van Dijk, T.A., and Kintsch, W. (1977). Cognitive psychology and discourse: Recalling and summarizing stories. In W. U. Dressler (Ed.), *Current trends in text-linguistics* (pp. 61–81). New York: DeGruyter.

Van Dongen, R., and Westby, C.E. (1986). Building the narrative mode of thought through children's literature. *Topics in Language Disorders, 7*(1), 70–83.

Vygotsky, L. (1962). *Thought and language*. Cambridge, MA: MIT Press.

Vygotsky, L.S. (1978). *Mind in society: The development of higher psychological processes*. Cambridge, MA: Harvard University Press.

Westby, C.E. (1990). The role of the speech-language pathologist in whole language. *Language, Speech, and Hearing Services in Schools, 21*, 228–237.

Westby, C.E. (1991). Learning to talk—talking to learn: Oral-literate language differences. In C. S. Simon (Ed.), *Communication skills and classroom success: Assessment and therapy methodologies for language and learning disabled students* (pp. 334–355). Eau Claire, WI: Thinking Publications.

WGBH Television (Producer). (1984). *NOVA: Signs of the apes, songs of the whales* [Videotape]. New York: Ambrose Video.

Whitehurst, G.J., Falco, F.L., Lonigan, C.J., Fischel, J.E., DeBaryshe, B.D., Valdez-Menchaca, M. C., and Caulfield, M. (1988). Accelerating language development through picture book reading. *Developmental Psychology, 24*, 552–559.

Wisconsin Department of Public Instruction. (1989). *Strategic learning in the content areas*. Madison, WI: Author.

Wollman-Bonilla, J. (1989). Reading journals: Invitations to participate in literature. *The Reading Teacher, 42*, 112–119.

Zoller, M.B. (1991). Use of music activities in speech-language therapy. *Language, Speech, and Hearing Services in Schools, 22*, 272–276.

INDEXES

THEMATIC/TOPICAL INDEX

GRADE LEVEL	THEME/TOPIC	TREATED IN
	Animals as Characters	
Early Grades	Bear	*Great White Bear*
	Goats	*Gregory, the Terrible Eater*
	Jungle Animals	*"Stand Back," Said the Elephant. . .*
	Bear	*The Biggest Bear*
	Jungle Animals	*The Proud and Fearless Lion*
	Dog	*The Puppy Who Wanted a Boy*
	Fish	*The Rainbow Fish*
	Frog	*The Show-and-Tell Frog*
Middle Grades	Cow	*Rude Giants*
	Cat	*Sam, Bangs & Moonshine*
	Bat	*Stellaluna*
	Donkey	*Sylvester and the Magic Pebble*
Upper Grades	Whale	*Humphrey the Lost Whale*
	Snake	*Mufaro's Beautiful Daughters*
	Guinea Pig	*Professor Puffendorf's Magic Potions*
	Jungle Animals	*The Eleventh Hour*
	Horses	*The Girl Who Loved Wild Horses*
	Rain Forest Animals	*The Great Kapok Tree*
	Family as Characters	
Early Grades	Siblings; Father; Stepmother	*Sam Is My Half Brother*
Middle Grades	Grandmother; Mother	*Amazing Grace*
	Mother; Children	*Heckedy Peg*
	Father	*Sam, Bangs & Moonshine*
	Adoptive Parents	*The Rainbabies*
	Cousins	*Too Many Tamales*
Upper Grades	Grandfather	*A Day's Work*
	Grandmother	*Annie and the Old One*
	Siblings	*Mufaro's Beautiful Daughters*

(continued)

THEMATIC / TOPICAL INDEX — *Continued*

GRADE LEVEL	THEME/TOPIC	TREATED IN
	Feelings and Emotions	
Early Grades	Anxiety	*Great White Bear*
	Anxiety	*Gregory, the Terrible Eater*
	Jealousy	*Sam Is My Half Brother*
	Fear of Danger	*"Stand Back," Said the Elephant…*
	Curiosity	*Strega Nona*
	Affection	*The Biggest Bear*
	Pride; Fear of Danger	*The Proud and Fearless Lion*
	Loneliness	*The Puppy Who Wanted a Boy*
	Loneliness	*The Rainbow Fish*
	Sadness; Surprise	*The Show-and-Tell Frog*
Middle Grades	Determination	*Amazing Grace*
	Pride	*Eyes of the Dragon*
	Anxiety	*Heckedy Peg*
	Hunger; Fear of Danger	*Rude Giants*
	Guilt	*Sam, Bangs & Moonshine*
	Loneliness	*Sylvester and the Magic Pebble*
	Greed	*The Baker's Dozen*
	Love; Fear of Danger	*The Rainbabies*
	Anxiety	*Too Many Tamales*
Upper Grades	Guilt	*A Day's Work*
	Fear of Death	*Annie and the Old One*
	Jealousy	*Mufaro's Beautiful Daughters*
	Greed	*Professor Puffendorf's Magic Potions*
	Hunger; Disappointment	*The Eleventh Hour*
	Love	*The Girl Who Loved Wild Horses*
	Confusion	*The Story of Wali Dad*
	Fear of Unknown	*The Widow's Broom*

(continued)

THEMATIC/TOPICAL INDEX—*Continued*

GRADE LEVEL	THEME/TOPIC	TREATED IN
Magic		
Early Grades		*Strega Nona*
Middle Grades		*Eyes of the Dragon*
		Heckedy Peg
		Sylvester and the Magic Pebble
Upper Grades		*Mufaro's Beautiful Daughters*
		Professor Puffendorf's Magic Potions
		The Widow's Broom
Multicultural		
Early Grades	Native American-Alaskan	*Great White Bear*
Middle Grades	African-American	*Amazing Grace*
	Chinese	*Eyes of the Dragon*
	Spanish-American	*Too Many Tamales*
Upper Grades	Spanish-American	*A Day's Work*
	Native American	*Annie and the Old One*
	African	*Mufaro's Beautiful Daughters*
	Native American	*The Girl Who Loved Wild Horses*
	Indian	*The Story of Wali Dad*
Mystery		
Upper Grades		*The Eleventh Hour*
		The Widow's Broom
Personal Values		
Early Grades	Friendship; Loyalty	*Great White Bear*
	Family	*Sam Is My Half Brother*
	Obedience	*The Biggest Bear*
	Friendship; Loyalty	*The Proud and Fearless Lion*
	Family	*The Puppy Who Wanted a Boy*
	Kindness	*The Rainbow Fish*

(continued)

THEMATIC / TOPICAL INDEX — *Continued*

GRADE LEVEL	THEME/TOPIC	TREATED IN
	Personal Values — *Continued*	
Middle Grades	Self-confidence; Tolerance	*Amazing Grace*
	Humility	*Eyes of the Dragon*
	Obedience	*Heckedy Peg*
	Cleanliness; Politeness	*Rude Giants*
	Honesty	*Sam, Bangs & Moonshine*
	Family; Tolerance	*Stellaluna*
	Family	*Sylvester and the Magic Pebble*
	Generosity	*The Baker's Dozen*
	Family	*The Rainbabies*
Upper Grades	Honesty; Integrity	*A Day's Work*
	Acceptance of Death	*Annie and the Old One*
	Generosity; Kindness	*Mufaro's Beautiful Daughters*
	Honesty	*Professor Puffendorf's Secret Potions*
	Generosity	*The Story of Wali Dad*
	Friendship	*The Widow's Broom*
	Rhyme	
Early Grades		*Great White Bear*
		"Stand Back," Said the Elephant…
Middle Grades		*The Baker's Dozen*
Upper Grades		*The Eleventh Hour*
	Science	
Early Grades	Preservation	*The Biggest Bear*
Middle Grades	Mammals; Birds	*Stellaluna*
Upper Grades	Preservation	*Humphrey the Lost Whale*
	Inventions	*Professor Puffendorf's Secret Potions*
	Preservation	*The Girl Who Loved Wild Horses*
	Preservation	*The Great Kapok Tree*

(continued)

THEMATIC/TOPICAL INDEX—*Continued*

GRADE LEVEL	THEME/TOPIC	TREATED IN
	Social/Pragmatics Issues	
Early Grades	Overeating; Picky Eating	*Gregory, the Terrible Eater*
	Etiquette	*"Stand Back," Said the Elephant…*
	Respecting Others' Belongings	*Strega Nona*
	Sensitivity to Others	*The Proud and Fearless Lion*
	Politeness	*The Puppy Who Wanted a Boy*
	Sharing	*The Rainbow Fish*
	Show and Tell	*The Show-And-Tell Frog*
Middle Grades	Refusing a Bribe	*Heckedy Peg*
	Etiquette	*Rude Giants*
	Lying	*Sam, Bangs & Moonshine*
	Making Friends	*Stellaluna*
	Cheating	*The Baker's Dozen*
	Sensitivity to Others	*The Great Kapok Tree*
	Respecting Others' Belongings	*Too Many Tamales*
Upper Grades	Lying	*A Day's Work*
	Sensitivity to Others	*Mufaro's Beautiful Daughters*
	Respecting Others' Belongings	*Professor Puffendorf's Magic Potions*
	Problem Solving	*The Eleventh Hour*
	Teasing	*The Widow's Broom*
	Special Occasions/Seasons	
Early Grades	Christmas	*The Puppy Who Wanted a Boy*
Middle Grades	Halloween	*Heckedy Peg*
	Christmas	*The Baker's Dozen*
	Mothers' Day	*The Rainbabies*
	Christmas	*Too Many Tamales*
Upper Grades	Wedding	*Mufaro's Beautiful Daughters*
	Birthday	*The Eleventh Hour*
	Wedding	*The Story of Wali Dad*
	Halloween	*The Widow's Broom*

TEACHING-STRATEGIES INDEX

STRATEGIES	Early-Grade (E) Units										Middle-Grade (M) Units										Upper-Grade (U) Units									
	1	2	3	4	5	6	7	8	9	10	1	2	3	4	5	6	7	8	9	10	1	2	3	4	5	6	7	8	9	10
Art Activities	★	★		★	★		★	★	★	★	★		★	★		★	★		★			★		★	★	★				
Compare/Contrast Charts or Diagrams													★		★	★					★			★		★	★			
Directed Reading/Thinking Activities		★		★		★		★		★	★	★	★		★		★				★				★	★	★		★	★
Discussion Webs					★			★		★		★				★						★						★		★
Dramatic Play			★	★			★	★	★	★	★					★									★	★	★			
Episode Maps		★							★		★	★									★		★		★	★				
Extensions	★	★	★	★	★	★	★	★	★	★	★		★	★	★	★	★	★	★	★	★		★	★		★	★	★	★	★
Flow Charts				★		★													★			★								★
Internal-States Charts	★	★	★	★	★			★			★	★		★	★		★	★		★		★	★		★				★	★
Journals	★	★		★					★	★				★	★	★	★	★				★	★	★	★		★		★	★
Music								★	★	★										★		★	★	★			★		★	

STRATEGIES	Early-Grade (E) Units										Middle-Grade (M) Units										Upper-Grade (U) Units									
	1	2	3	4	5	6	7	8	9	10	1	2	3	4	5	6	7	8	9	10	1	2	3	4	5	6	7	8	9	10
Preparatory Sets	★	★	★	★	★	★	★	★	★	★	★	★	★	★	★	★	★	★	★	★	★	★	★	★	★	★	★	★	★	★
Question-Answer Relationships	★	★	★	★	★	★	★	★	★	★	★	★	★	★	★		★	★	★	★	★	★	★		★	★	★	★	★	★
Questioning	★	★	★	★	★	★	★	★	★		★	★	★		★		★		★	★	★	★	★		★	★	★	★	★	★
Semantic-Word Maps	★	★	★	★	★	★	★		★	★		★	★	★			★	★				★	★	★	★			★	★	
Story Generation		★				★	★					★	★			★			★		★			★						★
Story-Grammar Cue Charts												★		★				★		★	★	★	★			★		★		★
Story Maps							★	★		★			★			★	★										★		★	
Story Retelling	★	★		★	★	★				★	★	★	★	★	★	★	★	★	★	★	★			★		★	★		★	
Summarizing	★		★			★	★			★	★		★		★				★								★	★		
Think Alouds	★	★	★	★	★	★	★	★	★	★	★	★	★	★	★	★	★	★	★	★	★	★	★	★	★	★	★	★	★	★
Word Substitutions		★	★					★	★	★		★	★	★			★	★			★		★		★			★	★	